1847

GROSSE ÎLE:
a Record of Daily Events

André CHARBONNEAU
André SÉVIGNY

1847

GROSSE ÎLE:
a Record of Daily Events

Canadian   Patrimoine
Heritage   canadien

Parks   Parcs
Canada   Canada

1997

Writing : André Charbonneau and André Sévigny

Research Supervision : André Charbonneau and André Sévigny

Project Supervision : Michel P. de Courval

Art Direction
and Printing Supervision : Pierre Demers

Drawings : Bernard Duchesne and Daniel Rainville

Cartography : Christiane Hébert and François Pellerin

Data Capture
and Word Processing : Noëlla Gauthier

Translation : Alison McGain and Jane Macaulay

Proofreading : Johanne Lachance and Irène Halikas

Graphics Design : Norman Dupuis inc.

Printing : Imprimerie La Renaissance

Cover : *"Waiting to Board Ship at Cork"*
(Illustrated London News, May 10, 1851, McGill
University, McLellan Library, illustration
electronically colored by Marc Duplain and
reproduced from *The Irish in Québec* by
Robert J. Grace with the gracious authorization
from Les Éditions de l'IQRC and Les Presses de
l'université Laval.)

Canadian Cataloguing in Publication Data

Charbonneau, André, 1950-

1847, Grosse Île: a Record of Daily Events

Issued also in French under title: 1847, Grosse-Île au fil des jours.

ISBN 0-660-16878-2

Cat. no. R64-198/2-1997E

1. Irish — Quebec (Province) — Grosse Île (Montmagny) — Mortality.
2. Quarantine — Quebec (Province) — Grosse Île, (Montmagny).
3. Grosse Île, (Montmagny, Quebec) — History — 19th century.
I. Sévigny, André. II. Parks Canada. III. Title.

FC2908.1C42 1997   971.4'735   C97980148-6   F1035.16C42 1997

Printed on recycled
and alkaline paper

Legal deposit (Québec and Ottawa)
2nd trimester 1997

Published under the authority of the Minister of Canadian
Heritage, Ottawa, 1997.

Printed in Canada

CONTENTS

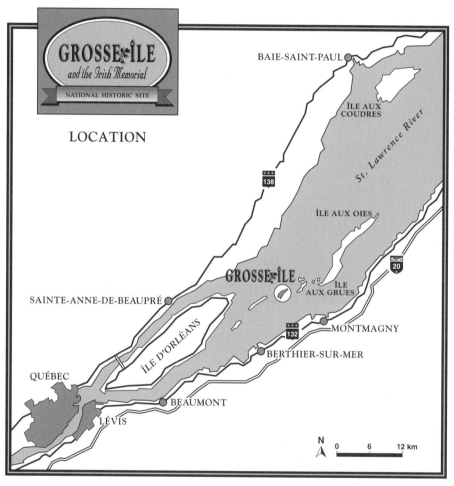

ACKNOWLEDGEMENTS

At several points in its production, this publication benefited in various ways by the efforts of a number of different people. Historians Christine Chartré and Doris Drolet-Dubé, members of the Grosse Île research team, inevitably contributed very useful knowledge and recommendations, as did our colleague Yvan Fortier.

Both in Quebec City and in Ottawa, researchers Joanne Lachance and Odette Vincent worked on the basic documentary material, while at Laval University student trainees from the Department of Anthropology pored over Québec City newspapers from 1847. As for historian Robert Grace, in addition to his archival research, he acted as an Irish history adviser to the project.

Others, such as Rose Dompierre, Marianna O'Gallagher, Fernand Harvey, Marc Lafrance, Pierre Lessard, Louis R. Richer and Pierre Thibodeau, graciously agreed to proofread this book in manuscript and offer us their comments and advice, for which we sincerely thank them. We also drew great inspiration from Rose Dompierre and Marianna O'Gallagher, who pioneered the Grosse Île development project.

As regards its physical production, this publication profited by the expertise and judicious advice of many colleagues. We particularly want to stress the friendly and professional help given by Michel de Courval, Pierre Demers, Norman Dupuis and our translators, Alison McGain and Jane Macaulay.

Lastly, we wish to express our heartfelt thanks to Noëlla Gauthier, who, in often trying conditions, ensured that our manuscript would be correctly presented. Her hard work and vigilance, particularly with respect to the many tables the work contains, were essential to the completion of the project.

We hope that all the persons mentioned above, as well as any we may have omitted, will accept our very sincere thanks.

ANDRÉ CHARBONNEAU   ANDRÉ SÉVIGNY

Foreword

This book is intended to shed light on the tragedy that took place at Grosse Île in 1847 and the intense activity it entailed. For this purpose, we have decided to present the results of our research in a very simple format, that of a chronicle. Through this record of daily events, readers will discover the frequency at which emigrants arrived at the quarantine station and the rate at which they left it as their ships were authorized to proceed to the port of Québec. Through the administrative decisions made by the various authorities and other players involved, they will gradually realize the scope of the tragedy which struck the quarantine station in 1847. They will also gain insight into the doubts and questions raised and find out what solutions were proposed to offset the impact of a terrible disease, typhus.

Readers will be presented with firsthand reports by emigrants, priests, civil servants and others who witnessed these troubled times. They will also be provided with extracts from Québec City newspapers, which discussed the events from their particular perspective. At the end of each day described in the chronicle, they will find a summary of the entries for that date in the baptismal, marriage and burial registers of the Catholic and Anglican chapels on Grosse Île.

Readers will be able to consult weekly statistics on the number of emigrants who arrived through the port of Québec, the number of patients admitted to quarantine hospitals and the number of deaths. These figures are based on those submitted to the government authorities by the station's medical superintendent and the emigration agent in Québec City.

Several sources were consulted to prepare this publication, including the archives of the civil secretary, military and religious archives, Québec City newspapers and correspondence between the Governor General of Canada and the Colonial Office in London. Inevitably, presenting the events of 1847 in chronicle format required certain analyses, interpretations and choices, some of which are discussed below.

In-Depth Statistical Analyses

Tables showing the daily arrival and departure of ships were prepared by compiling information from two major sources: the list of ships that were inspected at Grosse Île and the list of those that arrived in the port of Québec. These two sources complement each other quite well, but errors were detected in the first. In general, we allowed for a day's difference between dates, since the day on which a ship was registered may have depended on whether the vessel arrived late at night or early in the morning.

We had to correct the dates on which some 80 vessels were reported to have arrived at and left Grosse Île because they did not tally with the information given in the register of the port of Québec regarding the time these ships had taken to cross the Atlantic and were detained in quarantine. However, we believe that the various sources we used, including the official correspondence of the authorities of the period, have enabled us to reach a fairly accurate assessment of arrival and departure dates.

This book contains several statistical tables whose data are sometimes incomplete or may even seem contradictory. Because of the disparities between the various accounts of what happened and the crisis situation in which the data were recorded, it is almost impossible to be totally accurate. Nevertheless, the data from the different sources are generally consistent and provide a reasonably exact picture of the situation.

When faced with contradictory information on the number of sick or dead, we have always chosen the highest figures so as to avoid underestimating the seriousness of the situation at Grosse Île in 1847. On the other hand, the many sources at our disposal minimized the risk of exaggerating.

Québec City Newspapers in 1847

This chronicle is based largely on information gleaned from newspapers of the period. Given that a few days often elapsed between the time events took place and the moment they were reported in the newspaper, we have tried, when possible, to describe the events presented here on the date they actually occurred. Comparisons with other documents of the period have helped us to achieve this goal.

Readers will note that some newspapers, such as the *Quebec Mercury,* are quoted more frequently than others. This reflects the importance this newspaper attached to emigration activities at Grosse Île and Québec City in 1847. In general, the *Quebec Mercury* was the first to obtain the most accurate reports about the situation; other contemporary newspapers often took information from it and published it a day or two later. The *Canadien,* on the other hand, is the most reliable source of information on the movements of the Roman Catholic clergy who came to the assistance of the emigrants at Grosse Île.

Readers will note that the term emigration, rather than immigration, has been used almost exclusively in this book about Grosse Île. This usage reflects a reality of the period. Since Canada was still a British colony in the mid-19th century, migration to North America was governed exclusively by the policies of the mother country. Therefore, in the eyes of the London authorities, this phenomenon was emigration. This perception is also reflected in the title of Québec emigration agent assigned to A. C. Buchanan, the person responsible for dealing with emigrants in Québec City. Correspondence from the period and all the other sources consulted also use the term emigration.

We are aware that this book has not explored all possible avenues, in that some themes have not been discussed and many analyses remain to be done. Perhaps readers will feel that certain questions have been left unanswered. Nevertheless, until a more in-depth study of the tragic days of 1847 is available, we hope that this chronicle will shed light on what happened at Grosse Île that year. It begins with a brief introduction summarizing the main events of that very long season.

The Typhus Epidemic at Grosse Île in 1847: Establishing the Facts

Tragedy Strikes

ON FRIDAY, MAY 14, 1847, a sailing ship, the *Syria*, anchored off Grosse Île in an area known since 1832 as the *quarantine pass.* It had taken Captain Cox and his 245 passengers 46 days to travel from the large port of Liverpool, England, to this small island and its quarantine station, 34 kilometres east of the port of Québec. On reaching Grosse Île, the captain declared that nine emigrants had already died, while 52 others were suffering from dysentery and the terrible disease known as ship fever, or typhus. Two weeks later, over half of the vessel's passengers were in hospital on the island.

The sinister procession of sick and dying emigrants had begun. Involving mostly frail, destitute Irish, it came to an end 171 days later, on Monday, November 1, when the *Lord Ashburton* left the quarantine station for Québec City. All the tragic events of the 1847 navigation season took place during this six-month period, when about 400 vessels unwittingly took part in this ghastly cortege. They transported a good portion of the some 100 000 emigrants who left that year for Québec City, the gateway to Canada.

In 1847, nearly 2 emigrants in 10 died on ships crossing the Atlantic or sailing up the St. Lawrence, or even after they reached Grosse Île or major Canadian cities. This singularly tragic odyssey, involving mainly Irish emigrants, made a lasting impression on individuals and society as a whole. The massive influx of newcomers not only had an immediate impact on the history of the communities along the river, but eventually took on legendary proportions on account of its evocative power and its place in people's memories. No other location in Canada is so closely associated with this sad, but memorable period than the Grosse Île quarantine station — that isolated outpost to which the authorities entrusted the impossible mission of averting a nation-wide health catastrophe.

Memories and History

The year 1997 marks the 150th anniversary of the terrible battle waged by a handful of devoted people at Grosse Île to release thousands of emigrants from the clutches of typhus and dysentery. However, 150 years of history have not eliminated the following paradox: although the events of the 1847 navigation season constitute one of the most famous episodes of the 19th century, our knowledge of what really happened is still fairly limited. The human chaos of that deadly summer has given rise to so many legends, clichés and contradictory opinions that it is very difficult to determine the facts. As always in such situations, the true story can only be uncovered through documentary research as well as critical analysis and comparison of the data collected.

Our sole objective in preparing this book on the events at Grosse Île in 1847 has been to paint a realistic picture of daily life on the island. For this purpose, we have attempted to shatter the myths about the quarantine station and to eliminate misconceptions and emotional judgments. This chronicle presents raw, but factual, data, which will provide the basis for a true understanding of the 1847 migratory crisis and its impact on Grosse Île. It introduces numerous players and witnesses and, inevitably, often divergent viewpoints and conclusions.

A major advantage of presenting the events of 1847 in the form of a chronological record is that it allows readers to gradually realize that life on the island was not constantly chaotic and cruel during the six-month period the station was open. From May 3 to November 3, activities at the quarantine station went through a number of different phases, marked by quite different conditions. A brief description of these phases will make it easier to understand the events discussed in this book.

DR GEORGE M. DOUGLAS (1809-64), A SCOT, WAS MEDICAL SUPERINTENDENT OF GROSSE ÎLE FROM 1836 TO 1864. THIS ENERGETIC, DEVOTED PHYSICIAN EARNED GREAT RESPECT. (BERNARD DUCHESNE, PARKS CANADA, 1997.)

1. A Sudden, Unexpected Crisis (May 1847)

At the end of the 1846 navigation season, Dr. George M. Douglas, medical superintendent of the Grosse Île quarantine station, warned the Governor General of Canada that a greater number of emigrants, including many sick, would be arriving in Canada in 1847 on account of the almost total failure of potato harvests in Ireland over the past two years. However, since Douglas had no idea of the magnitude of the impending influx of emigrants, he believed that the situation could be controlled by simply adjusting or slightly expanding quarantine facilities and hiring more personnel. In addition, he did not expect to have to cope with the ravages of typhus, a contagious disease — also known as ship fever, famine fever or prison fever — associated with human misery and poor sanitary conditions.

A Seemingly Ordinary Season

When Douglas moved into his seasonal quarters at Grosse Île on May 3, 1847, he was accompanied by regular hospital personnel as well as a steward[1], an orderly and a nurse. Before leaving Québec City, he had ordered 50 additional beds and the construction of another emigrant shelter, or "shed" as these buildings were called at the time. In his opinion, the 200 beds reserved for the sick would be sufficient, given that, in previous years, there had never been more than about 100 patients on the island at a time. The medical superintendent was also counting on the fact that emigration usually peaked in July and August, which would leave him enough time to make necessary adjustments.

Dr. Douglas was soon confronted with a situation that was quite different from any encountered previously. In just a few days, from May 14 to 19, 285 sick passengers were let off at the quarantine station by the first four vessels obliged to stop there. Over 1 200 healthy passengers also arrived, while the island's sheds could accommodate only 800. Two days later, five emigrants ships anchored off Grosse Île with more than 1 700 passengers aboard, nearly 500 of whom were ill. The situation was so serious that the medical superintendent had to rapidly convert the sheds for healthy people into hospitals. Day after day, other sailing ships appeared in the quarantine pass and the number of sick continued to rise. Even with the new hospitals, there was not enough room to accommodate everyone who was ill. Priority had to be given to bringing the worst cases ashore, while the other passengers were obliged to remain on the ships.

Preliminary assistance

On May 24, tents were requested for lodging 10 000 people. At the time, 50 to 60 people were being buried every day, and 32 ships were lined up off Grosse Île waiting for help. Although Dr. Douglas could now count on the assistance of three more doctors

---

1. At the time, the term steward referred to a kind of managing director, responsible for the day-to-day operation of a hospital.

and nurses, his team was overworked. From a logistical standpoint, the emergency was twofold: all sick passengers had to be taken ashore and provided with accommodations and treatment; however, in addition, all healthy passengers on ships with cases of illness aboard had to be detained for a period of 10 days by law. Moreover, it was advisable to keep convalescent patients separate from healthy people and those who were still hospitalized. It was proposed, although to no avail, that convalescent emigrants be housed at the east end of the island while healthy passengers be sent to Cliff Island, a small island nearby, now known as Île de la Sottise.

Near the end of May 1847, a few more hospitals were built, and several hundred tents, including marquees and hospital tents, were delivered to Grosse Île. There was not enough manpower, however, to erect the canvas shelters, since many workers refused to approach the hospitals. On May 31, the hospitals and various other buildings in the western part of the island were crowded with 1 300 patients. Meanwhile, there were just as many sick on the ships anchored in the St. Lawrence. In all, over 12 000 people were detained at Grosse Île, including about 100 orphans.

2. Reaction and Organization (June 1847)

In early June, the quarantine station was the scene of chaos and suffering. A few more doctors had just arrived to assist their exhausted colleagues, and kitchens had been hastily set up to feed all the emigrants. Under the circumstances, however, these initiatives were disorganized and generally ineffective. Since it was impossible to pitch tents for healthy passengers on Cliff Island, owing to its rocky ground, these passengers had to remain on board next to the sick and dead until they were authorized to disembark. Meanwhile, up to 86 people were buried per day, and Grosse Île's Catholic and Anglican chapels had to be converted into hospitals.

Medical Commission

The time had come for sweeping, well-organized, decisive action. Effective measures were finally implemented in early June. The Governor General ordered the construction of sheds for 2 000 sick emigrants, and a steamer was chartered for transporting supplies to the island and the quarantined vessels. The Governor General also sent a commission of three doctors to visit Grosse Île in order to inquire into the situation at the quarantine station and the state of the people detained there. The commission soon made recommendations, which were adopted immediately. For example, it advocated the massive recruitment of doctors, nurses, domestics

4

and workers skilled in various trades. It also declared that all sick passengers still on board ship had to be taken ashore and provided with accommodations. For this purpose, it recommended that all workers on the island as well as sailors and craftsmen from the ships be entrusted with erecting as quickly as possible all the tents received.

Other measures implemented on the recommendation of the commission targeted the 12 000 to 15 000 healthy people who were in danger of contracting typhus or dysentery at any time. First, the large fields at the east end of the island were placed at their disposal, and hundreds of tents with room for 3 000 to 4 000 people were soon set up at this spot. In accordance with the commission's wishes, it was also decided that healthy emigrants, after being quarantined for 10 days on land or for 15 days aboard ship, would be rapidly evacuated from the station and sent directly to Montréal on steamers, which would pick them up at the island. This measure meant that healthy passengers would no longer have to wait for their ocean-going vessel to be disinfected to proceed to their destination. On June 5, over 2 100 passengers left Grosse Île, followed by 4 000 to 5 000 others the next day. These departures no doubt helped to reduce overcrowding at the quarantine facility. However, Dr. Douglas was no fool; he predicted that at least half of those who had left would fall ill within three weeks.

Hospitals and Additional Accommodations

Throughout June and early July, construction contracts were negotiated and seven hospitals and a number of sheds were built. Forty-five labourers on the island were assigned to the construction work, whose completion became increasingly urgent every day. No less than 91 ships stopped at the quarantine station in June 1847 and, during that period, there were never less than about 15 000 emigrants, including 2 000 sick, at Grosse Île. The concentration of so many sick people in a single location created such an unhealthy, even lethal, environment that the station employees had little chance of not falling ill. The high risk of infection seriously complicated the operation of the quarantine facility as, one after the other, the doctors, nurses, orderlies, policemen, workers and priests took sick. Dr. Douglas found it extremely difficult to keep medical staff on the island.

When the new hospitals became operational in late June or early July, the situation at Grosse Île improved dramatically. Patients who had been living in small tents, which were particularly unsanitary in rainy weather, finally had access to appropriate

accommodations. On July 1 or 2, all those still confined to the ships were granted permission to land and were provided with necessary treatment. Meanwhile, medical superintendent Douglas was relieved to note a substantial improvement in sanitary conditions on vessels that had arrived recently, no doubt on account of more stringent inspections of ships from Ireland in the port of Liverpool. However, although there was definitely a change for the better at the quarantine station, it remained to be seen whether the situation was permanent.

3. Construction of New Facilities in the Eastern and Western Parts of Grosse Île (July - August 1847)

Inevitably, the government and Grosse Île administrators gave priority to battling disease in 1847. Available energy and resources were devoted largely to the reception and treatment of the sick, which was fortunate, since the season promised to be a long one and the average number of patients in hospital per day was increasing rapidly (e.g. from 1 454 in July to 2 021 in August). Once again, tents and chapels had to be placed at the disposal of the emigrants, and passengers had to wait to go ashore. The main problem was that the typhus epidemic had not abated; on the contrary, Grosse Île authorities were faced with a new outbreak of the disease and witnessed the death of 225 to 325 people per week throughout the month of August. More hospitals were erected in August and September in an effort to cope with the situation.

Efforts to Check the Spread of Typhus

On July 13, just when the authorities began to think that accommodations for the sick were quite sufficient at Grosse Île, other facilities had to be set up for the reception of healthy emigrants. As Dr. Douglas had predicted, many of the so-called healthy people who had left the quarantine station had fallen ill on their way to the port of Montréal or soon after landing there. The Montréal

Board of Health immediately questioned the effectiveness of administrative procedures at Grosse Île and demanded that newcomers, particularly those declared healthy, be subject to much stricter quarantine rules. On July 15, the Governor General announced that Solicitor General Cameron would visit the island in order to establish more stringent measures regarding the release of emigrants from the quarantine station in the St. Lawrence River.

The proposed measures were rapidly adopted. One of them required that emigrants disembarking from ships with sick passengers aboard be quarantined either for 20 days or for 7 days after the last case of illness was reported on their vessel. Obviously, this new rule meant that a large number of healthy emigrants would be detained at Grosse Île in the stifling, often unsanitary tents at the east end of the island. Therefore, Dr. Douglas was immediately authorized to have sheds for 3500 people built in that sector.

Prefabricated Sheds for Healthy People

On July 26, contracts were signed with various Québec City contractors for the rapid construction and delivery of six prefabricated sheds, to be assembled and erected on the island. Six more buildings of this type were ordered soon afterwards. In addition, it was finally decided that two convalescent hospitals with 150 beds would be erected in the eastern part of the quarantine station, away from the other facilities. Recovering patients had to be kept at a fair distance from the sick and, on account of the space needed for constructing new hospitals in the western part of Grosse Île, such patients would have to be transferred to the east end of the island "as soon as possible." By August 6, some 150 workers were engaged in the construction of sheds and hospitals at both ends of the island.

The 12 sheds for healthy people in the eastern sector were not all finished until September 14. Nevertheless, by late August, a sufficient number had been erected for the tents to be taken down. The last few weeks had been particularly difficult, with the medical staff constantly having to cope with at least 2 000 patients at a time, several hundred of whom were lodged in tents or even on board ship. In addition, hundreds of people who had been classified as healthy had perished in overheated, unsanitary canvas shelters. It is hard to believe that, in mid-July, Douglas and his assistants had thought such problems were a thing of the past.

4. Finally, an End to the Crisis (September - October 1847)

In early September, when construction work was still under way on the island, the number of emigrants arriving at Grosse Île finally began to decline. That month, only 40 ships put in at the quarantine station, and the average number of people in hospital per day fell to 1 330. At long last, the situation had begun to improve. On September 7, the chapels resumed their original function, and the next day, the old sheds in the western part of the island, which had been converted into hospitals in late May, were evacuated. Meanwhile, convalescent patients were transferred to the east end of Grosse Île. On September 11, Douglas reduced the facility's medical personnel.

Paradoxically, it was when needs were the least pressing that the quarantine establishment finally met the medical superintendent's expectations: it boasted hospitals with 2 000 beds, including two convalescent hospitals with room for 300 patients in the eastern part of the island, about 12 sheds for 3 500 healthy travellers, kitchens, wash houses, police headquarters, doctors' and civil servants' residences and so forth. The only thing lacking was a wharf at the east end of Grosse Île for embarking and disembarking healthy emigrants and their luggage. However, far from being plagued with regrets, Dr. Douglas viewed the future with optimism.

Evacuating Remaining Patients and Closing the Quarantine Station

In August, the authorities began to wonder what to do with all the sick and convalescent emigrants when the navigation season ended in late October. Should they be kept on the island and provided with suitable accommodations for the winter or be hospitalized in Québec City? In early October, when several hundred emigrants were still on the island and other ships were expected to arrive, the authorities decided, at the suggestion of the medical superintendent, to evacuate around 400 sick and convalescent patients to Montréal every week. People whose life would be endangered by the journey were taken to the Marine and Emigrant Hospital in Québec City.

By October 12, there were only about 400 emigrants left at Grosse Île. In preparation for closing the station at the end of the month, the medical superintendent convinced the authorities to leave the island under the supervision of four caretakers during the winter on account of the many buildings located there. By October 21,

PLAN OF THE HEALTHY DIVISION

GROSSE ISLE.

Scale of English Feet.

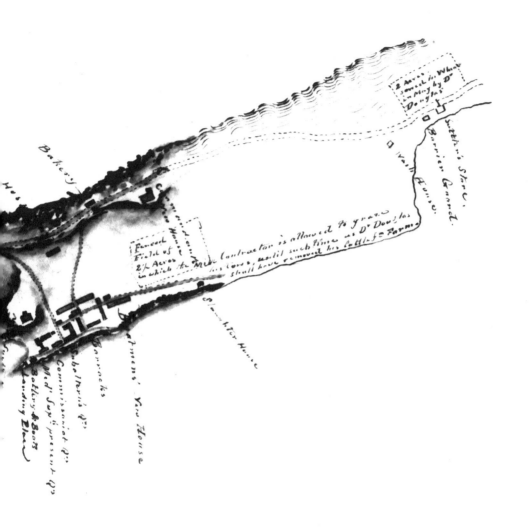

MAP OF THE WEST AND CENTRAL SECTORS OF THE QUARANTINE STATION IN 1848.
THE NAME THEN GIVEN TO THE WESTERN DIVISION SHOWS THAT IMMEDIATELY AFTER
THE 1847 SEASON, HEALTHY EMIGRANTS WERE ACCOMMODATED IN THE SICK PER-
SONS' AREA AND VICE-VERSA. ("PLAN OF THE HEALTHY DIVISION, GROSSE ISLE",
JUNE 24, 1848. NAC, RG4, C1, VOL. 231, #2020.)

all the emigrants and almost all the personnel had left the station. Soon afterwards, a notary inventoried the personal effects and sums of money left by the emigrants who had died on the island. On November 3, medical superintendent Douglas officially closed the station for the winter and returned to Québec City.

5. Grim Statistics

Number of Emigrants

Based on an official assessment by emigration agent Buchanan, 98 649 people set sail for Québec City in 1847 (Tables 1, 2, 3 and 4). To calculate the total number of arrivals in the port of Québec, it is necessary to subtract the number of deaths that occurred during the crossing or in quarantine and to add the number of births at sea. Buchanan set the number of arrivals at 90 150, i.e. 696 cabin passengers, 84 583 steerage passengers and 4 871 infants aged 0 to 1.

ALEXANDER C. BUCHANAN (1808-68), AN IRISHMAN, SERVED AS BRITISH EMIGRATION AGENT IN QUÉBEC CITY FROM 1838 UNTIL HIS DEATH. THE POSITION WAS ALL THE MORE IMPORTANT IN THAT, AT THE TIME, QUÉBEC CITY WAS BY FAR THE MOST IMPORTANT PORT OF ENTRY TO CANADA FOR EMIGRANTS. (NAC, C-117427.)

The steerage passengers comprised 58 976 adults (33 110 men and 25 866 women) and 25 607 children aged 1 to 14. Buchanan prepared his assessment in the winter of 1848 and submitted it along with his report on emigration through the port of Québec in 1847. According to a preliminary estimate, prepared in November 1847, the total number of departures was 98 106: 32 328 from England, 54 329 from Ireland, 3 752 from Scotland and 7 697 from Germany, consisting of 684 cabin passengers, 91 882 steerage passengers and 5 540 infants aged 0 to 1.

Arrivals at the port of Québec in 1847 were three times higher than the total for 1846 and the average for previous seasons. The vast majority of emigrants were Irish, and many had passed through British ports, especially Liverpool. According to Buchanan, over six emigrants in seven were of Irish origin in 1847. Given their extreme poverty and the high disease rate on emigrant ships, we can readily assume that most, if not all, of these emigrants stopped at the Grosse Île quarantine station.

Ships

In 1847, 398 ships were officially inspected at Grosse Île and 441 registered in Québec City. Seventy-seven carried over 400 passengers each. Seventy-two of the vessels were from Liverpool, England, which was the main port of departure, while 50 hailed from Limerick, Ireland. Another 33 were from Cork, Ireland, 30 from Glasgow, Scotland, 27 from Dublin, Ireland, 26 from Sligo, Ireland, 26 from Bremen, Germany, and 21 from Belfast, Ireland (Table 5). Although it normally took an average of 45 days to make the crossing, 26 of these vessels took over 60 days to reach Grosse Île; 24, however, managed to complete the journey in less than 30 days, probably by taking advantage of favourable winds. It should be noted that all were sailing ships.

EMIGRANT SHIP BEING TOWED OUT OF A BRITISH PORT BY A TUGBOAT. (*ILLUSTRATED LONDON NEWS*, APRIL 13, 1844, McGILL UNIVERSITY, McLELLAN LIBRARY.)

The difference between the number of vessels inspected at Grosse Île and the number registered in the port of Québec may be attributed to, among other things, the fact that certain ships carried only a few passengers, usually cabin passengers. Since they generally had no sick on board, these ships did not stop at the quarantine station.

Quarantine Period

Although several vessels were quarantined for over 20 days at Grosse Île in 1847, most were detained for no more than about 6 days. Such a short quarantine period may be attributed to the exceptionally large influx of emigrants in 1847. The station authorities were overworked, and many ships were released from quarantine rapidly to make way for the ever-increasing number of incoming vessels.

The time ships spent in quarantine does not reflect how long emigrants stayed at the station. In accordance with regulations adopted in July, healthy emigrants had to be detained either for 20 days or for 7 days after the last case of illness was detected on their ship. They were then taken directly to Québec City or Montréal aboard steamers chartered for that purpose.

Owing to the lack of facilities on the island, emigrants were often kept there for less than the official quarantine period, with the result that many fell ill after leaving Grosse Île and reaching Québec City, Montréal or cities and towns elsewhere in Canada, or while travelling on ships to various destinations in the colony. For the time being, we are unable to determine how long sick emigrants were usually hospitalized at Grosse Île.

Number of Sick Passengers on Ships

Based on data concerning the number of deaths that occurred during the crossing and the number of sick that were on the ships when they reached the quarantine station, it is clear that vessels from Liverpool and Cork had some of the highest disease and death rates. In contrast, emigrant ships from German ports, although often just as overcrowded, usually arrived with relatively healthy passengers and stopped at Grosse Île only long enough to be inspected (Table 5).

These observations tend to confirm statements made by Douglas and Buchanan at the end of the 1847 season. In their opinion, the high sickness and death rates of 1847 were not only attributable to overcrowding, unsanitary conditions and lack of food on vessels, but to emigrants' state of health prior to departure and to the fact that some were already harbouring certain diseases. Ships from Liverpool and Cork transported mainly Irish emigrants, already seriously weakened by famine.

EMIGRANTS HUDDLE TOGETHER ABOARD A SHIP LEAVING THE PORT OF LIVERPOOL. (*ILLUSTRATED LONDON NEWS*, JULY 6, 1850, McGILL UNIVERSITY, McLELLAN LIBRARY.)

Number of Emigrants Hospitalized

The number of emigrants hospitalized in Canada in 1847 was also very high, i.e. nearly 50 percent of total arrivals (Table 6). In Québec City and Montréal, hospitals admitted 3313 and 13189 emigrants respectively. A total of 8691 people were hospitalized at the quarantine station alone; according to Douglas, this represented an average of about 1307 people in hospital per day. This was a sharp increase in comparison with 1846, when only 892 people were admitted to hospital on Grosse Île (Table 7). In 1847, men accounted for the majority of patients, i.e. 3534, while women and children represented 2763 and 2394 respectively (Table 8). Dysentery and especially typhus were among the most prevalent illnesses in 1847.

Number of Deaths and Burials

Around 18 percent (17477) of the 98649 emigrants who boarded vessels for Québec City in 1847 died before reaching their final destination (Table 9). A total of 5293 people perished on board ship, either during the crossing or in quarantine, and 3452 while they were detained on Grosse Île. Of the latter, 3238 died in hospital and 214 in accommodations for healthy emigrants (Table 10). Deaths on ships (20 percent) and on the island (30 percent) accounted for nearly 50 percent of total emigrant deaths in 1847. The remainder occurred in Québec City, Montréal and other major Canadian cities.

A SHIP'S CAPTAIN SAYING THE CUSTOMARY PRAYERS DURING A BURIAL AT SEA. WHEN THERE WERE DEATHS ON SHIPS COMING UP THE ST LAWRENCE, THE BODIES WERE KEPT ON BOARD UNTIL ARRIVAL AT GROSSE ÎLE. (DANIEL RAINVILLE, PARKS CANADA, 1997.)

It is more difficult to determine the exact number of burials at Grosse Île. However, the figure inscribed on the monument to physicians, i.e. 5424, seems to be the highest possible (Table 11). The problem stems mainly from the inaccuracy of the figures for deaths on quarantined ships, since it is hard to establish how many bodies were actually taken ashore for burial in the island's cemetery.

Based on the statistics furnished by medical superintendent Douglas between December 1847 and February 1848, a total of 4294 people were buried on Grosse Île in 1847: 3452 died on the island and 842 on quarantined ships. According to the data for individual vessels, derived from the list of ships that were inspected at Grosse Île and the list of those that arrived in Québec City, 3501 people died in the island's hospitals and 1190 on quarantined vessels, for a total of 4691 burials.

Number of Sick Employees

For the time being, it is difficult to determine exactly how many people worked on Grosse Île at different times during the season. Based on certain data, we know that 13 physicians assisted Dr. Douglas in late June and that the medical personnel, comprising hospital stewards, nurses and orderlies, totalled 77. Obviously, this does not take into account the many other employees assigned to various tasks, such as police officers, cooks, carters, sailors and domestics.

Station personnel also included soldiers, civilian Commissariat employees, and emigration and customs office staff. Sutlers[2] and their employees were present as well, not to mention contractors and the many workers involved in the intense construction activity of 1847. Lastly, we must not forget the many Anglican and Roman Catholic clergy who took turns providing spiritual assistance to the emigrants, a service that was highly appreciated, particularly by the Irish.

According to a record of illness among Grosse Île personnel, 320 employees fell ill in 1847 (Table 12). However, this is probably only a very small proportion of the total number of people who worked at the quarantine station that year. Although most were likely recruited in the Québec City region, many were also hired among the emigrants themselves.

An Expensive Season

The operation of the quarantine station entailed a total investment of £ 45 342.14 in 1847, nearly 27 percent of the colony's total emigration expenditures for the year (Table 13). Obviously, expenditures related to running the hospitals and the sheds for convalescent and healthy emigrants accounted for a large share, i.e. around 46 percent.

To a large extent, it was in 1847 that Grosse Île's emigrant reception infrastructure was developed. While at the beginning of the season, the station was able to accommodate 200 sick and convalescent patients and 800 people under medical observation, by the end of the summer, it had room for 2000 sick people, 300 convalescents and 3500 healthy people.

---

2. Persons responsible for supplying food and beverages.

This is the general sequence of events that we have been able to establish using the documents found thus far. They will be presented in much more detail in the following pages, which focus not only on the major events at Grosse Île in 1847 but also on the ordinary day-to-day activities of that very unusual season. We must reiterate that since this book is not a critical analysis, it would be futile to seek comprehensive questions and definite answers in it. The sole objective of our research over the past few years has been to establish, once and for all, what really happened during the six-month period that has inspired so many legends. We hope, therefore, that readers will approach our work from this perspective alone.

Regardless of the very grim statistics for 1847, particularly with respect to sickness and death among both emigrants and station employees, and despite errors, indecision, haste and even attempts by certain individuals to profit from the situation, the Grosse Île quarantine station witnessed outstanding humanitarian efforts by men and women who strove to relieve suffering of an extent that defies the imagination.

Table 1
DEPARTURES FOR THE PORT OF QUÉBEC

Country*	No. of ships	Cabin passengers	Steerage passengers				Infants aged 0 - 1**	Total
			Adults		Children aged 1 - 14			
			M	F	M	F		
England	140	217	12101	8692	4927	4585	2349	32871
Ireland	224	295	19082	16037	8432	7817	2869	54532
Scotland	42	175	1195	996	636	562	163	3727
Germany	36	9	3449	2003	899	933	226	7519
TOTAL	442	696	35827	27728	14894	13897	5607	98649

March 31, 1848

* This table identifies the location of ports of departure and not emigrants' country of origin.
** Since infants travelled free of charge, they were counted separately.

Table 2
BIRTHS AND DEATHS DURING THE CROSSING AND IN QUARANTINE

Country*	Deaths during crossing						Deaths in quarantine						Births		
	Adults		Children aged 1 - 14		Infants aged	Total	Adults		Children aged 1 - 14		Infants aged	Total			
	M	F	M	F	0 - 1		M	F	M	F	0 - 1		M	F	Total
England	556	397	667	541	351	2512	659	470	235	248	86	1698	31	33	64
Ireland	741	500	516	492	356	2605	719	471	211	187	71	1659	47	45	92
Scotland	14	7	17	15	16	69	10	6	7	4	4	31	0	1	1
Germany	18	10	23	21	24	96	0	1	0	0	0	1	7	8	15
TOTAL	1329	914	1223	1069	747	5282	1388	948	453	439	161	3389	85	87	172

March 31, 1848

* This table identifies the location of ports of departure and not emigrants' country of origin.

Table 3
ARRIVALS IN QUÉBEC CITY

Country*	Cabin passengers	Steerage passengers				Infants aged	Total
		Adults		Children aged 1 - 14		0 - 1 **	
		M	F	M	F		
England	217	10886	7825	4025	3796	1976	28725
Ireland	295	17622	15066	7705	7138	2534	50360
Scotland	175	1171	983	612	543	144	3628
Germany	9	3431	1992	876	912	217	7437
TOTAL	696	33110	25866	13218	12389	4871	90150

March 31, 1848

* This table identifies the location of ports of departure and not emigrants' country of origin.
** Since infants travelled free of charge, they were counted separately.

Table 4
EMIGRATION THROUGH THE PORT OF QUÉBEC IN 1847

Departures	98649
Deaths during crossing	-5282
Deaths in quarantine	-3389
Births at sea or in quarantine	+172
TOTAL	90150

March 31, 1848

A VIEW OF THE QUARANTINE STATION FROM THE GUN BATTERY IN THE CENTRAL SECTOR. ON JUNE 4, 1847, THE GOVERNOR GENERAL OF CANADA PROMULGATED ADDITIONAL QUARANTINE REGULATIONS WHICH, IN PARTICULAR, AUTHORIZED THE MILITARY ON GROSSE ÎLE TO USE ANY MEANS NECESSARY, INCLUDING FORCE, TO ENSURE THAT SHIPS COMPLIED WITH QUARANTINE MEASURES. (WATERCOLOUR BY H. PERCY, BEFORE 1850. NAC, C-13656).

BARRACKS IN THE CENTRAL PART OF THE ISLAND. THE ARMY WAS CALLED UPON THAT SUMMER TO SUPPLY TENTS FOR THE EMIGRANTS ON GROSSE ÎLE, TO ERECT THESE CANVAS SHELTERS, TO MAINTAIN ORDER AT THE STATION AND TO ENFORCE THE QUARANTINE REGULATIONS. (HENRI DELATTRE, 1850. NAC, C-120285).

Table 5
SICKNESS AND DEATH RATES BY PORT OF DEPARTURE IN 1847

Port	Country	No. of ships	Total passengers	Average No. of passengers per ship	Average No. of sick on arrival	Average No of deaths at sea per ship
Aberdeen	Scotland	4	372	93	0	0
Aberystwyth	Wales	1	243	243	0	1
Ballyshannon	Ireland	1	66	66	0	0
Belfast	Ireland	21	6913	329.19	10.05	6.67
Benicarló	Spain	1	3	3	0	0
Bideford	England	2	19	9.50	0	0
Bremen	Germany	24	5433	226.38	0.08	2.21
Bremerhaven	Germany	2	531	265.50	1	3
Bridgwater	England	1	55	55	0	0
Bristol	England	5	157	31.40	0	0
Cardiff	Wales	2	9	4.5	0	0
Chepstow	England	1	1	1	0	0
Cork	Ireland	33	10322	312.79	50.27	26.91
Donegal	Ireland	5	836	167.20	0.20	3
Dublin	Ireland	27	6568	243.26	18.78	8.93
Dundee	Scotland	2	72	36	0	0
Falmouth	England	2	319	159.5	0	0
Galway	Ireland	4	749	187.25	9.50	3.50
Glasgow	Scotland	30	2019	67.30	2.73	2.03
Greenock	Scotland	5	1142	228.40	12.20	1.80
Hamburg	Germany	10	1646	164.60	0.90	3.30
Hull	England	4	350	87.50	0	0.25
Killala	Ireland	5	1388	277.60	19.60	6.60
Kilrush	Ireland	1	119	119	0	0
Limerick	Ireland	50	9174	183.48	3.96	4.22
Liverpool	England	72	27039	375.54	43.44	25.76
Loch Saxford	Scotland	1	279	279	0	0
London	England	19	1985	104.47	0.32	1.68
Londonderry	Ireland	11	3526	320.55	18.36	5.64
Maryport	England	2	31	15.50	0	0
Milford	Wales	1	32	32	0	0
New Ross	Ireland	15	4395	293	16.07	7.80
Newport	England	1	364	364	43	5
Newry	Ireland	5	1502	300.40	3.20	4.20
Padstow	England	3	684	228	0	0.67
Penzance	England	1	66	66	0	0
Plymouth	England	7	1025	146.43	0	0.43
Poole	England	2	10	5	0	0
Saint Helier	Jersey	1	19	19	0	0
Saint Ives	England	2	66	33	0	0
Sligo	Ireland	26	5732	220.46	14.85	14.23
Southampton	England	2	252	126	0	0
Stockton	England	2	7	3.50	0	0
Sunderland	England	2	7	3.50	0	0
Torquay	England	2	13	6.50	0	0
Waterford	Ireland	14	3050	217.86	4.64	2.64
Westport	Ireland	2	74	37	0	0.50
Weymouth	England	1	4	4	0	0
Whitehaven	England	1	2	2	0	0
Youghal	Ireland	3	318	106	1.33	0.67

Table 6
EMIGRANTS HOSPITALIZED IN 1847

Quarantine station	8691
Québec City (Marine and Emigrant Hospital, as at January 1, 1848)	3313
Montréal (Point St. Charles Hospital)	13189
Saint-Jean (Québec)	172
Lachine	342
Toronto (Emigrant Hospital, as at February 2, 1848)	4355
Various cities in Upper Canada	12478
TOTAL PATIENTS	42540

March 31, 1848

Table 7
COMPARISON OF HOSPITALIZATION, SICKNESS AND DEATH RATES
AT GROSSE ÎLE IN 1846 AND 1847

Year	Total arrivals	Patients admitted to hospital	% of total arrivals	Deaths	% of total admissions	Cholera	%	Typhus and dysentery	%	Smallpox	%	Other diseases	%
1847	98106	8691	8.86	3238	37.26	0	0	8574	8.74	92	0.09	25	0.03
1846	32753	892	2.72	66	7.40	0	0	613	1.87	106	0.32	173	0.53

December 27, 1847

Table 8
HOSPITALIZATION, SICKNESS AND DEATH RATES AT GROSSE ÎLE IN 1847

Emigrants	Patients admitted to hospital	Patients discharged	Deaths	Typhus and dysentery	Smallpox	Other diseases*
Men	3534	2173	1361	3515	15	4
Women	2763	1794	969	2730	20	13
Children	2394	1486	908	2329	57	8
TOTAL	8691	5453	3238	8574	92	25

December 27, 1848

* On account of the prevalence of typhus and dysentery, it was necessary, according to Dr. Douglas, to limit as much as possible the number of patients admitted to hospital for smallpox and "other diseases."

Table 9
DEATHS AMONG EMIGRANTS ARRIVING THROUGH THE PORT OF QUÉBEC IN 1847

In quarantine on Grosse Île	3452
On ships during crossing and in quarantine	5293*
At the Marine and Emigrant Hospital in Québec City	1041
At the Point St. Charles Hospital in Montréal (as at January 1, 1848)	3579
In Saint-Jean (Québec)	71
In Lachine	130
At the Emigrant Hospital in Toronto (as at February 2, 1848)	863
In various cities in Upper Canada	3048
GRAND TOTAL	17477

December 1847 and March 1848

* Includes 842 deaths on quarantined ships. The bodies were buried in the cemetery on Grosse Île.

Table 10
WEEKLY BREAKDOWN OF DEATHS AT GROSSE ÎLE IN 1847

Week	No. of deaths
May 8 - 15	1
May 16 - 22	16
May 23 - 29	71
May 30 - June 5	119
June 6 - 12	154
June 13 - 19	202
June 20 - 26	156
June 27 - July 3	144
July 4 - 10	165
July 11 - 17	171
July 18 - 24	197
July 25 - 31	188
August 1 - 7	220
August 8 - 14	322
August 15 - 21	288
August 22 - 28	256
August 29 - September 4	191
September 5 - 11	143
September 12 - 18	133
September 19 - 25	121
September 26 - October 2	86
October 3 - 9	61
October 10 - 16	33
October 17 - 23	14
TOTAL	3452*

October 1847

* Includes 3238 deaths recorded in hospital and 214 others in the "healthy" camp at the east end of the island.

Table 11
BURIALS AT GROSSE ÎLE IN 1847

Sources	Deaths on Grosse Île	Deaths on quarantined ships	Total
Statistics published in the *Quebec Morning Chronicle* on October 28, 1847	3452	1282	4734
Statistical data provided by Douglas (December 1847 - February 1848)	3452	842	4294
List annexed to 1897 hospital admissions register	3226*	2198**	5424
Figure on commemorative monument in Grosse Île cemetery			5424
Cumulative data for each ship	3501	1190	4691

* Includes only deaths that occurred in hospital.
** Includes deaths that occurred on quarantined ships or as emigrants were taken ashore (i.e. prior to registration in hospital).

Table 12
HOSPITALIZATION, SICKNESS AND DEATH RATES AMONG
QUARANTINE STATION PERSONNEL AND CLERGY IN 1847

Occupation	Admitted to hospital	Suffering from typhus	Deaths
Roman Catholic priests	42	19	4
Anglican missionaries	17	7	2
Physicians	26	22	4
Hospital stewards	29	21	3
Nurses, orderlies, cooks	186*	76	22
Police officers	10	8	3
Carters employed to transport the sick, dead and dying	6	5	2
Clerks, bakers and domestics of Mr. Ray, a sutler	0	15	3
Clerks, bakers and domestics of Mr. Bradford, a storekeeper	0	4	1
Deputy emigration agent	1	1	0
Clerk of deputy emigration agent	1	1	0
Customs officers in charge of inspecting baggage	2	1	0
TOTAL	320	180	44

December 1847

* Several nurses, orderlies and cooks were emigrants, who were employed after recovering from typhus. They were thought to be immunized.

Table 13
TOTAL EXPENDITURES AT THE GROSSE ÎLE QUARANTINE STATION IN 1847

Construction of hospitals, sheds and other buildings	£ 10682.19.11
Hospital operating expenses, salaries and wages of medical personnel, cost of medicine and other supplies	£ 21019.14.3
Food and other provisions for destitute emigrants	£ 3117.9.4
Expenditures related to the medical commission appointed to inquire into the situation at Grosse Île	£ 130.0.0
Maintenance expenses for Roman Catholic and Anglican clergy and their missions on Grosse Île	£ 1270.15.10
Cost of transportation from Grosse Île	£ 9121.14.8
TOTAL	£ 45342.14.0

March 1848

MAP OF IRELAND AND THE BRITISH ISLES

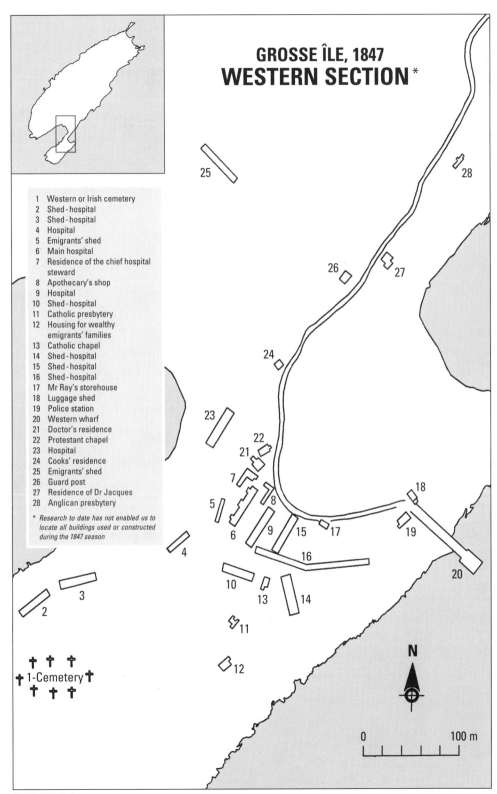

GROSSE ÎLE, 1847
WESTERN SECTION *

1 Western or Irish cemetery
2 Shed-hospital
3 Shed-hospital
4 Hospital
5 Emigrants' shed
6 Main hospital
7 Residence of the chief hospital steward
8 Apothecary's shop
9 Hospital
10 Shed-hospital
11 Catholic presbytery
12 Housing for wealthy emigrants' families
13 Catholic chapel
14 Shed-hospital
15 Shed-hospital
16 Shed-hospital
17 Mr Ray's storehouse
18 Luggage shed
19 Police station
20 Western wharf
21 Doctor's residence
22 Protestant chapel
23 Hospital
24 Cooks' residence
25 Emigrants' shed
26 Guard post
27 Residence of Dr Jacques
28 Anglican presbytery

* Research to date has not enabled us to locate all buildings used or constructed during the 1847 season

1-Cemetery

N

0   100 m

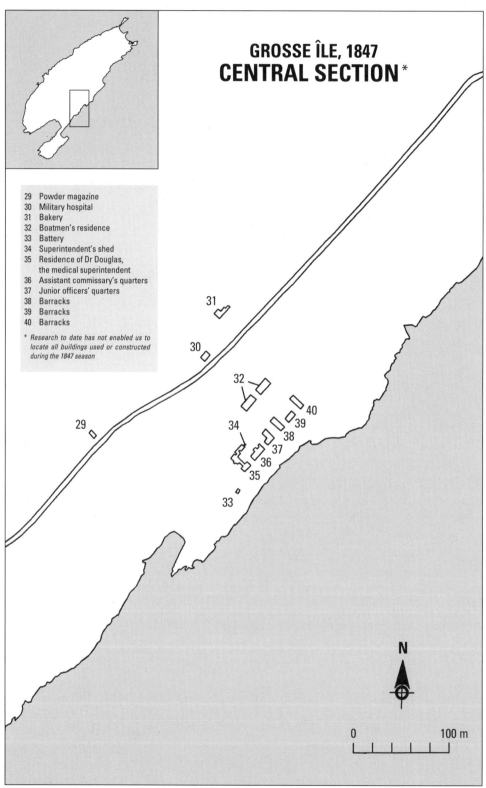

GROSSE ÎLE, 1847
CENTRAL SECTION *

29 Powder magazine
30 Military hospital
31 Bakery
32 Boatmen's residence
33 Battery
34 Superintendent's shed
35 Residence of Dr Douglas,
   the medical superintendent
36 Assistant commissary's quarters
37 Junior officers' quarters
38 Barracks
39 Barracks
40 Barracks

* Research to date has not enabled us to
  locate all buildings used or constructed
  during the 1847 season

N

0   100 m

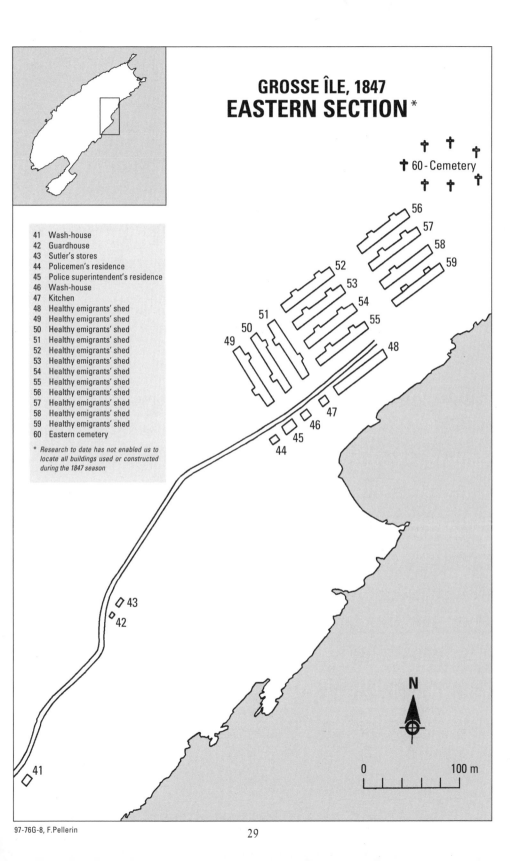

GROSSE ÎLE, 1847
EASTERN SECTION *

† 60 - Cemetery

56
57
58
59
52
53
54
55
48
51
50
49

41 Wash-house
42 Guardhouse
43 Sutler's stores
44 Policemen's residence
45 Police superintendent's residence
46 Wash-house
47 Kitchen
48 Healthy emigrants' shed
49 Healthy emigrants' shed
50 Healthy emigrants' shed
51 Healthy emigrants' shed
52 Healthy emigrants' shed
53 Healthy emigrants' shed
54 Healthy emigrants' shed
55 Healthy emigrants' shed
56 Healthy emigrants' shed
57 Healthy emigrants' shed
58 Healthy emigrants' shed
59 Healthy emigrants' shed
60 Eastern cemetery

* Research to date has not enabled us to
  locate all buildings used or constructed
  during the 1847 season

47
46
45
44

43
42

N

41

0   100 m

JANUARY

S	M	T	W	T	F	S
					1	2
3	4	5	6	7	8	9
10	11	12	13	14	15	16
17	18	19	20	21	22	23
24	25	26	27	28	29	30
31						

FEBRUARY

S	M	T	W	T	F	S
	1	2	3	4	5	6
7	8	9	10	11	12	13
14	15	16	17	18	19	20
21	22	23	24	25	26	27
28						

MARCH

S	M	T	W	T	F	S
	1	2	3	4	5	6
7	8	9	10	11	12	13
14	15	16	17	18	19	20
21	22	23	24	25	26	27
28	29	30	31			

APRIL

S	M	T	W	T	F	S
				1	2	3
4	5	6	7	8	9	10
11	12	13	14	15	16	17
18	19	20	21	22	23	24
25	26	27	28	29	30	

MAY

S	M	T	W	T	F	S
						1
2	3	4	5	6	7	8
9	10	11	12	13	14	15
16	17	18	19	20	21	22
23	24	25	26	27	28	29
30	31					

JUNE

S	M	T	W	T	F	S
		1	2	3	4	5
6	7	8	9	10	11	12
13	14	15	16	17	18	19
20	21	22	23	24	25	26
27	28	29	30			

JULY

S	M	T	W	T	F	S
				1	2	3
4	5	6	7	8	9	10
11	12	13	14	15	16	17
18	19	20	21	22	23	24
25	26	27	28	29	30	31

AUGUST

S	M	T	W	T	F	S
1	2	3	4	5	6	7
8	9	10	11	12	13	14
15	16	17	18	19	20	21
22	23	24	25	26	27	28
29	30	31				

SEPTEMBER

S	M	T	W	T	F	S
			1	2	3	4
5	6	7	8	9	10	11
12	13	14	15	16	17	18
19	20	21	22	23	24	25
26	27	28	29	30		

OCTOBER

S	M	T	W	T	F	S
					1	2
3	4	5	6	7	8	9
10	11	12	13	14	15	16
17	18	19	20	21	22	23
24	25	26	27	28	29	30
31						

NOVEMBER

S	M	T	W	T	F	S
	1	2	3	4	5	6
7	8	9	10	11	12	13
14	15	16	17	18	19	20
21	22	23	24	25	26	27
28	29	30				

DECEMBER

S	M	T	W	T	F	S
			1	2	3	4
5	6	7	8	9	10	11
12	13	14	15	16	17	18
19	20	21	22	23	24	25
26	27	28	29	30	31	

1847

FEBRUARY

S	M	T	W	T	F	S
		1	2	3	4	5	6
7	8	9	10	11	12	13
14	15	16	17	18	19	20
21	22	23	24	25	26	27
28						

33

FRIDAY,
FEBRUARY 19, 1847

Dr. George M. Douglas, medical superintendent of the Grosse Île quarantine station, began to prepare for the coming navigation season. All reports indicated that the season would witness a large influx of emigrants and an increase in the number of sick people needing accommodation on the island. Therefore, Douglas asked the Governor General to announce quarantine regulations and to organize the inspection and detention centre on Grosse Île without delay. The medical superintendent reminded the Governor General that numerous sick and dying emigrants had arrived in Canada in 1832, a year after the failure of harvests in Ireland.

Douglas anticipated another, but much larger, influx of sick and dying emigrants in 1847, given the famine that had been ravaging Ireland for some time. He noted that an even greater number of poor and needy would land on Canadian shores owing to the measures taken by the Americans to prevent emigrants from disembarking in U.S. ports. In his opinion, appropriations of at least £ 3000 would have to be earmarked for quarantine expenditures in 1847.

Dr. Douglas requested permission to invite tenders for steamer service between Grosse Île and Québec City. In addition, he sought authorization to hire a managing director, or "steward," for the hospital at 3s. 6p. a day. About two years earlier, when there were not very many patients in hospital, the medical superintendent had entrusted the duties of apothecary and steward to a single person. For the past year, however, the apothecary had been required to devote all his time and energy to preparing medicine and administering it to the sick (See Executive Council committee's recommendation of March 8.)

1847

MARCH

S	M	T	W	T	F	S
		1	2	3	4	5	6
7	8	9	10	11	12	13
14	15	16	17	18	19	20
21	22	23	24	25	26	27
28	29	30	31			

MONDAY,
MARCH 8, 1847

An Executive Council committee, which was responsible for advising the Governor General on administrative decisions, recommended the approval of the requests made by Douglas on February 19 regarding the announcement of quarantine regulations and the implementation of measures for opening the Grosse Île quarantine station. The committee specified, however, that no expenditures should be incurred for hiring a hospital steward unless absolutely necessary. (The Governor General ratified this decision on March 10.)

The medical superintendent requested additional wages for the months of April, November and December of each year. Previously, he had been remunerated for his services at Grosse Île for only part of the year, i.e. from May to October, or during the navigation season. Dr. Douglas pointed out that, in April, he hired police officers, boatmen and nurses, looked after supplies, chartered a steamer and so forth, while in November and December, he paid employees' wages, closed the books for the season and wrote an annual report. He could not carry out other professional duties during those periods. He also said that, on account of the health risks associated with his work and to provide for the material needs of his family, he had to take out a life insurance policy of £ 1 000, whose premiums cost him 20 percent of his annual salary. In addition, he had to have a house in Québec City. Lastly, Douglas stressed that, for the past seven years, he had been performing single-handed the duties previously entrusted to five people. (See answer of March 30.)

THURSDAY,
MARCH 11, 1847

Public Works commissioners approved work that Dr. Douglas had said was necessary at Grosse Île, notably, the completion of the wharf. They requested that the sum of £ 250 be placed at his disposal, and entrusted him with supervising and approving the work. (On March 24, the Executive Council committee recommended that this expenditure be authorized.)

WEDNESDAY,
MARCH 17, 1847

Tenders were invited for a steamer to make one trip per week between Québec City and Grosse Île. The deadline for receiving bids was April 10.

SATURDAY,
MARCH 27, 1847

It was officially announced that quarantine regulations would be enforced for the next eight months. These regulations identified the location of the quarantine facility and specified which ships would have to stop there. They also established quarantine procedures at Grosse Île and in Québec City, and defined the roles and responsibilities of the personnel involved, including the medical superintendent, the harbour master for the port of Québec, the boarding officer and the police. In addition, the regulations included certain provisions pertaining to merchants, sutlers and grocers working on the island, outlined the responsibilities of pilots and passengers and established ship disinfection procedures. Additional regulations were announced on June 4.

A hurricane destroyed a section of the wharf under construction in the western part of Grosse Île. The news was related by William Patton, the person responsible for building the wharf.

TUESDAY,
MARCH 30, 1847

A report by the Executive Council committee, approved by the Governor General, recommended that medical superintendent Douglas, who received £ 50 per month in summer, also be paid a salary for April, November and December, when he wrapped up the activities of the past season and prepared for those of the next.

1847

APRIL

S	M	T	W	T	F	S
				1	2	3
4	5	6	7	8	9	10
11	12	13	14	15	16	17
18	19	20	21	22	23	24
25	26	27	28	29	30	

THURSDAY,
APRIL 15, 1847

A tender offering the services of the steamer *St. George*, submitted by W. Stevenson, was accepted. This boat would provide transportation between Grosse Île and Québec City when the quarantine station was open, at a cost of £ 17 10s. per trip, or £ 449 for the entire season. In addition, in accordance with the wish expressed by Dr. Douglas and Dr. Parant, inspecting physician for the port of Québec, a sailing ship would be chartered for no more than £ 50 for the season.

FRIDAY,
APRIL 23, 1847

A reader of the *Canadien* sent a letter to the editor about the anticipated arrival of emigrants in 1847. Signing himself simply "A Citizen," he reminded the editor that Ireland and Scotland would be casting their starving and dying on our shores within a few weeks. He said that a serious crisis was imminent and wondered who was going to deal with it. According to recent reports, the number of emigrants would be three, if not four, times higher than in previous years. What would become of Québec City and Montréal, he asked, if as was probably the case, these newcomers brought the germs of contagious diseases with them? Steps had to be taken to avoid a repetition of the disaster of 1832; otherwise, unfortunate emigrants would be dying on the wharves and in the streets again.

The reader proposed six measures that might avert another human catastrophe:

1. All emigrants, whether they were sick or not, should be required to disembark at Grosse Île and stay there for eight days.

2. The emigration agent should have his office at Grosse Île in 1847.

3. Emigrants headed for western Canada or the United States should not be allowed to land in Québec City or Montréal, but should be picked up by steamer at Grosse Île and taken to the Lachine Canal.

4. All emigrants who insisted on disembarking in Québec City or Montréal should be forewarned that they would not be allowed to deal with the emigration agent.

5. The government should be prepared to erect temporary shelters, or "sheds," for 10 000 to 20 000 emigrants on Grosse Île, if necessary. Although there was no need to incur such expenditures or even to buy the necessary materials beforehand, steps should be taken to find out where workers, planks, beams, nails and so forth could be obtained within the space of 24 hours.

6. If a large number of emigrants arrived at Grosse Île, a medical assistant should be sent to the island to ensure that no one suffering from a contagious illness boarded ships for Québec City or Montréal, or even left Grosse Île.

THURSDAY,
APRIL 29, 1847

The civil secretary informed Dr. Parant and Father Charles-Félix Cazeau, secretary of the archdiocese, that a Catholic missionary would be posted to Grosse Île again in 1847.

FRIDAY,
APRIL 30, 1847

Dr. Parant and Dr. Douglas signed an agreement, on behalf of the government, chartering the steamboat *St. George* for one trip per week between Québec City and Grosse Île from March 1 to October 31. Under the agreement, which was concluded before Archibald Campbell, a Québec City notary, the steamer could be used for transporting passengers, merchandise and provisions.

1847

MAY

S	M	T	W	T	F	S
						1
2	3	4	5	6	7	8
9	10	11	12	13	14	15
16	17	18	19	20	21	22
23	24	25	26	27	28	29
30	31					

MONDAY,
MAY 3, 1847

Medical superintendent G. M. Douglas arrived at the quarantine station aboard the *St. George* accompanied by nurses, boatmen and police officers. They immediately began to prepare the hospital for receiving patients, to whitewash the buildings and to ready the boats for visiting the ships that would soon come up the St. Lawrence.

Dr. Douglas hired four policemen (one sergeant and three subordinates) to work on the island until October 31, 1847. They were responsible for providing 24-hour service and were prohibited from drinking spirits or wine. They also had to perform certain tasks, such as whitewashing buildings, chopping wood, maintaining roads and so forth.

TUESDAY,
MAY 4, 1847

The Archbishop of Québec, Joseph Signay, placed a Catholic missionary, Father Bernard McGauran, in charge of the Catholics staying on Grosse Île and all those obliged to stop there under the Quarantine Act. In accordance with an agreement between the Archbishop and the civil authorities, Father McGauran could, when necessary, use the steamer or any other boat to travel between Québec City and Grosse Île.

SUNDAY,
MAY 9, 1847

SHIPS ARRIVING IN QUÉBEC CITY WITHOUT A STOP-OVER AT GROSSE ÎLE

Name of ship	Port of departure	Passengers	
		Steerage	Cabin
Cambria	Glasgow (Scotland)	0	19
Coeur-de-Lion	Liverpool (England)	0	3
TOTAL		0	22

MONDAY,
MAY 10, 1847

Douglas mentioned that several structures needed repairs: the hospital kitchen, the wash house, the head nurse's room, the hospital wards and the passengers' sheds. Another room also had to be built for the hospital steward and his wife.

THURSDAY,
MAY 13, 1847

SHIPS ARRIVING IN QUÉBEC CITY WITHOUT A STOP-OVER AT GROSSE ÎLE

Name of ship	Port of departure	Passengers	
		Steerage	Cabin
Canada	Glasgow (Scotland)	0	3

FRIDAY,
MAY 14, 1847

SHIPS ARRIVING AT GROSSE ÎLE

Name of ship	Captain	Port of departure	Crossing time (in days)	Passengers		No. of sick on arrival	No. of deaths during crossing
				Steerage	Cabin		
Syria	M. B. Cox	Liverpool (England)	46	243	2	125	9

SHIPS ARRIVING IN QUÉBEC CITY WITHOUT A STOP-OVER AT GROSSE ÎLE

Name of ship	Port of departure	Passengers	
		Steerage	Cabin
Sophia Moffatt	London (England)	0	4

SATURDAY,
MAY 15, 1847

According to the *Journal de Québec*, the temporary sheds being erected on the India Wharf in Québec City, on the orders of emigration agent A. C. Buchanan, were arousing concern among the population.

There were 64 sick people at Grosse Île.

Catholic baptism of Owen Wood, born at sea on April 21 to Henry Wood, a pit sawyer, and Ann Duffy, from County Monaghan, Ireland. Father B. McGauran drew up the baptismal certificate.

According to a list published in the *Quebec Morning Chronicle*, one person had died at Grosse Île during the week of May 8 to 15.

SHIPS ARRIVING IN QUÉBEC CITY WITHOUT A STOP-OVER AT GROSSE ÎLE

Name of ship	Port of departure	Passengers	
		Steerage	Cabin
Ann	Liverpool (England)	0	3
Pearl	London (England)	11	0
TOTAL		11	3

NUMBER OF PEOPLE IN HOSPITAL ON GROSSE ÎLE DURING THE WEEK OF MAY 8 TO 15 *

Emigrants	Patients admitted	Deaths	New total
	(+)	(-)	
Men	20	0	20
Women	23	0	23
Children	22	1	21
TOTAL	65	1	64**

* Based on the first report of the season.

** All patients had typhus.

MONDAY, MAY 17, 1847

Faced with the arrival of an ever-increasing number of sick emigrants and passengers that would have to be placed under medical observation, Dr. Douglas requested, in the first of a series of weekly reports, that additional accommodations be erected. More precisely, he recommended the construction of a 100- by 25-foot hospital, with a capacity of 60 beds, and a 120- by 25-foot shed.

One burial was recorded in the register of the Catholic chapel.

SHIPS ARRIVING AT GROSSE ÎLE

Name of ship	Captain	Port of departure	Crossing time (in days)	Passengers		No. of sick on arrival	No. of deaths during crossing
				Steerage	Cabin		
Jane Black	T. Gorman	Limerick (Ireland)	46	425	1	20	13

TUESDAY, MAY 18, 1847

Catholic baptism of Mary Ryan, born May 5 to Edward Ryan, a labourer, and Harriett Pole, from County Tipperary, Ireland. Father B. McGauran drew up the baptismal certificate.

SHIPS ARRIVING AT GROSSE ÎLE

Name of ship	Captain	Port of departure	Crossing time (in days)	Passengers Steerage	Cabin	No. of sick on arrival	No. of deaths during crossing
Ocean Queen	R. Williams	Bristol (England)	46	82	1	0	0

SHIPS LEAVING GROSSE ÎLE FOR QUÉBEC CITY

Name of ship	Quarantine time (in days)	Deaths in Grosse Île hospitals	Deaths on quarantined ships
Ocean Queen	A few hours	1	0

SHIPS ARRIVING IN QUÉBEC CITY WITHOUT A STOP-OVER AT GROSSE ÎLE

Name of ship	Port of departure	Passengers Steerage	Cabin
Mahaica	Liverpool (England)	0	1
Sarah	Liverpool (England)	0	2
TOTAL		0	3

WEDNESDAY,
MAY 19, 1847

The Governor General approved Douglas' suggestion of building a hospital and an additional shed for an estimated cost of £ 150 and £ 135 respectively.

Four burials were recorded in the register of the Catholic chapel.

SHIPS ARRIVING AT GROSSE ÎLE

Name of ship	Captain	Port of departure	Crossing time (in days)	Passengers Steerage	Cabin	No. of sick on arrival	No. of deaths during crossing
Perseverance	H. Secas	Dublin (Ireland)	36	311	0	62	9
Wandsworth	G. Dunlop	Dublin (Ireland)	42	527	0	78	51
TOTAL				838	0	140	

SHIPS ARRIVING IN QUÉBEC CITY WITHOUT A STOP-OVER AT GROSSE ÎLE

Name of ship	Port of departure	Passengers Steerage	Cabin
Caledonia	Glasgow (Scotland)	15	0
Delia	Poole (England)	4	0
Rainbow	Southampton (England)	0	2
TOTAL		19	2

THURSDAY,
MAY 20, 1847

Two burials were recorded in the register of the Catholic chapel.

No more burials were recorded in this register until June 16.

SHIPS ARRIVING AT GROSSE ÎLE

Name of ship	Captain	Port of departure	Crossing time (in days)	Passengers Steerage	Cabin	No. of sick on arrival	No. of deaths during crossing
Glenswilly	T. Henderson	Glasgow (Scotland)	40	40	3	1	0

SHIPS LEAVING GROSSE ÎLE FOR QUÉBEC CITY

Name of ship	Quarantine time (in days)	Deaths in Grosse Île hospitals	Deaths on quarantined ships
Syria	6	40	0

FRIDAY,
MAY 21, 1847

Dr. Douglas informed the Governor General about the deplorable state of emigrants disembarking from the crowded vessels that had arrived since the beginning of the season. The hospitals were full of sick emigrants, including 212 from the *Syria*. Two hundred and sixteen others were still aboard four ships owing to a lack of room on land. The medical superintendent had barely been able to accommodate up to 200 patients the previous year. In view of the current and impending influx of emigrants, Douglas suggested that all the sheds for healthy passengers be converted temporarily into hospitals to house nearly 500 people. In addition, he requested permission to hire Dr. Jacques and Dr. McGrath, reputable, highly talented men, and to place them in charge of the new hospitals. A steward, a cook and four nurses would have to be assigned to the hospitals as well.

The medical superintendent said that, with the proposed arrangement, it would be impossible to lodge healthy passengers on Grosse Île. Instead, the former would have to remain on the ships, where a physician would visit them daily. Douglas would ensure that their clothes, personal effects and bedding were disinfected on board. He admitted that such procedures did not comply with the Quarantine Act, which stipulated that all passengers had to disembark at the island with their luggage. However, if he followed the law to the letter, he would have to accommodate 12 000 to 15 000 people on land. Dr. Douglas added that he could count temporarily on the assistance of Dr. John Benson, a passenger aboard the *Wandsworth* from Dublin, who had already worked in a "fever" hospital in Ireland.

Father McGauran, who was stationed at Grosse Île, informed the Archbishop of Québec, Joseph Signay, that Father John C. O'Grady wished to leave the island on account of his infirmities, which prevented him from being of help at the quarantine station. McGauran said that the death rate continued to rise: 52 people had been buried on May 20 and 59 on May 21. In addition, over 14 000 passengers were waiting on ships anchored off the station.

The *Canadien* announced the arrival of three vessels from Ireland, one of which reported over 40 deaths at sea. The newspaper also mentioned that 150 people, mostly Irish Catholics, were already hospitalized on Grosse Île. Another member of the Catholic clergy would have to go to the island to assist the chaplain, who was overworked.

Two burials were recorded in the register of the Protestant chapel.

SHIPS ARRIVING AT GROSSE ÎLE

Name of ship	Captain	Port of departure	Crossing time (in days)	Passengers Steerage	Cabin	No. of sick on arrival	No. of deaths during crossing
Agnes	T. McCawley	Cork (Ireland)	41	428	2	190	39
George	J. Simpson	Liverpool (England)	39	397	0	180	40
John Francis	H. Deaves	Cork (Ireland)	42	257	3	98	16
Royalist	T. [Burridge]	Liverpool (England)	28	437	0	12	26
Try Again	J. Barry	Cork (Ireland)	41	182	0	11	10
TOTAL				1701	5	491	

SHIPS LEAVING GROSSE ÎLE FOR QUÉBEC CITY

Name of ship	Quarantine time (in days)	Deaths in Grosse Île hospitals	Deaths on quarantined ships
Glenswilly	1	0	0

SHIPS ARRIVING IN QUÉBEC CITY WITHOUT A STOP-OVER AT GROSSE ÎLE

Name of ship	Port of departure	Passengers Steerage	Cabin
Colloony	Glasgow (Scotland)	0	6

SATURDAY, MAY 22, 1847

According to the *Quebec Mercury*, three more physicians were on their way to Grosse Île. The newspaper also reported that steamer service between Québec City and Grosse Île would soon be available twice a week.

Three burials were recorded in the register of the Protestant chapel.

According to a list published in the *Quebec Morning Chronicle*, 16 people had died at Grosse Île during the week of May 16 to 22.

SHIPS ARRIVING AT GROSSE ÎLE

Name of ship	Captain	Port of departure	Crossing time (in days)	Passengers Steerage	Cabin	No. of sick on arrival	No. of deaths during crossing
Celeste	D. Mulhay	Limerick (Ireland)	39	199	0	0	1
Douglas	J. Douglas	London (England)	47	32	15	0	0
Dunbrody	J. Baldwin	New Ross (Ireland)	40	307	5	6	5
Earl Powis	W. Walker	Dundee (Scotland)	49	43	9	0	0
Ellen Thompson	J. Grays	Londonderry (Ireland)	36	371	0	0	4
Fergus	R. Martin	Hull (England)	43	131	0	0	0
Ganges	T. Dron	Cork (Ireland)	41	411	1	24	4
Jane	R. Dunn	Limerick (Ireland)	49	200	1	0	1
Jessie	H. McGee	Sligo (Ireland)	28	243	0	4	6
Lady Seaton	W. Morrison	London (England)	52	20	1	0	0
Lord Seaton	W. Talbot	Belfast (Ireland)	41	299	2	46	20
Scotland	W. Thompson	Cork (Ireland)	40	564	0	160	60
Tottenham	E. Evans	Youghal (Ireland)	47	228	0	4	2
Urania	R. Mills	Cork (Ireland)	44	199	1	55	11
Wallace	R. Morton	Liverpool (England)	31	417	0	0	4
TOTAL				3664	35	299	

SHIPS LEAVING GROSSE ÎLE FOR QUÉBEC CITY

Name of ship	Quarantine time (in days)	Deaths in Grosse Île hospitals	Deaths on quarantined ships
Earl Powis	A few hours	0	0
Fergus	A few hours	0	0
Jane Black	5	6	0

SHIPS ARRIVING IN QUÉBEC CITY WITHOUT A STOP-OVER AT GROSSE ÎLE

Name of ship	Port of departure	Passengers Steerage	Cabin
Bellona	Glasgow (Scotland)	10	0
Mersey	Torquay (England)	5	0
TOTAL		15	0

An April 1847 flyer announcing the sailing of the *Jane* from Ireland for Québec City. The ship arrived at Grosse Île on May 22 carrying 201 passengers, all healthy. Only one death had occurred during the crossing. The *Jane* reached the port of Québec on May 23. (In Liam Kelly et al., *Blennerville, Gateway to Tralee's Past*, Training & Employment Authority, Tralee, Co. Kerry, Ireland, 1989, p. 148.)

NUMBER OF PEOPLE IN HOSPITAL ON GROSSE ÎLE DURING THE WEEK OF MAY 16 TO 22

Emigrants	Patients hospitalized as at last report	Patients admitted (+)	Patients discharged (-)	Deaths (-)	New total
Men	20	135	0	4	151
Women	23	128	7	3	141
Children	21	106	6	9	112
TOTAL	64	369	13	16	404*

* All 404 patients had typhus.

SUNDAY,
MAY 23, 1847

Anglican baptism of Edward Andrews, born April 28 to Vincent Andrews, a "surgeryman" at Grosse Île, and Mary Anne Holloway. The Reverend Armine W. Mountain drew up the baptismal certificate.

Five burials were recorded in the register of the Protestant chapel.

SHIPS ARRIVING AT GROSSE ÎLE

Name of ship	Captain	Port of departure	Crossing time (in days)	Passengers Steerage	Cabin	No. of sick on arrival	No. of deaths during crossing
Aberdeen	M. McGrath	Liverpool (England)	23	411	0	65	9
Constitution	R. Neil	Belfast (Ireland)	33	394	0	15	6
TOTAL				805	0	80	

SHIPS LEAVING GROSSE ÎLE FOR QUÉBEC CITY

Name of ship	Quarantine time (in days)	Deaths in Grosse Île hospitals	Deaths on quarantined ships
Celeste	1	0	0
Jane	1	0	0
Lady Seaton	A few hours	0	0
Perseverance	4	10	0

SHIPS ARRIVING IN QUÉBEC CITY WITHOUT A STOP-OVER AT GROSSE ÎLE

Name of ship	Port of departure	Passengers Steerage	Cabin
Marchioness of Queensbury	Glasgow (Scotland)	11	3
Victoria	Saint Ives (England)	19	3
TOTAL		30	6

MONDAY,
MAY 24, 1847

In his weekly report, Dr. Douglas mentioned that he had hired two medical assistants, Dr. Jacques and Dr. McGrath, but that he needed at least two more. The newly recruited assistants were already caring for over 300 sick people and would not be able to look after the many emigrants about to arrive at Grosse Île or still waiting to disembark. Douglas declared that he was fully occupied with inspecting incoming vessels, identifying sick passengers and caring for those who could not be taken ashore.

The civil secretary, Major T. E. Campbell, asked the military secretary to immediately provide tents and other camping equipment for the many sick emigrants who would soon land at Grosse Île. Specifying that 10 000 people would have to be accommodated, Campbell requested as many hospital tents and large tents as possible. He also asked that a detachment of troops be sent to erect and look after these installations.

DETAIL OF ARMY QUARTERS IN THE CENTRE OF THE ISLAND.
(JOHN F. COMER, 1849. COLLECTION OF THE AGNES ETHERINGTON
ART CENTER, QUEEN'S UNIVERSITY, KINGSTON, ONTARIO).

THE BATTERY OVERLOOKING THE
QUARANTINE PASS. APPARENTLY,
THE MILITARY MADE NO USE OF THESE
GUNS IN ENFORCING THE QUARANTINE
REGULATIONS IN 1847, IN SPITE OF
ORDERS THAT AUTHORIZED THEM TO
DO SO. (JOHN F. COMER, 1849.
COLLECTION OF THE AGNES
ETHERINGTON ART CENTRE, QUEEN'S
UNIVERSITY, KINGSTON, ONTARIO).

DETAIL OF ARMY QUARTERS IN THE CENTRE OF THE ISLAND.
(JOHN F. COMER, 1849. COLLECTION OF THE AGNES ETHERINGTON
ART CENTER, QUEEN'S UNIVERSITY, KINGSTON, ONTARIO).

A FRANTIC SCENE ON WATERLOO DOCKS, LIVERPOOL, AS EMIGRANTS BOARD A SHIP. EMIGRANTS, PARTICULARLY THOSE ARRIVING FROM IRELAND, WERE OFTEN BILKED ON THE LIVERPOOL DOCKS BY UNSCRUPULOUS TICKET VENDORS IN THE PAY OF SHIP BROKERS. (*ILLUSTRATED LONDON NEWS*, JULY 6, 1850, McGILL UNIVERSITY, McLELLAN LIBRARY.)

Medical superintendent Douglas reported that there had never been such an influx of sick, wretched emigrants into this country, even during the cholera outbreaks of 1832 and 1834. All ships with Irish passengers, especially those from Liverpool and Cork, had large numbers of sick on board and reported a deplorable number of deaths from typhus and dysentery. Seventeen vessels loaded with Irish emigrants had recently arrived at Grosse Île: five were from Cork, four from Liverpool and the remainder from Sligo, Limerick, Belfast, Londonderry and New Ross.

Of the 5 607 passengers who had embarked on these vessels, 260 had perished during the crossing and over 700 had been hospitalized on Grosse Île or treated on board ship until hospital beds became available on land. According to the weekly report from the quarantine station, 695 people were currently in hospital on the island and 164 were receiving care on four vessels. The latter would be brought ashore as soon as the sheds for healthy passengers were converted into hospitals.

At the request of Dr. Parant, inspecting physician for the port of Québec, the Executive Council authorized the *St. George* to make two trips to Grosse Île per week, instead of only one as previously.

In response to requests by Dr. Douglas and emigration agent Buchanan, the Executive Council committee recommended that the government

EMIGRANTS' SHED MADE INTO A HOSPITAL IN THE WESTERN PART OF THE QUARANTINE STATION (D. A. MCLAUGHLIN, CA. 1905. NAC, PA-135716.)

erect more buildings and accommodations on the island. It also approved the hiring of additional personnel.

Father McGauran informed Archbishop Signay of the dreadful situation on Grosse Île. He reported that 700 people were in hospital and that Douglas did not want any more passengers to land owing to lack of room. Since the medical superintendent obliged captains to keep the sick on board, the 32 vessels waiting offshore had become floating hospitals, where the sick and the healthy were crowded together and everyone eventually fell ill. McGauran wrote that Douglas should be forced to pitch tents on his farm so that at least healthy emigrants could come ashore. The situation was extremely wearing for the Catholic priests. Of the 700 patients in hospital, only 40 were Protestant.

According to McGauran, the station needed a priest for each ship. While the clergymen visited the vessels, emigrants died in hospital without the last rites; he himself had spent five hours that day in the hold of a ship administering the last rites to 100 people. McGauran added that people in need of spiritual assistance were encountered everywhere; some even lay dying on rocks or on the beach, where they had been left by sailors, who could not keep up with the numbers they had to carry to hospital. The first ship had arrived at Grosse Île only 10 days earlier and, already, 135 people were dead. McGauran reported that 28 people had been buried on May 23 and as many on May 24.

Two burials were recorded in the register of the Protestant chapel.

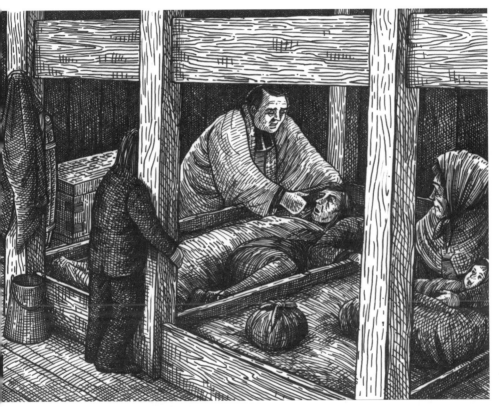

A CATHOLIC PRIEST ADMINISTERS THE LAST RITES TO A DYING MAN IN STEERAGE QUARTERS ON AN EMIGRANT SHIP AT GROSSE ÎLE. AS SOON AS SHIPS REACHED THE QUARANTINE STATION, MISSIONARIES WENT ON BOARD TO MINISTER TO THE SICK PEOPLE WHO COULD NOT BE TAKEN ASHORE OWING TO LACK OF ROOM IN THE RECEPTION FACILITIES ON THE ISLAND. (DANIEL RAINVILLE, PARKS CANADA, 1997.)

SHIPS ARRIVING AT GROSSE ÎLE

Name of ship	Captain	Port of departure	Crossing time (in days)	Passengers Steerage	Cabin	No. of sick on arrival	No. of deaths during crossing
Achilles	W. Taylor	Liverpool (England)	39	413	0	0	42
Bee	T. Muir	Cork (Ireland)	37	373	0	157	77
Blonde	A. Crawford	Liverpool (England)	23	424	0	11	5
Clarendon	J. McFarlane	Liverpool (England)	52	286	1	128	18
Eagle	M. Pamel	Padstow (England)	39	115	14	0	0
Spermaceti	E. Moon	Plymouth (England)	42	248	3	0	1
Wolfville	D. Ritchie	Sligo (Ireland)	29	309	2	0	37
TOTAL				2168	20	296	

SHIPS LEAVING GROSSE ÎLE FOR QUÉBEC CITY

Name of ship	Quarantine time (in days)	Deaths in Grosse Île hospitals	Deaths on quarantined ships
*Douglas**	2	0	0
Dunbrody	3	0	0
Eagle	A few hours	0	0
Spermaceti	A few hours	0	0

* It is hard to understand why the *Douglas* was detained for two days, since none of its passengers or crew had died during the crossing or were sick when they reached Grosse Île.

TUESDAY, MAY 25, 1847

Dr. Douglas asserted that, contrary to the wishes of emigration agent Buchanan, all healthy emigrants could not come ashore. If all passengers disembarked, it would be impossible to keep the sick separate from the healthy, since the former occupied all available room. The medical superintendent proposed that the east end of the island be used for receiving convalescent patients as they left hospital. He also suggested that all healthy passengers be authorized to land on Cliff Island, a small island nearby, and that a detachment of 50 soldiers be sent to Grosse Île to maintain order among the many emigrants detained there.

The government was unable to provide municipal authorities or hospitals with money for caring for the emigrants. All funds available for that purpose were being allocated to the Grosse Île quarantine station.

The wharf at Grosse Île was flooded on account of strong winds. It had also been damaged by ice at the beginning of the navigation season.

A medical student, Mr. Barter, was hired as an apothecary to supply the island's 10 physicians with medicine.

The *Quebec Mercury* reported that the population of Québec City was alarmed by rumours about Grosse Île. The author of the article tried to reassure readers by saying that emigration agent Buchanan was on his way to the quarantine station armed with all the authority needed to meet various needs. Tents were to be pitched in the eastern part of the island for healthy and convalescent emigrants. In addition, a detachment of troops, reputed to be much more efficient than the civil police stationed at Grosse Île, would maintain order and assist the medical superintendent.

One burial was recorded in the register of the Protestant chapel.

SHIPS ARRIVING AT GROSSE ÎLE

Name of ship	Captain	Port of departure	Crossing time (in days)	Passengers Steerage	Passengers Cabin	No. of sick on arrival	No. of deaths during crossing
Aquamarine	S. Connolly	Liverpool (England)	34	24	3	0	0
Fame	W. Miller	Limerick (Ireland)	22	207	1	0	1
John Bolton	T. Samson	Liverpool (England)	43	578	0	98	74
Roslin Castle	W. Snoler	Falmouth (England)	45	212	2	0	0
Sir Colin Campbell	J. Campbell	Belfast (Ireland)	28	383	0	0	2
TOTAL				1 404	6	98	

SHIPS LEAVING GROSSE ÎLE FOR QUÉBEC CITY

Name of ship	Quarantine time (in days)	Deaths in Grosse Île hospitals	Deaths on quarantined ships
Aquamarine	A few hours	0	0
Ellen Thompson	3	1	0
Fame	A few hours	0	0
Ganges	3	1	0
Jessie	3	4	0
Roslin Castle	A few hours	0	0
Tottenham	3	1	0
Wallace	2	1	0
Wandsworth	6	54	0

SHIPS ARRIVING IN QUÉBEC CITY WITHOUT A STOP-OVER AT GROSSE ÎLE

Name of ship	Port of departure	Passengers Steerage	Passengers Cabin
Cherokee	Glasgow (Scotland)	10	4
Isabella	Whitehaven (England)	0	2
TOTAL		10	6

WEDNESDAY,
MAY 26, 1847

Three more "hospital sheds" were under construction. In addition, plans were being made to reserve the east end of Grosse Île for convalescents leaving hospital.

Emigration agent A. C. Buchanan informed the Governor General about the situation on the island, which he had left the night before. He reported that the vessels already there had a large number of sick passengers, many of whom were obliged to remain on board since the station's hospitals were full. Steps were taken immediately to erect new hospitals. Thirty ships, carrying over 10 000 people, were moored off the quarantine station; more than 400 of their passengers had died prior to the vessels' arrival. A total of 660 people had been admitted to hospital, and of that number, at least 43 were dead. Since Sunday, May 23, 3 000 passengers had reached the port of Québec. According to Buchanan, most were joining friends. Douglas requested that troops be sent to the island to help maintain order among the emigrants, all of whom would have to be taken ashore and disinfected before being authorized to proceed to Québec City.

Dr. John Benson died from typhus at about age 45. This physician, from Castle Comer, Ireland, was a surgeon aboard the *Wandsworth*, which put in at Grosse Île on May 19. He had offered to stay at the quarantine station to help Dr. Douglas attend the sick.

According to the *Quebec Gazette*, 35 vessels were anchored off Grosse Île. The newspaper also reported that over 50 orphans were already at the station, and said it hoped that the government would take charge of these children.

One burial was recorded in the register of the Protestant chapel.

SHIPS ARRIVING AT GROSSE ÎLE

Name of ship	Captain	Port of departure	Crossing time (in days)	Passengers Steerage	Cabin	No. of sick on arrival	No. of deaths during crossing
Araminta	J. Rogers	Liverpool (England)	24	412	4	89	13
Belleisle	J. Reid	Glasgow (Scotland)	60	35	0	0	1
Caithness-shire	T. Leggate	Belfast (Ireland)	46	249	1	57	10
Chieftain	W. McGowan	Belfast (Ireland)	44	267	0	0	1
Concord	H. Burden	Dublin (Ireland)	26	183	0	0	3
Eliza Caroline	J. Briggs	Liverpool (England)	22	540	0	46	16
Estafette	D. H. Heyon	Bremen (Germany)	34	126	1	0	0
Favourite	W. Crawford	Glasgow (Scotland)	51	79	2	3	1
Henry	H. McFell	Donegal (Ireland)	44	169	1	0	10
Ninian	D. Fittock	Limerick (Ireland)	42	258	3	24	20
Ottawa	G. Thrift	Bridgwater (England)	44	55	0	0	0
Souvenir	J. [Dadeaster]	Limerick (Ireland)	25	120	4	1	1
TOTAL				2493	16	220	

SHIPS LEAVING GROSSE ÎLE FOR QUÉBEC CITY

Name of ship	Quarantine time (in days)	Deaths in Grosse Île hospitals	Deaths on quarantined ships
Belleisle	A few hours	0	0
Chieftain	A few hours	0	1
Concord	A few hours	0	0
Estafette	A few hours	0	0
Ottawa	A few hours	0	0
Sir Colin Campbell	1	0	1

THURSDAY,
MAY 27, 1847

Dr. Douglas received permission to hire two medical assistants, in addition to the two recruited earlier.

The Governor General's secretary informed the military authorities that, as in previous years, a detachment of 50 soldiers was required to maintain order at Grosse Île. They could be taken to the station aboard the government steamer. These soldiers, who would be commanded by an officer, would be responsible for pitching tents supplied by the army and for helping the medical superintendent to enforce the Quarantine Act and its attendant regulations.

The Executive Council accepted Douglas' proposal of May 25 to disembark healthy emigrants on Cliff Island and to send 50 soldiers to Grosse Île to maintain order.

One captain's tent, 8 hospital tents and 266 Flanders tents were requisitioned for Grosse Île.

Dr. Parant drew up a list of supplies needed for the hospitals at the quarantine station, including medicine, medical instruments, tools, stationery, coffin construction materials and a cart for hauling water and transporting bodies to the cemetery.

> Summary of an eyewitness account by John Roberts, an emigrant aboard the *Clio*, which had been anchored off Grosse Île all night:
>
> Around 5:00 a.m., Roberts went on deck to view the surrounding countryside; he made out several houses, a hospital and soldiers' barracks on the island. Thirty-six vessels, including barques and brigs, were anchored in the St. Lawrence. Most of their passengers were Irish or Scottish and many were sick. Roberts mentioned that 50 people had been buried on the island the day before, and that 25 others had died in hospital and several on board ship that day. He also said that recent reports about the situation at the quarantine station were truly horrible.
>
> Around 3:00 p.m., a physician boarded the *Clio*, and all passengers were ordered to line up on deck in front of the main mast. After counting the passengers, the doctor went down into the ship's hold and then returned, saying that he was satisfied with the situation. He announced that he would come back the next day to release the ship from quarantine. Sailors took ashore a child who had died the day before; they brought a bit of snow with them when they returned.

The *Quebec Mercury* informed its readers that a large number of tents would be delivered to Grosse Île to house healthy passengers placed in quarantine. These passengers would be sent to neighbouring Cliff Island to prevent them from coming into contact with sick emigrants.

According to the *Quebec Mercury*, 25 emigrant ships were anchored off Grosse Île.

Nine burials were recorded in the register of the Protestant chapel.

A NUMBER OF VESSELS LIE AT ANCHOR IN THE QUARANTINE PASS OFF GROSSE ÎLE. THERE WERE MOMENTS WHEN DOZENS OF SHIPS AT A TIME WERE WAITING TO SEND THEIR PASSENGERS ASHORE AND BE DISINFECTED BEFORE GOING ON TO QUÉBEC CITY. (DANIEL RAINVILLE, PARKS CANADA, 1997.)

SHIPS ARRIVING AT GROSSE ÎLE

Name of ship	Captain	Port of departure	Crossing time (in days)	Passengers Steerage	Cabin	No. of sick on arrival	No. of deaths during crossing
Ajax	R. Scott	Liverpool (England)	41	258	1	86	36
Albion	C. Daly	Galway (Ireland)	24	211	0	1	3
Annie	W. Mearns	Belfast (Ireland)	29	429	0	0	1
Argo	A. Mitchell	Liverpool (England)	23	593	0	56	11
Christiana	D. Kenyon	Londonderry (Ireland)	49	480	0	18	10
Clio	R. Easthorpe	Padstow (England)	47	320	8	0	2
Congress	W. Carwin	Sligo (Ireland)	33	219	0	9	38
Dykes	J. Sewell	Sligo (Ireland)	35	170	0	44	16
Gilmour	J. J. Parkeham	Cork (Ireland)	33	368	0	45	19
Industry	J. Stevens	Dublin (Ireland)	38	295	6	4	3
Phoenix	D. Kerr	Liverpool (England)	44	279	7	12	4
Robert and Isabella	R. Jordan	Hamburg (Germany)	41	170	0	0	2
Sisters	T. Christian	Liverpool (England)	35	507	0	86	58
Tay	H. Brennan	Sligo (Ireland)	22	301	2	0	11
Transit	C. Ferguson	Sligo (Ireland)	27	158	0	1	6
TOTAL				4758	24	362	

SHIPS LEAVING GROSSE ÎLE FOR QUÉBEC CITY

Name of ship	Quarantine time (in days)	Deaths in Grosse Île hospitals	Deaths on quarantined ships
Annie	A few hours	0	0
Favourite	1	0	2
Industry*	A few hours	3	0
Robert and Isabella	A few hours	0	1
Souvenir	Nearly a day	0	0

* Since this ship had sick people on board, it seems odd that it left for Québec City the same day it arrived.

SHIPS ARRIVING IN QUÉBEC CITY WITHOUT A STOP-OVER AT GROSSE ÎLE

Name of ship	Port of departure	Passengers	
		Steerage	Cabin
Nestor	Maryport (England)	7	0

EMIGRANTS ARRIVING IN THE PORT OF QUÉBEC

Country of origin	Steerage passengers	Cabin passengers	Total
England	1515	12	1527
Ireland	3727	0	3727
Scotland	137	28	165
Germany	127	0	127
TOTAL	5506	40	5546*

* According to Buchanan, this represented an increase of 214 emigrants compared with the total reported for the same period in 1846. Thirty-five ships were still anchored off Grosse Île.

FRIDAY, MAY 28, 1847

An article in the *Canadien* blamed people for spreading wild rumours about the situation at the quarantine station: "It is true that sickness and death have struck many of the emigrants arriving at Grosse Île, [but] most of the ravages caused to date have been wrought by dysentery." [*Translation*]

The *Canadien* also reported that the government had ordered the shipment of 1000 tents to Grosse Île since there were not enough buildings to keep the sick separate from people who were merely detained in quarantine. The steamer *St. George* left for Grosse Île with supplies for the emigrants and for the carpenters who had been hired to erect a large number of sheds. The military authorities agreed to station an officer and 50 soldiers on the island to maintain order.

The *Canadien* announced that nearly 10 000 emigrants were detained at Grosse Île. Since the number would soon rise, the newspaper said that all small islands in the vicinity of the quarantine establishment should be leased to accommodate healthy emigrants and thus ensure that station authorities would not be caught unprepared.

Two burials were recorded in the register of the Protestant chapel.

SHIPS ARRIVING AT GROSSE ÎLE

Name of ship	Captain	Port of departure	Crossing time (in days)	Passengers Steerage	Cabin	No. of sick on arrival	No. of deaths during crossing
Bryan Abbs	W. Wood	Limerick (Ireland)	44	194	0	1	5
Constitution	J. Wilson	Sligo (Ireland)	43	166	0	15	16
Rankin	Lawrence	Liverpool (England)	24	579	0	0	5
TOTAL				939	0	16	

SHIPS LEAVING GROSSE ÎLE FOR QUÉBEC CITY

Name of ship	Quarantine time (in days)	Deaths in Grosse Île hospitals	Deaths on quarantined ships
Clio	1	0	1

SATURDAY,
MAY 29, 1847

Since the adoption of an Order-in-Council on May 25, requiring that healthy passengers be taken ashore and enough tents be sent to accommodate them, Dr. Douglas had received only 8 marquees and 266 other tents. Although the marquees had been pitched on the hospital grounds, the others, which were for sick and convalescent emigrants, would be erected only when help was available, given that the military authorities in Québec City had refused to provide the necessary assistance. However, since the station personnel were fully occupied with the exhausting task of helping the sick and dying, it would take time to finish putting up the tents.

The night before, Douglas had identified 856 cases of typhus and dysentery in the hospitals, sheds and tents. Another 470 people, still waiting to go ashore, were also suffering from these illnesses. During the past week, 70 people had died on the island and twice as many on the ships. Thirty-six vessels with over 13 000 passengers aboard were anchored off the quarantine station.

The ground on Cliff Island was too rocky for pitching tents and, on Grosse Île, there were only enough accommodations for the sick. Bringing healthy people ashore would condemn many to death, since most were already weakened by lack of food and other hardships. On the ships, the emigrants had a bed, a place to cook and access to water for washing. They could even get fresh air circulating in the hold by opening the fore and aft portholes. Douglas asked the Governor General to rescind the Order-in-Council, saying he could not comply with it. He argued that enforcing the order would bring at least 20 000 people, or the population of a large city, onto Grosse Île before the end of the week. Even if a sufficient number of tents were available, there would not be enough room to erect them all on the island.

According to Buchanan, there were over 12 000 emigrants at Grosse Île, and most were on board the ships. There was not enough food for everyone. Recently, about 40 to 50 deaths had been recorded per day.

Buchanan suggested that a commission of three reputable doctors be sent to Grosse Île to inquire into the situation of the emigrants detained there and to adopt necessary measures.

According to Buchanan's report of May 29, 36 ships with 12 450 people aboard were moored off Grosse Île; 662 of their passengers had perished at sea.

Eight burials were recorded in the register of the Protestant chapel.

According to a list published in the *Quebec Morning Chronicle*, 71 people had died at Grosse Île during the week of May 23 to 29.

SHIPS ARRIVING AT GROSSE ÎLE

Name of ship	Captain	Port of departure	Crossing time (in days)	Passengers Steerage	Cabin	No. of sick on arrival	No. of deaths during crossing
Nerio	W. Gibson	Limerick (Ireland)	45	132	0	3	3

SHIPS LEAVING GROSSE ÎLE FOR QUÉBEC CITY

Name of ship	Quarantine time (in days)	Deaths in Grosse Île hospitals	Deaths on quarantined ships
Albion	2	1	2

SHIPS ARRIVING IN QUÉBEC CITY WITHOUT A STOP-OVER AT GROSSE ÎLE

Name of ship	Port of departure	Passengers Steerage	Cabin
Constance	Bristol (England)	15	0
Lord Ramsay	Bideford (England)	10	0
TOTAL		25	0

NUMBER OF PEOPLE IN HOSPITAL ON GROSSE ÎLE DURING THE WEEK OF MAY 23 TO 29

Emigrants	Patients hospitalized as at last report	Patients admitted (+)	Patients discharged (-)	Deaths (-)	New total
Men	151	115	10	28	228
Women	141	98	4	19	216
Children	112	109	1	24	196
TOTAL	404	322	15	71	640*

* Of this number, 627 (228 men, 215 women and 184 children) had typhus and 12 (all children) had smallpox. One woman had been hospitalized to give birth.

SUNDAY, MAY 30, 1847

In a letter to Archbishop Signay, Father Elzéar-Alexandre Taschereau described the situation on Grosse Île. He reported that some forty ships were waiting at the quarantine station, but only about a dozen, at most, had been visited. He added that, according to Mr. Robert Symes, the deputy emigration agent posted on the island, almost 1 200 sick people were hospitalized at the quarantine station and nearly half were awaiting the last rites. Most died immediately after receiving them and their places were taken by other patients. Taschereau reported that 55 people had been buried the day before. The total number of emigrants was estimated at 10 000, including about 1 000 sick people aboard the ships, almost all of which had passengers who had fallen ill.

Father Taschereau said that the church would be occupied by sick people the next day, and that 36 tents were already full. Heart-rending scenes could be observed in the hospitals. Father Hugh McGuirk was well, Father Bernard McGauran a bit less so and Father James McDevitt too weak to last much longer. In Taschereau's opinion, six energetic missionaries would be able to meet the spiritual needs of the emigrants detained on the island once the current backlog of work was eliminated. Taschereau implored Archbishop Signay to do his utmost to send three more priests, at least for a few days, until he and his colleagues had met the most pressing needs and caught up on their work.

Father McGauran told Archbishop Signay that he was delighted about the impending arrival of Father James F. McDonnell, but that he could not lodge a fourth clergyman in the Catholic priests' residence since it was already full. He reported that mortality was increasing on the ships and, to support this assertion, mentioned that 50 people had died on board that day.

Four burials were recorded in the register of the Protestant chapel.

SHIPS ARRIVING AT GROSSE ÎLE

Name of ship	Captain	Port of departure	Crossing time (in days)	Passengers Steerage	Cabin	No. of sick on arrival	No. of deaths during crossing
Ann	A. McFee	Limerick (Ireland)	47	119	0	0	4
Columbia	J. Aim	Sligo (Ireland)	29	250	0	20	15
Pursuit	W. Spence	Liverpool (England)	27	472	0	130	37
TOTAL				841	0	150	

MONDAY,
MAY 31, 1847

Buchanan noted that a large number of newcomers suffered from an acute shortage of food. Therefore, he decided to send oatmeal, pork, biscuits and bread to Grosse Île. These provisions were sold at cost price to those who could afford to pay and handed out free of charge to destitute emigrants. Buchanan also chartered a small steamer for £ 12 a day and placed it at the disposal of Dr. Douglas at Grosse Île. The medical superintendent could use it to bring the sick ashore, transport supplies and so forth.

It was decided that a Commissariat officer would go to Grosse Île to look after food supplies for the emigrants at the quarantine station and on Cliff Island.

Dr. Joseph Parant, inspecting physician for the port of Québec, suggested that the east end of Grosse Île be used for the reception of healthy emigrants, since it was impossible to accommodate them on Cliff Island. Grosse Île's eastern sector was occupied by a large farm, where tents could be erected, as during the cholera epidemic of 1834. In Parant's opinion, using the land for purposes other than farming would be of little importance under the circumstances. Emigration agent Buchanan's idea of prefabricating additional sheds in Québec City and sending them to Grosse Île seemed very expensive. Moreover, such an initiative was the responsibility of the Executive Council and the Board of Works.

Medical superintendent Douglas reported that sick emigrants continued to throng to the quarantine station. Since Saturday, he had brought 420 more sick passengers ashore and placed them in tents, sheds and the island's two chapels. All available buildings were crowded with patients and no more passengers could land. There were 1050 sick people on the island, but far too few nurses and cooks to look after them. Douglas added that the lower classes of Irish were so afraid of fever that they readily abandoned their closest relatives, without even trying to help them and without any remorse.

According to the medical superintendent, the four doctors who had come to assist him were so exhausted and disgusted by what they had to do to care for these people, who were often filthy, that they refused to stay at the quarantine station unless their salary was increased to 25s. per day. Douglas recommended that they be granted the raise. At the time, 40 ships were anchored off the island, over an area nearly two miles long, and the medical superintendent wanted to hire two assistants to visit them. His health was already seriously impaired and he could no longer carry out the never-ending task of inspecting the vessels on his own.

The Executive Council committee, on learning about the presence of over 12000 emigrants, many of whom were sick, at the Grosse Île quarantine station, recommended the adoption of a proposal put forward by emigration agent A. C. Buchanan. The latter had suggested that a commission of three doctors be sent to the island to inquire into the nature and prevalence of the diseases diagnosed there and to determine the best way of checking their progress and preventing them from spreading.

A. C. Buchanan and Dr. Douglas hired another small steamboat, also known as the *St. George*, owned by Mr. Poiré and Mr. Barras, two navigators from Pointe-Lévy. For £ 12 a day, they would have access to this boat either in Québec City or at Grosse Île, and could use it from "dawn to dusk" for as long as necessary.

According to the *Quebec Gazette*, the latest reports from Grosse Île were alarming. There were 1300 sick people on the island and about 13000 passengers on the vessels in quarantine. Death and hunger were as prevalent as in Ireland. One hundred children were now orphans at the station.

A steam-powered ferryboat brought various provisions to Grosse Île that evening.

Death of John Davis, a cook aboard the *Aberdeen*, at age 50.

One burial was recorded in the register of the Protestant chapel.

According to Dr. Douglas, an average of 451 people were in hospital per day from May 15 to 31 inclusively.

SHIPS ARRIVING AT GROSSE ÎLE

Name of ship	Captain	Port of departure	Crossing time (in days)	Passengers Steerage	Cabin	No. of sick on arrival	No. of deaths during crossing
Abbotsford	W. Gibson	Dublin (Ireland)	38	382	0	86	9
Elizabeth	W. Thompson	Liverpool (England)	38	347	0	27	12
Pacha	W. Allen	Cork (Ireland)	27	218	0	5	11
TOTAL				947	0	118	

SHIPS LEAVING GROSSE ÎLE FOR QUÉBEC CITY

Name of ship	Quarantine time (in days)	Deaths in Grosse Île hospitals	Deaths on quarantined ships
Constitution	3	0	2

A RECONSTRUCTION OF THE WESTERN SECTOR OF GROSSE ÎLE IN 1847. IN EARLY JULY, NEARLY 2000 PATIENTS AND NUMEROUS CONVALESCENTS WERE OCCUPYING THIS PART OF THE STATION, WHERE, DESPITE A CONCERTED EFFORT TO BUILD SHEDS AND HOSPITALS, SEVERAL HUNDRED TENTS WERE STILL IN USE. (BERNARD DUCHESNE, PARKS CANADA, 1995.)

1847

JUNE

S	M	T	W	T	F	S
		1	2	3	4	5
6	7	8	9	10	11	12
13	14	15	16	17	18	19
20	21	22	23	24	25	26
27	28	29	30			

TUESDAY,
JUNE 1, 1847

A shed, measuring 150 feet long by 25 feet wide, was under construction at Grosse Île. Another 100-foot building was being prefabricated in Québec City and was supposed to be shipped to the island.

Two more doctors arrived at the quarantine station. The deputy commissary general also went there to determine how his department could assist the emigrants.

The Executive Council committee approved various relief measures for the emigrants at Grosse Île. It recommended that the commissary general be asked to provide supplies for them and that the east end of Grosse Île, like Cliff Island, be used for housing healthy people. The committee also recommended that barges from Québec City be authorized to travel to Grosse Île to pick up rigging and merchandise for local merchants from the ships anchored there. It stipulated, however, that these goods could be transferred to the barges only once the emigrants had disembarked.

Henceforth, emigrants would be authorized to proceed to Québec City and their final destination on steamers hired for that purpose after spending 10 days in quarantine on Grosse Île or 15 days in quarantine on board ship. All ships would have to be fumigated before a customs officer on the island could issue a permit for them to continue on to Québec City. The Executive Council committee also approved the construction of sheds for 2000 sick people and the use of another small steamboat for bringing the sick ashore.

Father Taschereau noted an improvement in the situation at Grosse Île. Most of the ships at the station had been visited by a priest and, in general, there were few sick aboard, except on one of the vessels, where Father McDonnell had spent seven hours. Taschereau himself had visited 10 ships that day, two of which had no sick on board, a situation the passengers attributed to the care provided by the captains. The *Elizabeth* was the filthiest vessel of all, and the missionary stressed the complaints he had heard about the captain's hard-heartedness. Priests had already spent over 12 hours aboard the *Agnes*, and, in Taschereau's opinion, they would have to spend as many more unless the situation improved. The captain, who was already sick, and all the passengers were in danger of dying.

To save time, Taschereau and Father McGauran agreed to reorganize the activities of the Catholic priests: two would visit the hospitals and three the ships, while the remaining priest would look after and record the burials and be available for emergencies. Taschereau also expressed his hope that Father McDevitt would recover and stay at Grosse Île.

Summary of an eyewitness account of the situation at Grosse Île by Alexander Mitchell, captain of the *Argo* (from a letter written on Grosse Île and published in the *Quebec Morning Chronicle* on June 4):

Mitchell affirmed that the situation was deteriorating daily. Owing to a lack of room on the island, no sick passengers had been removed from his ship, or from several other vessels. He noted that about 35 ships, with at least 12000 emigrants aboard, were waiting at the quarantine station. There were several cases of typhus on his vessel, and five of his crew members were infected. He could not count on the medical assistance of Dr. Douglas, even though the latter was doing his utmost under the circumstances. Mitchell feared that famine would make matters worse, given that many emigrants had nothing to eat other than the pound of bread provided by their ship. Nineteen of his passengers had already died.

The *Quebec Mercury* reported that at least 13000 emigrants were at Grosse Île, and of that number, 12000 were still afloat. There was not enough room at the quarantine station even for all the sick, who totalled 1500. In addition, the vessels were starting to run out of food. The newspaper said, however, that there was no cause for alarm since the most prevalent disease was dysentery, not typhus. The author of the article praised Douglas for his unflagging efforts, noting that he needed more personnel. Meanwhile, in Québec City, Buchanan was trying to prepare for all possible contingencies. He had already chartered another steamer, the *St. George*, to meet Douglas' needs. He had also hired Dr. Jackson to care for the emigrants in the sheds in Québec City.

Anglican baptism of Rosanne Conway, born May 23 to William Conway, a labourer, and Maria McGhee, from County Kilkenny, Ireland. The Reverend Charles Forest drew up the baptismal certificate.

Seven burials were recorded in the register of the Protestant chapel.

SHIPS ARRIVING AT GROSSE ÎLE

Name of ship	Captain	Port of departure	Crossing time (in days)	Passengers Steerage	Passengers Cabin	No. of sick on arrival	No. of deaths during crossing
Argent	J. Allison	Limerick (Ireland)	30	127	0	0	0
Dominica	G. Storach	Cork (Ireland)	32	254	0	7	0
TOTAL				381	0	7	

WEDNESDAY, JUNE 2, 1847

The Governor General appointed three physicians, Dr. Painchaud from Québec City and Dr. McDonnell and Dr. Campbell from Montréal, to the medical commission responsible for inquiring into the situation of the emigrants at Grosse Île and the nature and prevalence of their diseases.

Mr. Laidley, the deputy commissary general, wrote from Grosse Île that six large sheds were needed immediately to supplement the existing one, which measured 150 feet long by 25 feet wide. He hoped that they would be built by the following Friday. Another shed was under construction in Québec City. Laidley also identified one of the other major inconveniences on the island: the lack of kitchen utensils. The emigrants had a few iron kettles, but that was not enough. The main problem, however, was the shortage of nurses. Despite the high wages offered, few wanted to work at the quarantine station.

Dr. Douglas wrote to the editors of the *Quebec Mercury* and the *Quebec Gazette* to dispute the exaggerated reports of distress and misery among the emigrants at Grosse Île. Douglas asserted that there was no lack of food on board the ships at the island. Every day, the vessels provided each of their passengers with "a pound of biscuit, flour, oatmeal or soft bread," in accordance with the provisions of the Imperial Passenger Act. To support his claims, Douglas said that, on June 1, 22 ships that had been quarantined for the past eight days were visited by Mr. Robert Symes, the deputy emigration agent at Grosse Île, aboard a small steamer loaded with tea, sugar, pork, bread, oatmeal and biscuits. These provisions, which had been sent by Buchanan, were distributed free of charge to the most destitute emigrants.

Douglas added that, despite the large number of sick and dead at the quarantine station, there was no need to exaggerate the situation. All told, 116 people had died in hospital since the beginning of the season (i.e. as at May 29), and most were young children suffering from dysentery. There were no more than 20 orphans at Grosse Île, and the medical superintendent had hired convalescent emigrants to look after them and provide them with milk and food. At the time, there were less than 1400 patients in the island's hospitals, sheds, chapels and tents, and six doctors were attending them. Douglas noted, however, that nurses were lacking and the sick were often abandoned by their next of kin. He concluded his letter with the wish that navigation regulations would be amended to limit the number of passengers allowed on vessels, as in the United States. He believed that this would prevent Irish landlords from sending too many poor emigrants overseas.

The *Canadien* wrote that although the reports from Grosse Île were disheartening, there were still no cases of so-called contagious diseases at the island. A total of 13000 people were in quarantine and 10 percent were sick; 50 to 60 people, and often more, died per day. The newspaper disagreed with the Board of Trade's recommendation that only sick emigrants be detained at Grosse Île, while healthy ones be allowed to proceed to Québec City. Instead, it argued, the authorities should accept the offer of certain steamship owners to transport the emigrants from Grosse Île to Montréal.

The *Quebec Gazette* expressed concern about the situation on Grosse Île, where the number of sick was increasing daily. Dysentery appeared to be the most prevalent disease, but typhus and smallpox were also present. The newspaper had received a letter from a cabin passenger on one of the emigrant ships relating the dangers to which healthy passengers were exposed when they could not go ashore because of a lack of accommodations.

Death of Randolph Fisher, a cook aboard the *Constitution*, at age 29.

Eight burials were recorded in the register of the Protestant chapel.

SHIPS LEAVING GROSSE ÎLE FOR QUÉBEC CITY

Name of ship	Quarantine time (in days)	Deaths in Grosse Île hospitals	Deaths on quarantined ships
Ann	3	0	0
Argent	1	1	0
Bryan Abbs	5	1	0
Nerio	4	1	0
Transit	6	0	0

THURSDAY,
JUNE 3, 1847

The Governor General informed medical superintendent Douglas that relief measures had been adopted for the emigrants at Grosse Île. The east end of the island was to be used for the reception of healthy emigrants, while Cliff Island, originally reserved for that purpose, would be evacuated. Healthy passengers, after being quarantined for 10 days on shore or for 15 days on board ship, would be authorized to proceed to their destination on steamers sent to Grosse Île. The ocean-going vessels would have to be fumigated before continuing their journey. Sheds capable of lodging 2000 sick people were to be built and a small steamer used for disembarking the sick.

Father E.-A. Taschereau informed the Archbishop of Québec that the Catholic chapel had been occupied since the day before by sick passengers from the *Agnes*, "the most plague-ridden ship of all and in danger of losing everyone aboard." [*Translation*] The large tent erected by Douglas behind the sacristy for saying Mass housed other sick people from the same vessel. Henceforth, the Catholic priests celebrated Mass in the sacristy amidst the moans of the dying. Fifty people had been buried on June 2 and 86 on June 3.

Taschereau repeated the comments of a captain of one of the vessels to Archbishop Signay: "It would be better to simply send a battery of artillery from Québec City to sink these ships to the bottom, than to let all these poor people suffer such a slow, agonizing death. Unless the situation improved, everyone will perish." [*Translation*]. Some captains confided to the priests that three to ten times more passengers had died on board their vessels since they arrived at the quarantine station than during the voyage across the ocean.

In Taschereau's opinion, the situation was hopeless for many emigrants, who breathed the foul air of the between decks, walked on floors littered with refuse, ate unwholesome food and drank dirty water. Most slept on planks or a few filthy wisps of straw. After a month and a half on board, many emigrants were still wearing the same clothes and shoes they had on when they first embarked; moreover, they had been wearing them day and night. Taschereau had seen people whose socks were so stuck to their feet that he was unable to anoint them.

Father McGauran complained of weakness and went to bed with a high fever. Dr. Douglas recommended that he be sent to Québec City the next day. Taschereau himself and Father William

Moylan offered to stay longer at the quarantine station. Father McGuirk, who was in charge of most of the hospitals, displayed admirable, although perhaps, excessive zeal, since he was exhausted.

A large number of orphans were now at Grosse Île and, unfortunately, the station authorities had no alternative but to entrust them to a few mothers and give the latter money for food. According to Taschereau, most of these children would die like the others. He described the apathy of some emigrants, caused by too much suffering and misfortune. Several appeared indifferent to the dead bodies beside them.

The *Quebec Mercury* noted an improvement in the situation of emigrants who had received medical treatment on Grosse Île. However, there were still a great many sick people on the vessels. The newspaper questioned certain changes in the quarantine station's *modus operandi*. Apparently, healthy emigrants would now be offered a choice of being quarantined for 10 days on land or for 15 days on board ship. Since Cliff Island would no longer be used for accommodating healthy emigrants because it was impossible to pitch tents there, the east end of Grosse Île would be prepared for that purpose. Bringing both healthy and sick passengers ashore would make it possible to fumigate the ships, which could then be authorized to pursue their journey. A customs officer would be stationed at Grosse Île to give emigrants permission to proceed to their destination in Canada. After healthy emigrants were released from quarantine, they would be taken directly to Montréal aboard steamers. Sheds capable of housing over 2000 sick people were supposed to be built on Grosse Île within the near future.

Seven burials were recorded in the register of the Protestant chapel.

FRIDAY,
JUNE 4, 1847

Additional quarantine regulations were announced by the Governor General. Essentially, they stipulated that a detachment of troops, commanded by an officer, would be integrated into the quarantine station's staff. These soldiers, who would be under the authority of the medical superintendent, were to help the police officers already stationed at Grosse Île to enforce the Quarantine Act and its attendant regulations. They were to use all necessary means, including force and armed intervention, to oblige vessels subject to the Act to anchor at Grosse Île and comply with the quarantine measures. In accordance with the new legislation, the soldiers were to allow passengers to re-embark only when the medical superintendent so authorized; the latter could grant such permission only after ensuring that ships, luggage and passengers had been thoroughly disinfected and that there were no longer any cases of contagious illness on board. The soldiers would also be responsible for helping to maintain order among healthy emigrants.

Dr. McGrath was reported to have fallen ill from fatigue and exhaustion.

The medical commission left for Grosse Île aboard the *St. George* and was not expected to return until the following evening at the earliest. It was anticipated that bad weather would impede the commission's investigation.

Based on an eyewitness account of the situation at Grosse Île, the *Canadien* wrote that the illnesses encountered on the ships were not contagious, but resulted mainly from the filthy conditions in the vessels' between decks. Such conditions in turn stemmed from the greed of navigation company agents and shipowners. Nevertheless, sickness and death rates were gradually falling, and steamers were to be sent to the island to take healthy emigrants to Montréal. Sick emigrants or those whose health was in doubt would be left at Grosse Île and placed in the island's hospitals, sheds or tents.

The *Canadien* noted that there were at least 1 100 sick people at the quarantine station and that 700 to 800 had died aboard ship and on land since the beginning of the season. It also mentioned that the government had appointed a commission of three doctors to suggest appropriate health measures. At the time, seven Catholic priests were working on Grosse Île, but two were supposed to return to Québec City in the near future. An emigration agent and a customs officer left to spend the summer on the island in order to accelerate the departure of disinfected vessels and send emigrants who did not want to stay in the Québec City region on to Montréal.

According to the *Journal de Québec*, the Commissariat had announced that it would receive tenders until June 5 for the daily or regular supply of a sufficient quantity of bread and fresh beef for the emigrants at Grosse Île for the duration of the navigation season. The newspaper also mentioned that Dr. Parant, inspecting physician for the port of Québec, had announced that 20 well-paid nursing positions were available on the island.

SHIPS ARRIVING AT GROSSE ÎLE

Name of ship	Captain	Port of departure	Crossing time (in days)	Passengers Steerage	Cabin	No. of sick on arrival	No. of deaths during crossing
Dew Drop	J. Burke	Westport (Ireland)	44	33	0	0	0

SHIPS LEAVING GROSSE ÎLE FOR QUÉBEC CITY

Name of ship	Quarantine time (in days)	Deaths in Grosse Île hospitals	Deaths on quarantined ships
Dew Drop	A few hours	0	0
Phoenix	8	3	0

SATURDAY, JUNE 5, 1847

The deaths of emigrants from the *Cistus* were recorded in the burial register of the Anglican chapel. This vessel is not mentioned in either the list of ships that were inspected at Grosse Île or the list of those that arrived in Québec City.

According to A. C. Buchanan, the steamers *Queen, Quebec* and *Rowland Hill* had left Québec City that morning to pick up over 2100 healthy passengers on Grosse Île and take them directly to Montréal. The *Quebec Mercury* added that the steamers carried an ample supply of basic provisions, which would be sold to the emigrants at Québec City prices.

According to the *Journal de Québec,* the three physicians making up the commission appointed to inquire into the situation at Grosse Île had returned to Québec City that morning. The newspaper urged that their report be made public, stressing that the entire province was eager to hear the results: "People have to know about the situation at the quarantine station, no matter how terrible it is." [*Translation*]

The *Quebec Morning Chronicle* published a letter informing its readers about the presence of Protestant missionaries at Grosse Île. Although the Reverend C. Forest was in charge of the missionaries' activities for the season, he had not been able to assume his duties at the station until May 25. In the meantime, he was replaced by the Reverend A. W. Mountain from Québec City. The number of sick Protestant emigrants was very small in 1847, amounting to no more than 50. Nevertheless, Anglican clergymen visited the island occasionally to perform necessary services for the emigrants.

According to the *Quebec Mercury*, 65 people who had died on quarantined ships and 40 who had passed away in hospital were buried in the Catholic cemetery; 10 others were buried in the Protestant cemetery.

At the time, there were 110 Protestant emigrants on the island.

An article was written for the *Quebec Morning Chronicle* (published June 12) describing the situation at Grosse Île since the beginning of the navigation season. By June 5, 25 400 emigrants had arrived at the quarantine station. All told, 1 097 people had died at sea and 900 in hospital on Grosse Île or on quarantined ships. On June 4, there were 1 150 sick emigrants in the island's hospitals and 1 200 others aboard the vessels in quarantine; in addition, 43 ships were anchored offshore. Around three hundred of the emigrants authorized to leave the quarantine station and proceed to Québec City had been admitted to the Marine Hospital.

The *Quebec Gazette* reported that it was difficult to find nurses to work at Grosse Île, saying that they demanded overly high wages. Some asked for 3s. 6d. a day, and others 6s.

An eyewitness informed the readers of the *Quebec Gazette* that 21 000 passengers had arrived at Grosse Île since the opening of the navigation season. A total of 960 had died during the crossing and 700 others at the quarantine station. At the time, there were 1 500 sick people aboard ship and 1 100 on shore. Ninety people passed away on June 5.

Eight burials were recorded in the register of the Protestant chapel.

According to a list published in the *Quebec Morning Chronicle*, 117 people had died at Grosse Île during the week of May 30 to June 5.

SHIPS ARRIVING AT GROSSE ÎLE

Name of ship	Captain	Port of departure	Crossing time (in days)	Passengers Steerage	Passengers Cabin	No. of sick on arrival	No. of deaths during crossing
Erin	J. McDonald	New Ross (Ireland)	54	120	0	0	2

SHIPS ARRIVING IN QUÉBEC CITY WITHOUT A STOP-OVER AT GROSSE ÎLE

Name of ship	Port of departure	Passengers Steerage	Passengers Cabin
Albion	Glasgow (Scotland)	0	18
Marquis of Bute	Cardiff (Wales)	8	0
Norna	Sunderland (England)	4	0
Victory	Bristol (England)	5	0
TOTAL		17	18

EMIGRANTS ARRIVING IN THE PORT OF QUÉBEC DURING THE WEEK OF MAY 28 TO JUNE 5

Country of origin	Number
England	621
Ireland	2304
Scotland	77
Germany	113
Canadian ports downstream from Québec City	20
Total	3135
Previous total (as at May 27)	5546
GRAND TOTAL	8681*

* This represents a decrease of 2342 emigrants compared with the total reported by Buchanan up to the same period in 1846, i.e. 11023.

SUNDAY, JUNE 6, 1847

Dr. Douglas informed Buchanan that around 4000 to 5000 emigrants had left Grosse Île that day. He predicted that at least 2000 would fall ill within three weeks. He suggested, therefore, that accommodations be built for 2000 sick people in Montréal.

The *Quebec Mercury* reported that 55 people had been buried in the Catholic cemetery and 12 in the Protestant one, for a total of 67 burials that day. There were 137 Protestants on the island.

The *Quebec Morning Chronicle* mentioned that a number of emigrants had died on the *Hibernia* during the week of June 6 to 12, 1847. This ship is not mentioned in either the list of vessels that were inspected at Grosse Île or the list of those that arrived in Québec City.

Anglican baptism of Isabella Stanfield, born April 15 to Thomas Stanfield, a weaver, and Sarah Orr, passengers aboard the *Caithnessshire*, from County Down, Ireland. The Reverend C. Forest drew up the baptismal certificate.

Death of John Boyes, a sailor aboard the *Scotland*, at age 21.

Thirteen burials were recorded in the register of the Protestant chapel.

SHIPS ARRIVING AT GROSSE ÎLE

Name of ship	Captain	Port of departure	Crossing time (in days)	Passengers Steerage	Cabin	No. of sick on arrival	No. of deaths during crossing
British Queen	R. Errington	Limerick (Ireland)	40	189	1	0	1
Hope	A. Lester	Maryport (England)	35	24	0	0	0
Leveret	W. Robinson	Limerick (Ireland)	53	125	0	0	0
Lotus	J. Watson	Liverpool (England)	53	546	0	45	51
Mary	R. Ellis	Liverpool (England)	34	38	0	0	1
Orlando	W. Cockell	Newry (Ireland)	39	202	7	0	4
Princess Royal	J. [Duguid]	Liverpool (England)	32	599	0	12	14
TOTAL				1723	8	57	

SHIPS LEAVING GROSSE ÎLE FOR QUÉBEC CITY

Name of ship	Quarantine time (in days)	Deaths in Grosse Île hospitals	Deaths on quarantined ships
Erin	1	0	1
Henry	11	6	0
Leveret	A few hours	0	0
Try again	17	6	0

MONDAY, JUNE 7, 1847

A morgue, or "dead house," was reported to be under construction at Grosse Île; some 12 coffins were also being made.

The steamer, the *Queen*, passed Québec City with 600 passengers from Grosse Île on board and took them directly to Montréal.

Douglas informed the Public Works commissioners that the baggage storehouse and police sergeant's residence near the wharf was finished and occupied. He also mentioned that the fence between the wharf and the hospital had been erected. Douglas had already provided Mr. Laurencel, the construction superintendent, with funds for paying the contractors and workmen. He now requested the sum of £ 150 from the £ 250 approved on March 11, and an additional £ 300 for the construction of emigrant sheds.

Buchanan reported that two other steamers, the *Alliance* and the *Canada*, had left Québec City for Grosse Île to take healthy emigrants directly to Montréal and were expected to arrive there June 9. The emigration agent had arranged for a boat to travel from Québec City to Grosse Île daily to pick up healthy passengers. At the time, over 14000 emigrants were detained at the quarantine station; many were in a pitiful state and would eventually appeal to Buchanan's department for help.

Father Louis Huot, parish priest of Sainte-Foy, and Father Félix-Séverin Bardy, curate at Cacouna, arrived at Grosse Île.

Dr. J. Painchaud, Dr. G. W. Campbell and Dr. R. L. McDonnell, the three members of the medical commission appointed to inquire into the situation at the Grosse Île quarantine station and the state of the emigrants detained there, submitted their report to the government authorities. The report was published in the *Journal of the Legislative Assembly of the Province of Canada*. Although the journal did not specify the date on which the report was prepared, it was probably written on June 7 or perhaps June 6, based on when the events mentioned therein occurred. Essentially, the physicians recommended the following:

1. The number of policemen should be increased from 6 to 10, given that the soldiers had been ordered by their officers to keep away from the areas occupied by sick emigrants and to limit their activities to maintaining order among the healthy.

2. All sick passengers on board ship should be disembarked, since mortality rates were significantly higher among people confined to vessels than among those in hospital. All workers on the island, as well as the sailors and craftsmen from the ships, should be assigned to erecting tents for these passengers, and the small steam-powered ferryboat used to bring them ashore.

3. The number of doctors should be increased from 6 to 12 since, at the time, a single physician was sometimes required to care for up to 450 patients at once. All doctors should be paid 5 piastres per day, with rations. The commission also recommended that the number of boats be increased and that two doctors be placed in charge of daily visits to the sick on board the ships.

4. Fifty more nurses should be recruited immediately, at 3 louis per month with rations, through public notices and announcements placed in Québec City and Montréal newspapers. Twenty domestics should also be hired at the same salary.

5. Healthy emigrants on ships that had already been quarantined for several days should not be detained for the entire period currently prescribed by the Executive Council's regulations, but be allowed to embark on the steamboats that had just arrived from Québec City. The purpose of this recommendation was to rapidly reduce the very high number of emigrants at the quarantine station.

6. Healthy emigrants arriving on vessels with sick passengers aboard should henceforth be sent to their final destination only after being disinfected and remaining under medical observation for a few days.

7. Dr. Douglas should be authorized to hire Mr. Robert Symes to help send poor emigrants in need of assistance to their final destination. The commission also recommended that these emigrants be provided with wholesome food while they were on the island.

The *Quebec Mercury* reported that 75 people had been buried at Grosse Île on June 7: 65 in the Catholic cemetery and 10 in the Protestant one. At the time, there were 146 Protestant emigrants on the island. The newspaper added that, according to the Reverend C. Forest, the deceased Protestants included quite a few sailors, given that the crews were mostly Protestant. Forest mentioned that, since the Protestant patients were scattered throughout the station's hospitals, sheds and tents, they had to be visited individually. He went to see them on the vessels only if he had time or an opportunity to do so.

According to the *Journal de Québec*, the Catholic priests had witnessed the death of 327 people from June 3 to 7. On a daily basis, twice as many emigrants were dying on board ship than in hospital.

Death of Richard Fletcher, a sailor aboard the *Dykes*, at age 22.

Eleven burials were recorded in the register of the Protestant chapel.

SHIPS ARRIVING AT GROSSE ÎLE

Name of ship	Captain	Port of departure	Crossing time (in days)	Passengers Steerage	Cabin	No. of sick on arrival	No. of deaths during crossing
Lady Milton	J. Hayes	Liverpool (England)	33	445	0	60	21
Lord Glenelg	A. Martin	Limerick (Ireland)	32	264	0	1	7
TOTAL				709	0	61	

SHIPS LEAVING GROSSE ÎLE FOR QUÉBEC CITY

Name of ship	Quarantine time (in days)	Deaths in Grosse Île hospitals	Deaths on quarantined ships
Achilles	14	9	0
British Queen	1	0	0
Constitution	15	14	0
Hope	A few hours	0	0
Orlando	1	4	0
Royalist	17	10	0
Scotland	16	72	34

SHIPS ARRIVING IN QUÉBEC CITY WITHOUT A STOP-OVER AT GROSSE ÎLE			
Name of ship	Port of departure	Passengers	
		Steerage	Cabin
Jane and Ann	Stockton (England)	4	0

TUESDAY, JUNE 8, 1847

Repair work was under way on the wharf, which had been damaged by high tides: only 10 workers were assigned to the task, since the others had run away. A 150- by 25-foot shed was supposed to be ready Saturday, June 12, and would be used to house sick emigrants. A pre-fabricated building, measuring 100 feet long by 24 feet wide, had arrived from Québec City, and two other large buildings were under construction. About 45 labourers were working on these structures from five in the morning to seven at night.

Dr. Douglas said that emigrants on ships from Cork and Liverpool were extremely apathetic; he had never seen people so indifferent to life. Some even continued to share their berth with a dead person until the sailors or captain removed the body with boat hooks.

According to the *Quebec Mercury*, there were about 14 000 emigrants at Grosse Île.

According to the *Canadien*, Douglas mentioned in a letter written on June 8 that he was making arrangements for milk to be sold to the emigrants and the government at Québec City prices, since the inhabitants of the south shore refused to sell their milk for less than 8 cents a quart. Milk was always more expensive at Grosse Île than in Québec City.

The *Journal de Québec* was informed by a person arriving from Grosse Île that there were no cases of *Typhus Gravior* on the island and that the prevalent illnesses were rarely fatal as long as the sick were provided with fresh air and simple, wholesome food. These conditions were lacking, however, on Grosse Île. The newspaper added that, based on its information, over 25 000 emigrants had arrived at the quarantine station since the beginning of the season. More than 1 000 people had perished during the ocean voyage, and 700 more after reaching the island.

According to the *Journal de Québec*, a total of 2 360 sick people were now in quarantine: of that number, 1 150 were on shore and the rest on board the ships, 11 of which had still not been visited. The newspaper pointed out, however, that these figures only partially reflected the desperate situation at Grosse Île, where the sick and the dying were crowded into their ship's narrow hold next to the dead, who were removed only to be thrown into the water. In the newspaper's opinion, it was essential that "people who, under the cloak of humanity, sent their fellow citizens overseas, realize the state in which their compatriots arrived." [*Translation*]

One burial was recorded in the register of the Protestant chapel.

SHIPS ARRIVING AT GROSSE ÎLE

Name of ship	Captain	Port of departure	Crossing time (in days)	Passengers Steerage	Passengers Cabin	No. of sick on arrival	No. of deaths during crossing
Sobraon	J. Wilson	Liverpool (England)	32	602	5	52	31
Springhill	W. Gunn	Sligo (Ireland)	38	227	0	0	9
Thistle	P. Thomas	Waterford (Ireland)	53	175	1	0	0
Thompson	W. Benton	Sligo (Ireland)	34	159	0	11	7
Wave	R. Smallman	Dublin (Ireland)	39	389	7	0	5
TOTAL				1 552	13	63	

SHIPS LEAVING GROSSE ÎLE FOR QUÉBEC CITY

Name of ship	Quarantine time (in days)	Deaths in Grosse Île hospitals	Deaths on quarantined ships
Blonde	15	8	6
Clarendon	15	36	0
Mary	1	0	0
Tay	13	1	0

WEDNESDAY, JUNE 9, 1847

The Archbishop of Québec sent a letter to the archbishops and bishops of Ireland asking them to dissuade their compatriots from leaving their homeland as they had done in recent months. The Archbishop described the tragic situation of the poor Irish, who believed they could escape death by emigrating to America. However, contagious diseases crossed the Atlantic with them, and the emigrants died on reaching their destination. Archbishop Signay said that over 2 000 people were already on their sickbed at Grosse Île, where their ships were in quarantine. He believed that only about half would survive. More than 1 000 people had already perished since the first emigrant vessels arrived. The quarantine station, which usually employed only one clergyman, now had seven and, even so, the missionaries were exhausted. Two of the clergymen posted at the station were sick, and there was little hope that they would recover.

The Archbishop said that many emigrants, fortunate enough to leave Grosse Île in good health, soon fell ill in Québec City or Montréal. The hospitals in these two cities were crowded with patients and could not offer the necessary services. Amid the confusion, it was impossible to determine exactly how many orphans and families were now doomed to depend on public charity. Even those emigrants who escaped illness were poorly equipped to fulfil the dreams that had brought them to the shores of the St. Lawrence. Unable to find work, most lacked the resources they needed to achieve a comfortable, prosperous position.

According to the *Canadien*, people returning from Grosse Île brought news that outraged and alarmed the public. The number of sick was increasing rapidly, and they were detained in filthy conditions on board the ships. They received almost no treatment and often died of hunger. Some people even claimed that passengers were dragged on deck and thrown overboard when they were barely dead. The newspaper added that, despite the goodwill of the emigration agent and the quarantine officers, many sick emigrants were still landing in Québec City, where they were crowded into the Marine Hospital.

According to the *Quebec Gazette*, the Marine Hospital was admitting more and more sick emigrants from the vessels arriving from Grosse Île. To support its claims, the newspaper mentioned that six passengers had been taken to hospital from the *Blonde*, which had come in the night before (June 8), and that five others had been admitted that morning. It also reported that five of the 1 000 passengers crammed into the steamer *Canada* had died on their way to Montréal. According to the same newspaper, Father McGauran was at the General Hospital, after returning from Grosse Île with typhus. It also mentioned that 50 nurses and 20 orderlies were being recruited to work at the island's hospitals for £ 3 per month, with rations.

Death of John Robinson, a carpenter aboard the *Agnes*, at age 21.

SHIPS ARRIVING AT GROSSE ÎLE

Name of ship	Captain	Port of departure	Crossing time (in days)	Passengers Steerage	Cabin	No. of sick on arrival	No. of deaths during crossing
Despatch	R. Walsh	Waterford (Ireland)	47	244	11	0	5
Han Rumney	D. Hills	Hull (England)	61	178	0	0	1
Lady Gordon	T. Surr	Belfast (Ireland)	56	204	0	29	10
Magnet	O. Droste	Bremen (Germany)	40	202	0	0	1
Mail	W. Gordon	Cork (Ireland)	45	289	0	21	12
Mary	J. Harrison	Glasglow (Scotland)	34	30	2	0	3
Primrose	C. Irvine	Limerick (Ireland)	62	334	3	2	12
Standard	R. Ritchie	New Ross (Ireland)	49	365	4	12	6
Yorkshire	J. Synas	Donegal (Ireland)	39	230	5	0	2
TOTAL				2076	25	64	

SHIPS LEAVING GROSSE ÎLE FOR QUÉBEC CITY

Name of ship	Quarantine time (in days)	Deaths in Grosse Île hospitals	Deaths on quarantined ships
Agnes	18	96	35
Christiana	12	12	18
Dykes	12	6	3
Han Rumney	A few hours	0	0
John Francis	19	46	7
Lord Seaton	18	22	9
Magnet	A few hours	0	0
Marry	A few hours	0	0
Thistle	A few hours	0	0
Urania	18	20	5
Wave	1	0	0

THURSDAY,
JUNE 10, 1847

The *Henry*, commanded by Captain T. Johnstone, arrived at Grosse Île from Montrose with 25 steerage passengers who had been rescued from the *Imogene*, after it was shipwrecked off Cape Breton Island on its way from Liverpool England. Since no deaths or cases of illness were reported among its passengers or crew, the ship left the quarantine station that same day.

The government authorized Dr. Douglas to hire four more policemen.

The Executive Council accepted the recommendation made by the medical commission on June 3 to erect additional emigrant sheds on the island.

The *Journal de Québec* corrected information it had published earlier: "We believe that we should rectify our statement about bodies being thrown into the water at the quarantine station. All those who die on board ship are placed in coffins provided by the vessel's captain and then buried. There have been a few exceptions, however. For example, some captains have sent bodies ashore for burial wrapped in canvas bags, but this practice was stopped after the island's authorities got wind of it." [*Translation*]. The newspaper questioned the method of piling bodies in a large ditch and then covering them with only three inches of earth, with nothing to accelerate their decomposition. It asked "whether this should be tolerated in what is supposed to be a place of purification." [*Translation*]

The *Journal de Québec* also reported that notices had been posted on Québec City streets, offering 3 louis per month to women who wanted to work in the hospitals at Grosse Île. A maximum of 50 positions were available.

Anglican baptism of Robert Hazeltine, born September 4, 1846 to William Hazeltine, a labourer, and Eliza Burns, from County Tyrone, Ireland. The Reverend C. Forest drew up the baptismal certificate.

Death of William Andrews, mate aboard the *Abbotsford*, at age 36; of James Andrews, apprentice aboard the *Gilmour*; at age 18; and of Alexander Sutherland, steward aboard the *Agnes*, at age 35.

Six burials were recorded in the register of the Protestant chapel.

SHIPS ARRIVING AT GROSSE ÎLE

Name of ship	Captain	Port of departure	Crossing time (in days)	Passengers Steerage	Cabin	No. of sick on arrival	No. of deaths during crossing
Cape Breton	J. Murray	Dublin (Ireland)	35	176	0	9	0
Mary Brack	B. Smith	Limerick (Ireland)	38	184	0	2	7
Paragon	T. Dunstone	Falmouth (England)	57	105	0	0	0
St. Lawrence	W. Tullock	Aberdeen (Scotland)	55	208	4	0	0
TOTAL				673	4	11	

SHIPS LEAVING GROSSE ÎLE FOR QUÉBEC CITY

Name of ship	Quarantine time (in days)	Deaths in Grosse Île hospitals	Deaths on quarantined ships
Columbia	11	12	7
Congress	14	6	10
John Bolton	16	34	35
Paragon	A few hours	0	0
Springhill	2	0	0
St. Lawrence	A few hours	0	0
Wolfville	17	32	16
Yorkshire	1	0	0

FRIDAY,
JUNE 11, 1847

According to medical superintendent Douglas, the *Rose* reached Grosse Île with 14 dead aboard.

Father Edward John Horan, a priest from the Québec Seminary, arrived at the quarantine station.

The *Canadien* reported that the captains and crew of ships passing downwind from Grosse Île complained about the foul odour emanating from the island. They claimed it came from the decomposing bodies covered with only a few inches of earth.

According to the *Quebec Gazette*, Father McGuirk had returned from Grosse Île with typhus. The newspaper praised the zeal displayed by all the missionaries on the island.

One burial was recorded in the register of the Protestant chapel.

SHIPS ARRIVING AT GROSSE ÎLE

Name of ship	Captain	Port of departure	Crossing time (in days)	Passengers Steerage	Cabin	No. of sick on arrival	No. of deaths during crossing
Albion	H. Bowman	Limerick (Ireland)	54	189	0	2	17
Rose	D. McKinlay	Liverpool (England)	54	384	0	80	52
TOTAL				573	0	82	

SHIPS LEAVING GROSSE ÎLE FOR QUÉBEC CITY

Name of ship	Quarantine time (in days)	Deaths in Grosse Île hospitals	Deaths on quarantined ships
Bee	19	59	29
Caithness-shire	16	16	4
George	21	75	35

SATURDAY, JUNE 12, 1847

Summary of a letter written from Grosse Île by Bishop George Mountain to his son the Reverend Armine Mountain:

There were about 1 800 sick people at the quarantine station, and a growing number on the ships; 10 percent of these people were Protestants. The Reverend C. Forest was attending the patients in the tents, and Bishop Mountain the emigrants in the sheds and ships. Mountain was also in charge of burials. There was enough work, however, for three clergymen: one in the tents, one in the sheds and one on the vessels. At the time, the Anglican chapel was reserved for sailors. The 25-member crew of the *Gilmour*, which was in quarantine, had been decimated by sickness, death and the desertion of five men, who had escaped by stealing one of the ship's boats; only two crew members were left. Bishop Mountain described the Reverend C. Forest as being "exceedingly assiduous," adding that the latter had drawn up a list of all the sick Protestant emigrants in the sheds, who were sharing these accommodations with a large number of Roman Catholics.

According to the *Quebec Mercury*, the steamer *Neptune* left that morning for Grosse Île with provisions, and would return in the evening with passengers. The *Rowland Hill* also left in the morning to tow the *Aberdeen*.

The *Canadien* reported that there were 1 700 sick people at Grosse Île.

Death of John Jacques, second mate aboard the *Elizabeth*, at about age 22.

Three burials were recorded in the register of the Protestant chapel.

According to a list published in the *Quebec Morning Chronicle*, 155 people had died at Grosse Île during the week of June 6 to 12.

SHIPS ARRIVING AT GROSSE ÎLE

Name of ship	Captain	Port of departure	Crossing time (in days)	Passengers Steerage	Cabin	No. of sick on arrival	No. of deaths during crossing
Pacific	W. Walsh	Waterford (Ireland)	39	197	0	9	1
Resolution	W. T. Davis	Penzance (England)	58	66	0	0	0
TOTAL				263	0	9	

SHIPS LEAVING GROSSE ÎLE FOR QUÉBEC CITY

Name of ship	Quarantine time (in days)	Deaths in Grosse Île hospitals	Deaths on quarantined ships
Aberdeen	20	31	21
Argo	16	28	32
Mary Brack	2	1	1
Ninian	18	1	10
Resolution	1	0	0

EMIGRANTS ARRIVING IN THE PORT OF QUÉBEC DURING THE WEEK OF JUNE 6 TO 12

Country of origin	Number
England	3007
Ireland	6136
Scotland	258
Germany	202
Canadian ports downstream from Québec City	13
Total	9616
Previous total (as at June 5)	8681
GRAND TOTAL	18297

SICKNESS AND HOSPITALIZATION RATES AT GROSSE ÎLE DURING THE WEEK OF JUNE 6 TO 12

People admitted to hospital	1044
Sick passengers aboard ship	564
Sick captains and sailors	32
TOTAL	1640*

* During the same week, 156 people died in hospital and 93 on quarantined vessels.

SUNDAY, JUNE 13, 1847

In a letter to Archbishop Signay, Father E. J. Horan said that although the work had tapered off at Grosse Île, the clergy were still very busy. At the time, there were 1 300 to 1 400 sick emigrants on the island. Sixty-seven people had died on Friday, June 11, and even more the day before. A new hospital, with a capacity of 122 beds, had just been completed, and the sick were to be placed there on June 13 or 14. Two more hospitals were also being built. Services for the sick were better than before. However, although there were several cooks and nurses on the island, their number was still insufficient. Everywhere people clamoured for food and, in view of the gaunt features of most, their ill health no doubt stemmed mainly from lack of food.

According to Bishop Mountain, healthy emigrants were starting to be taken ashore. He took advantage of the good weather to officiate outdoors for the first time.

The *Quebec Morning Chronicle* reported that emigrants had died aboard the *Hercules* and the *Wanderer* during the week of June 13 to 19, 1847. Neither of these vessels is mentioned in the list of ships that were inspected at Grosse Île or in the list of those that arrived in Québec City.

Six burials were recorded in the register of the Protestant chapel.

SHIPS LEAVING GROSSE ÎLE FOR QUÉBEC CITY

Name of ship	Quarantine time (in days)	Deaths in Grosse Île hospitals	Deaths on quarantined ships
Dominica	12	6	5
Pacha	13	4	0

MONDAY, JUNE 14, 1847

The *Niger*, commanded by Captain W. McCleod, arrived at Grosse Île from Sydney with 104 steerage passengers who had been rescued from the *Imogene*, after it was shipwrecked off Cape Breton Island on its way from Liverpool, England. One person was reported to have died during the crossing and two others were said to be sick.

Douglas requested an additional boat with a crew of four to bring the sick ashore.

Destitute emigrants were provided with pots, kettles and other kitchen utensils by the Ordnance store in Québec City.

Sailors visiting shipmates hospitalized in the Anglican chapel informed Bishop George Mountain that people were ill on the *Lady Gordon*. After boarding the vessel, Mountain discovered 18 sick Protestants, all of whom were Presbyterians. He was delighted that the Reverend John Torrance had arrived.

In a letter to the editor of the *Quebec Gazette*, Richard Henderson, an emigrant aboard the *Achilles*, paid tribute to the ship's captain, Mr. Taylor, whose zeal and generosity towards his passengers had saved several lives.

Anonymous eyewitness account of the situation at Grosse Île, written on the island on June 14 and published in the *Journal de Québec* on June 17:

"I arrived here with about 250 tents on May 27. Forty sailing ships were in quarantine, with perhaps 10 000 passengers aboard, hundreds of whom were sick. They could not be taken ashore, however, because of a lack of sheds. I set to work pitching tents for sick people whose condition seemed most promising. Even if I had wanted to provide shelter for those whose recovery looked doubtful, I would not have had room for one tenth of them. It was impossible to enlist the help of enough women and domestics...so when I had time, I worked as a matron in the hospitals, giving the sick something to drink and washing their sores.

"I cannot describe the horrors and misery I saw...at least 13 000 terrible cases of typhus, in addition to smallpox and measles. People died right before our eyes at all hours of the day. The bodies were taken to the dead house in wheelbarrows, thrown on wood chips and left there until nightfall. They were then placed in coffins that were piled onto carts and transported to the cemetery. People perished in much greater numbers on the vessels than in the hospitals. Over 50 sailing ships with more than 15 000 passengers aboard were moored off the island.

"Steps have been taken to make the hospital more spacious, while additional sheds are being built with the help of the ships' crews....At the moment, there are 1 700 to 1 800 sick on shore, and the number of deaths is frightening. The weather is against us; a gale-force wind has been blowing for the past 48 hours, accompanied by heavy rain. Another large fleet of 12 to 14 ships has just arrived with perhaps another 4 000 miserable creatures on board...." [*Translation*]

Two burials were recorded in the register of the Protestant chapel.

SHIPS ARRIVING AT GROSSE ÎLE

Name of ship	Captain	Port of departure	Crossing time (in days)	Passengers Steerage	Cabin	No. of sick on arrival	No. of deaths during crossing
Jessie	D. Gorman	Limerick (Ireland)	56	479	10	56	26
Lady Flora Hastings	G. Wetherall	Cork (Ireland)	34	454	0	72	48
Sesostris	W. Dano	Londonderry (Ireland)	31	428	0	12	8
William Pirie	A. Agnew	Belfast (Ireland)	45	407	7	11	7
TOTAL				1 768	17	151	

SHIPS LEAVING GROSSE ÎLE FOR QUÉBEC CITY

Name of ship	Quarantine time (in days)	Deaths in Grosse Île hospitals	Deaths on quarantined ships
Eliza Carolline	20	30	33
Rankin	16	33	13
Thompson	6	0	5

SHIPS ARRIVING IN QUÉBEC CITY WITHOUT A STOP-OVER AT GROSSE ÎLE

Name of ship	Port of departure	Passengers Steerage	Cabin
Astrea	Weymouth (England)	4	0
Wellington	Bideford (England)	9	0
TOTAL		13	0

TUESDAY, JUNE 15, 1847

The *Quebec Gazette* reported that there were 2 200 sick people at Grosse Île, including 1 700 in hospital and 500 on board ship.

Death of James Adamson, mate aboard the *Argo*, at age 24, and of George Leveon, a sailor on the *Gilmour*, at age 20.

SHIPS ARRIVING AT GROSSE ÎLE

Name of ship	Captain	Port of departure	Crossing time (in days)	Passengers Steerage	Cabin	No. of sick on arrival	No. of deaths during crossing
Birman	J. Guthrie	London (England)	48	179	14	0	0
Matador	D. Panot	Bremen (Germany)	40	160	4	0	1
Sceptre	J. Robertson	Hamburg (Germany)	42	134	0	0	2
TOTAL				473	18	0	

SHIPS LEAVING GROSSE ÎLE FOR QUÉBEC CITY

Name of ship	Quarantine time (in days)	Deaths in Grosse Île hospitals	Deaths on quarantined ships
Matador	A few hours	0	0

WEDNESDAY, JUNE 16, 1847

Summary of an eyewitness account by P. O'Neil, a passenger aboard the *Birman*, which left London on April 29 and reached Grosse Île on June 15. (O'Neil claimed that he arrived at Grosse Île on June 16, but according to the list of ships inspected at the quarantine station, his vessel was registered on June 15.):

A PHYSICIAN EXAMINES EMIGRANTS ON THE DECK OF A SHIP ANCHORED OFF THE QUARANTINE STATION. MANY COM-PLAINTS WERE VOICED, IN 1847, ABOUT THE SUPERFICIAL NATURE OF THESE EXAMINATIONS. (DANIEL RAINVILLE, PARKS CANADA, 1997.)

O'Neil said that he and his fellow passengers waited all morning on June 16 for their ship to be inspected by doctors; the latter issued a health certificate immediately after visiting the vessel. At the time, there were about forty vessels waiting at the quarantine station. All the passengers and crew of the *Sisters* had typhus, and there were many other cases aboard the *Jessie*.

O'Neil mentioned that the water was covered with the bedding, kettles and other personal effects of the deceased. He described a horrible scene where sick people, who he felt had no chance of recovery, were taken ashore; several even died while they were being disembarked. On the island, where 150 people perished every day, O'Neil saw a village of white tents, which, he said, were used to house the sick. He described the exemplary behaviour of the Catholic priests, but qualified the medical services as mediocre. He left for Québec City on the morning of June 17 (or 16, according to the list of ships inspected at Grosse Île) aboard a steamer.

The *Canadien* revealed that the situation at the quarantine station was growing more alarming by the day. The report came a few days late, however, since the information was derived from a letter sent from

Grosse Île. When the informant first wrote to the newspaper, 34 ships were detained at the station. Their captains complained about slow inspections, unnecessary stop-overs and a lack of accommodations for the sick. As a result, many people in ill health remained on board and placed the lives of other passengers in danger. Apparently, there were 1 500 sick people on the island and 1 000 aboard the ships. The newspaper noted that four Catholic priests had returned in poor health from Grosse Île and that the Archbishop was asking all priests with a sufficient knowledge of English to be ready to go to the quarantine station to help the sick.

According to the *Quebec Mercury*, there were 25 ships at Grosse Île, 19 of which had just arrived.

Entries began to be made again in the burial register of the Catholic chapel.

Death of a man by the name of Hertle, a sailor aboard the *Abbotsford*.

Forty-seven burials were recorded in the register of the Catholic chapel and eight in that of the Protestant chapel.

SHIPS ARRIVING AT GROSSE ÎLE

Name of ship	Captain	Port of departure	Crossing time (in days)	Passengers Steerage	Passengers Cabin	No. of sick on arrival	No. of deaths during crossing
Lord Sandon	A. Feneran	Cork (Ireland)	36	246	0	0	17
Tay	J. Longwill	Liverpool (England)	45	371	0	15	9
Wilhelmina	J. Leslie	Belfast (Ireland)	39	276	0	4	4
TOTAL				893	0	19	

SHIPS LEAVING GROSSE ÎLE FOR QUÉBEC CITY

Name of ship	Quarantine time (in days)	Deaths in Grosse Île hospitals	Deaths on quarantined ships
Birman	1	0	0
Princess Royal	10	6	10

THURSDAY,
JUNE 17, 1847

The Catholic religious authorities asked the government to reimburse additional expenses incurred in sending a large number of priests to Grosse Île during the season. Previously, a single priest had been able to meet the spiritual needs of the emigrants detained there. The expenses included maintenance costs and accommodation and travelling expenses (e.g. for the transportation of priests to the island from various parts of the archdiocese), as well as costs related to caring for missionaries who had fallen ill. The Society for the Propagation of the Faith did not have any funds available to defray these extra expenses.

The *Quebec Mercury* reported that Douglas could count on the assistance of 11 physicians, an apothecary and a chief hospital steward.

According to the *Quebec Gazette* and the *Quebec Mercury*, all healthy passengers were housed in tents at the east end of Grosse Île. An additional shed had been erected for the sick in the western sector and was fully occupied the previous Saturday, June 12; another shed would be finished that week. Sick people on board ship were visited daily and treated by a doctor.

Five burials were recorded in the register of the Protestant chapel.

SHIPS ARRIVING AT GROSSE ÎLE

Name of ship	Captain	Port of departure	Crossing time (in days)	Passengers Steerage	Cabin	No. of sick on arrival	No. of deaths during crossing
Charlotte Harrison	A. McIntire	Greenoch (Scotland)	35	302	3	0	2
Josepha	H. Leitch	Belfast (Ireland)	39	301	0	0	2
TOTAL				603	3	0	

FRIDAY, JUNE 18, 1847

The *Catherine*, commanded by Captain T. Martel, arrived at Grosse Île from Sydney with 47 steerage passengers who had been rescued from the *Imogene*, after it was shipwrecked off Cape Breton Island on its way from Liverpool, England. Since no deaths or cases of illness were reported among its passengers or crew, the ship left the quarantine station that same day.

Legislation was adopted by the Legislative Assembly of the Province of Canada for the purpose of appointing a committee to inquire into the management of Grosse Île.

A new shed for sick emigrants, measuring 150 feet long by 25 feet wide, was finished, while another, measuring 100 feet by 24 feet, was being prefabricated in Québec City. The frame of a third 120- by 25-foot building, was already up and the rest of the structure was proceeding rapidly. A fourth building had also been ordered, and its framing was being prepared as quickly as possible.

The Executive Council committee approved Douglas' request for chartering an extra boat with a crew of four to take sick passengers ashore. It also approved the hiring, on May 25, of Mr. Barter, a fourth-year medical student, to work as an apothecary in the hospital. Barter's salary was set at 15s. per day, plus rations.

Besides the apothecary, the medical staff at Grosse Île included 12 physicians in addition to Dr. Douglas, namely, Drs. Jacques, Fenwick, Allen, Larocque, Malhiot, Damours, Dickinson, Jameson, Dease, Pinet and Johnston.

According to the *Canadien* and the *Quebec Gazette*, Father Phillippe-Honoré Jean, curate at Pointe-Lévy, was coming to attend the sick at Grosse Île.

The *Quebec Gazette* published a petition signed by numerous residents of Québec City, asking the mayor to hold a public meeting to form a society for the assistance and protection of emigrants.

The *Quebec Gazette* reported that many inhabitants of the parish of Saint-Joachim, on the north shore of the St. Lawrence nearly opposite Grosse Île, had come down with typhus.

Twenty-nine burials were recorded in the register of the Catholic chapel.

SHIPS ARRIVING AT GROSSE ÎLE

Name of ship	Captain	Port of departure	Crossing time (in days)	Passengers Steerage	Cabin	No. of sick on arrival	No. of deaths during crossing
Mountaineer	G. Flemming	Hull (England)	44	28	3	0	0
Thétis	W. Richmond	Limerick (Ireland)	40	161	0	0	3
Thomas Handford	A. Herbert	Limerick (Ireland)	38	155	0	0	1
TOTAL				344	3	0	

SHIPS LEAVING GROSSE ÎLE FOR QUÉBEC CITY

Name of ship	Quarantine time (in days)	Deaths in Grosse Île hospitals	Deaths on quarantined ships
Albion	8	0	2
Cape Breton	8	6	2
Charlotte Harrison	1	0	0
Despatch*	9	1	0
Gilmour	21	44	9
Josepha	1	0	0
Mountaineer	A few hours	0	0
Niger	4	0	0
Pacific	6	0	0
Primrose	9	2	1
Thomas Handford	A few hours	0	0

* It is hard to understand why this ship was quarantined for such a long period, since none of its passengers or crew were sick when it arrived at Grosse Île.

SATURDAY, JUNE 19, 1847

Forty-five burials were recorded in the register of the Catholic chapel and five in that of the Protestant chapel.

Death of Richard Bowes, a sailor aboard the *Lord Seaton*, at age 48.

According to a list published in the *Quebec Morning Chronicle*, 201 people had died at Grosse Île during the week of June 13 to 19.

SHIPS ARRIVING AT GROSSE ÎLE

Name of ship	Captain	Port of departure	Crossing time (in days)	Passengers Steerage	Cabin	No. of sick on arrival	No. of deaths during crossing
Jane Avery	C. Tate	Dublin (Ireland)	40	183	0	19	10
Maria and Elizabeth	W. Wood	Liverpool (England)	44	81	0	0	2
Mary and Harriett	J. Saxton	Limerick (Ireland)	62	177	1	0	9
TOTAL				441	1	19	

SHIPS LEAVING GROSSE ÎLE FOR QUÉBEC CITY

Name of ship	Quarantine time (in days)	Deaths in Grosse Île hospitals	Deaths on quarantined ships
Araminta	24	21	16
Elizabeth	19	4	10
*Lord Glenelg**	12	1	0
Mail	10	7	17
Sceptre	4	1	0
Sisters	14	17	44
Standard	10	2	4
Thetis	1	0	0

* It is hard to understand why this ship was quarantined for such a long period, since it had only one case of illness aboard when it arrived at Grosse Île.

SHIPS ARRIVING IN QUÉBEC CITY WITHOUT A STOP-OVER AT GROSSE ÎLE

Name of ship	Port of departure	Passengers Steerage	Cabin
Elizabeth	Liverpool (England)	2	0

SUNDAY, JUNE 20, 1847

Emigration agent Buchanan reported that a total of 116 ships had reached the port of Québec up to June 20 inclusively. Of the 28 452 passengers who had boarded these vessels, 3 877 had fallen ill and 1 579 had died. The sickness and death rates on these ships were thus 13.6% and 5.5% respectively.

The *Quebec Morning Chronicle* indicated that emigrants had died on the *Forrester*, the *Prince George* and the *Sovereign* during the week of June 20 to 26, 1847. None of these ships is mentioned in the list of vessels that were inspected at Grosse Île or in the list of those that arrived in Québec City.

Catholic baptism of Marguerite Elizabeth Langlois, born June 17 to Charles Langlois, a labourer at Grosse Île, and Hélène Chambers. Father Pierre Roy drew up the baptismal certificate.

Thirty-one burials were recorded in the register of the Catholic chapel and seven in that of the Protestant chapel.

SHIPS ARRIVING AT GROSSE ÎLE

Name of ship	Captain	Port of departure	Crossing time (in days)	Passengers Steerage	Cabin	No. of sick on arrival	No. of deaths during crossing
Louisa	J. McKinlay	Limerick (Ireland)	43	213	0	1	4

SHIPS LEAVING GROSSE ÎLE FOR QUÉBEC CITY

Name of ship	Quarantine time (in days)	Deaths in Grosse Île hospitals	Deaths on quarantined ships
Abbottsford	20	5	7
Lady Gordon	11	5	4
Wilhelmina	4	0	0
William Pirie	5	4	3

MONDAY,
JUNE 21, 1847

A committee of the Legislative Assembly, comprising Messrs. Aylwin, Boulton, Chabot, Cayley, Chauveau, Christie, De Witt, Moffatt and Murney, was appointed to inquire into the management of the quarantine station at Grosse Île.

According to Douglas, there were 1935 sick people in hospital and 260 aboard ship, for a total of 2195. All healthy emigrants had been taken to the tents at the east end of the island. Deaths during the week amounted to 199, and included two of the best nurses at the quarantine station. One had worked for 15 years in a "fever hospital" in Ireland. Three doctors had also fallen ill and left the station.

According to the *Canadien*, there were over 500 people at the Marine Hospital in Québec City. The newspaper also said that although the exact number of deaths at the hospital was unknown, it was very low compared with that at Grosse Île.

Catholic baptism of Ann Grace, born June 11 to Michael Grace, a labourer, and Bridget Duffy. Father Édouard Montminy drew up the baptismal certificate.

SHIPS ARRIVING AT GROSSE ÎLE

Name of ship	Captain	Port of departure	Crossing time (in days)	Passengers Steerage	Cabin	No. of sick on arrival	No. of deaths during crossing
Achsah	J. Monel	Limerick (Ireland)	42	174	0	1	2
Ross-shire	J. Teaster	Limerick (Ireland)	47	212	0	0	0
Trade	J. Pleves	Waterford (Ireland)	65	134	0	15	5
TOTAL				520	0	16	

EMIGRANTS ARRIVING IN THE PORT OF QUÉBEC DURING THE WEEK OF JUNE 13 TO 21

Country of origin	Number
England	4668
Ireland	5531
Scotland	311
Germany	290
Canadian ports downstream from Québec City	151
Total	10951
Previous total (as at June 12)	18297
GRAND TOTAL	29248*

* This represents an increase of 12432 emigrants compared with the total reported by Buchanan up to the same period in 1846, i.e. 16816.

TUESDAY,
JUNE 22, 1847

A public meeting of citizens from Québec City was held in the Legislative Assembly to form the Quebec Emigrant Society, a society for the assistance and protection of emigrants.

The *Canadien* and the *Quebec Gazette* reported that Father Pierre Beaumont, parish priest of Saint-Jean-Chrysostome, and Father Pierre-Télesphore Sax, curate at Québec City, had left for Grosse Île that day.

One burial was recorded in the register of the Catholic chapel.

SHIPS ARRIVING AT GROSSE ÎLE

Name of ship	Captain	Port of departure	Crossing time (in days)	Passengers Steerage	Passengers Cabin	No. of sick on arrival	No. of deaths during crossing
Agnes King	J. Ganson	Limerick (Ireland)	37	176	0	5	6
Ann	W. Johnston	Liverpool (England)	38	348	0	26	31
Eagle	W. Catterson	Dublin (Ireland)	41	211	0	0	6
Elizabeth	T. Dugget	Liverpool (England)	33	434	0	13	19
Helen	B. Hey	Bremen (Germany)	50	138	0	0	0
Jane Blane	P. Kelly	Sligo (Ireland)	37	225	0	4	6
TOTAL				1532	0	48	

SHIPS LEAVING GROSSE ÎLE FOR QUÉBEC CITY

Name of ship	Quarantine time (in days)	Deaths in Grosse Île hospitals	Deaths on quarantined ships
Achsah	1	0	0
Helen	A few hours	0	0
Mary and Harriett	3	0	0
Pursuit	23	30	7
Ross-shire	A few hours	0	0
Tay	6	0	4

SHIPS ARRIVING IN QUÉBEC CITY WITHOUT A STOP-OVER AT GROSSE-ÎLE

Name of ship	Port of departure	Passengers	
		Steerage	Cabin
Maid of the Mill	Glasgow (Scotland)	8	0

WEDNESDAY, JUNE 23, 1847

One hundred and fourteen burials were recorded in the register of the Catholic chapel and one in that of the Protestant chapel.

SHIPS ARRIVING AT GROSSE ÎLE

Name of ship	Captain	Port of departure	Crossing time (in days)	Passengers Steerage	Cabin	No. of sick on arrival	No. of deaths during crossing
Elliots	P. Gascoigne	Dublin (Ireland)	41	197	0	13	12
Herald	H. Auld	Dublin (Ireland)	34	559	10	0	26
Nelson's Village	J. McBerrine	Belfast (Ireland)	44	264	0	0	16
Swallow	C. Wright	Limerick (Ireland)	40	147	0	0	1
TOTAL				1 167	10	13	

SHIPS LEAVING GROSSE ÎLE FOR QUÉBEC CITY

Name of ship	Quarantine time (in days)	Deaths in Grosse Île hospitals	Deaths on quarantined ships
Ajax	27	18	33
Lotus	17	27	22
Maria and Elizabeth	4	0	2
Sesostris	9	5	4

SHIPS ARRIVING IN QUÉBEC CITY WITHOUT A STOP-OVER AT GROSSE ÎLE

Name of ship	Port of departure	Passengers	
		Steerage	Cabin
England	Stockton (England)	0	3

THURSDAY,
JUNE 24, 1847

The *Secret*, commanded by Captain J. Gowin, brought 26 steerage passengers to Grosse Île from Charlottetown. Since no deaths or cases of illness were reported, the ship left the quarantine station that same day.

Catholic baptism of Joseph Lavoie, born June 23 to Antonin Lavoie, a boatman at Grosse Île, and Josephte Lachance. Father P.-T. Sax drew up the baptismal certificate.

Forty-four burials were recorded in the register of the Catholic chapel and one in that of the Protestant chapel.

SHIPS ARRIVING AT GROSSE ÎLE

Name of ship	Captain	Port of departure	Crossing time (in days)	Passengers		No. of sick on arrival	No. of deaths during crossing
				Steerage	Cabin		
Sarah Maria	E. Faucett	Sligo (Ireland)	49	116	0	5	6

SHIPS LEAVING GROSSE ÎLE FOR QUÉBEC CITY

Name of ship	Quarantine time (in days)	Deaths in Grosse Île hospitals	Deaths on quarantined ships
Eagle	3	1	0
Jane Avery	5	14	0
Swallow	1	0	0

FRIDAY,
JUNE 25, 1847

The deaths of emigrants from the *Segastus* were recorded in the burial register of the Catholic chapel. This vessel is not mentioned in either the list of ships that were inspected at Grosse Île or the list of those that arrived in Québec City.

Three more sheds were finished and two others soon would be. The construction of new hospitals was proceeding rapidly; five of various sizes (150 by 25 feet, 120 by 24 feet, 120 by 25 feet, 100 by 24 feet, 120 by 25 feet) were already completed. Two others were supposed to be delivered in the near future.

Joseph Signay, the Catholic Archbishop of Québec, urged the Governor General, Lord Elgin, to speed up the work at Grosse Île, particularly, the construction of hospitals. This request complied with the wishes of all the Catholic priests who had been sent to the station, seven of whom were on their sickbed, suffering from typhus. They had contracted the disease "while offering spiritual comfort to the sick, especially to those unfortunate enough to be on board the ships." [*Translation*]

The *Journal de Québec* and the *Canadien* reported that tenders were requested for an additional steamer with accommodations for passengers to make one round trip per week between Québec City and Grosse Île.

According to the *Quebec Mercury*, the *Quebec Gazette* and the *Quebec Morning Chronicle*, there were 1830 sick people on the island and 114 aboard the ships.

The *Quebec Gazette* reported that 140 people had died on June 25. (It corrected this figure on June 30.)

Thirty-seven burials were recorded in the register of the Catholic chapel and two in that of the Protestant chapel.

SHIPS ARRIVING AT GROSSE ÎLE

Name of ship	Captain	Port of departure	Crossing time (in days)	Passengers Steerage	Cabin	No. of sick on arrival	No. of deaths during crossing
Juverna	J. Ledgewick	Waterford (Ireland)	36	180	2	0	1
Lawrence Forristal	J. Toole	Waterford (Ireland)	36	143	0	2	3
TOTAL				323	2	2	

SHIPS LEAVING GROSSE ÎLE FOR QUÉBEC CITY

Name of ship	Quarantine time (in days)	Deaths in Grosse Île hospitals	Deaths on quarantined ships
Juverna	A few hours	0	0
Lady Flora Hastings	12	19	15
Lawrence Forristal	A few hours	0	0
Lord Sandon	9	8	2
Louisa	5	0	0

SATURDAY,
JUNE 26, 1847

The deaths of emigrants from the *Sarah* [Ramin] were recorded in the burial register of the Catholic chapel. This vessel is not mentioned in either the list of ships that were inspected at Grosse Île or the list of those that arrived in Québec City.

> A letter written by the Anglican Bishop of Québec, George Mountain, who was posted to Grosse Île for a few days, described the tragic situation on the island and the problems encountered by the two Protestant ministers attending to the spiritual needs of the emigrants there. He noted the difficulty of locating and ministering to all 300 of the sick Protestants at the quarantine station, since they were scattered about the island and on quarantined ships and often placed in the same beds as Catholics.

According to the *Quebec Mercury*, the last 10 or 12 vessels that had reached Grosse Île had fewer sick on board than those that had arrived earlier in the season. Dr. Douglas hoped that matters were improving.

The *Quebec Mercury* and the *Quebec Gazette* reported that a third hospital would be finished at Grosse Île on June 26 and fully occupied the next day. Heavy rain over the past few days had seriously delayed work on the island. Three hundred sets of bedding, which had been washed and laid out to dry, would not be usable until fair weather returned. The newspapers also mentioned that three more physicians, namely, Dr. Jameson and Dr. Robillard, and another "Canadian professional gentleman," had gone to Grosse Île.

Fifty-five burials were recorded in the register of the Catholic chapel.

According to a list published in the *Quebec Morning Chronicle*, 156 people had died at Grosse Île during the week of June 20 to 26.

SHIPS ARRIVING AT GROSSE ÎLE

Name of ship	Captain	Port of departure	Crossing time (in days)	Passengers Steerage	Cabin	No. of sick on arrival	No. of deaths during crossing
Georgiana	J. Wilson	Dublin (Ireland)	42	184	0	17	2
Peruvian	J. Boyd	Glasgow (Scotland)	29	38	3	0	0
Progress	E. Abel	New Ross (Ireland)	52	555	0	68	27
TOTAL				777	3	85	

SHIPS LEAVING GROSSE ÎLE FOR QUÉBEC CITY

Name of ship	Quarantine time (in days)	Deaths in Grosse Île hospitals	Deaths on quarantined ships
Agnes King	4	3	0
Herald	3	3	1
Jane Blane	4	1	0
Jessie	13	22	10
Lady Milton	19	16	20
Nelson's Village	3	1	1
Peruvian	A few hours	0	0
Trade	5	2	0

SHIPS ARRIVING IN QUÉBEC CITY WITHOUT A STOP-OVER AT GROSSE ÎLE

Name of ship	Port of departure	Passengers	
		Steerage	Cabin
Wyke Regis	Poole (England)	0	6

EMIGRANTS ARRIVING IN THE PORT OF QUÉBEC DURING THE WEEK OF JUNE 22 TO 26

Country of origin	Number
England	2681
Ireland	3250
Scotland	9
Germany	138
Canadian ports downstream from Québec City	45
Total	6123
Previous total (as at June 21)**	26215
GRAND TOTAL	32338*

* This represents an increase of 10806 emigrants compared with the total reported by Buchanan up to the same period in 1846, i.e. 21532.

** According to Buchanan's last report, dated June 21, the number of emigrants totalled 29248. This would provide a grand total of 35371 arrivals in the port of Québec as at June 26. This error was not corrected in the emigration agent's subsequent reports.

NUMBER OF PEOPLE IN HOSPITAL ON GROSSE ÎLE DURING THE WEEK OF JUNE 20 TO 26

Emigrants	Patients admitted (+)	Deaths (-)	New total
Men	75	46	658
Women	89	59	642
Children	64	50	458
TOTAL	228	155	1758

SUNDAY, JUNE 27, 1847

The *Quebec Morning Chronicle* reported that emigrants had died aboard the *Courier* and the *St. George* during the week of June 27 to July 3, 1847. Neither of these vessels is mentioned in the list of ships that were inspected at Grosse Île or in the list of those that arrived in Québec City.

According to the *Quebec Mercury*, the Church Society would defray the expenses incurred in providing spiritual aid to Protestant emigrants at Grosse Île.

Burial of Alexander Prynne, a 19-year-old sailor aboard the *Aberdeen*.

Anglican baptism of George Scott, born May 18 to William Scott, a sawyer, and Elizabeth Shaw. The Reverend George Mackie drew up the baptismal certificate.

Three burials were recorded in the register of the Catholic chapel and three in that of the Protestant chapel.

SHIPS ARRIVING AT GROSSE ÎLE

Name of ship	Captain	Port of departure	Crossing time (in days)	Passengers Steerage	Cabin	No. of sick on arrival	No. of deaths during crossing
Agent	J. Mills	New Ross (Ireland)	39	387	0	0	8
Coromandel	M. Hubback	Dublin (Ireland)	45	446	0	17	10
John Bell	J. Carroll	New Ross (Ireland)	47	254	0	0	7
New York Packet	H. Kempt	Liverpool (England)	64	470	0	2	9
Panope	H. Lelly	Dublin (Ireland)	53	112	0	4	1
Solway	J. McLelland	New Ross (Ireland)	30	364	0	2	3
TOTAL				2033	0	25	

SHIPS LEAVING GROSSE ÎLE FOR QUÉBEC CITY

Name of ship	Quarantine time (in days)	Deaths in Grosse Île hospitals	Deaths on quarantined ships
Sarah Maria	3	8	0

MONDAY,
JUNE 28, 1847

The *Quebec Mercury* published a letter from Buchanan to the Québec Board of Health in which he described improvements made to emigrant reception services in Québec City. A large warehouse, known as the Blue Store, located near the Inclined Plan Wharf beneath the Citadel, had been rented for the sum of £ 100 to house the families of emigrants detained at Grosse Île or at the Marine Hospital in Québec City. Another building, on the India Wharf, was to be occupied temporarily by healthy emigrants waiting for the next ship inland.

According to the *Quebec Gazette*, five Catholic clergymen, who had recently returned sick from the Grosse Île quarantine station, were considered out of danger. However, two of their replacements, namely, Father James F. McDonnell, from Saint-Gilles, and Father Hubert Robson, from Saint-Thomas, had in turn fallen ill. The newspaper mentioned that the Archbishop of Québec had sent a circular letter to the clergy of his diocese, inviting those who were familiar with the English language to work at Grosse Île. It also reported that Mr. Robert Symes, the deputy emigration agent stationed on the island, had returned sick to Québec City a few days earlier.

According to the same newspaper, crew members of the steamers used for transporting emigrants were also falling ill. The *Rowland Hill* had lost one man.

Twenty-three burials were recorded in the register of the Catholic chapel and five in that of the Protestant chapel.

SHIPS ARRIVING AT GROSSE ÎLE

Name of ship	Captain	Port of departure	Crossing time (in days)	Passengers Steerage	Cabin	No. of sick on arrival	No. of deaths during crossing
Eliza Morrison	J. Leitch	Belfast (Ireland)	37	469	2	6	7
Junior	J. Gillis	Liverpool (England)	49	356	0	93	13
Margaret	J. Black	New Ross (Ireland)	40	528	3	20	10
TOTAL				1 353	5	119	

SHIPS LEAVING GROSSE ÎLE FOR QUÉBEC CITY

Name of ship	Quarantine time (in days)	Deaths in Grosse Île hospitals	Deaths on quarantined ships
Elizabeth	6	10	7
Georgiana	2	0	0
Sobraon	20	20	16

TUESDAY,
JUNE 29, 1847

The *Canadien* reported that the following priests had left for Grosse Île: Father Jean-Baptiste-Antoine Ferland, director of studies at the College of Nicolet, Father James Nelligan, parish priest of Saint-Sylvestre, and Father Étienne Payment, parish priest of Sainte-Marguerite.

The *Quebec Morning Chronicle* and the *Quebec Gazette* mentioned that two new hospitals, with a capacity of 260 beds, had been built. Another, with room for 120 beds, would probably be finished the following Friday, July 2. Two more hospitals were planned, but it was hard to find workmen willing to work in the vicinity of these buildings even for high wages. Tents able to accommodate 3000 people had been erected in the eastern part of the island, near the farm. Healthy passengers from ships with a large number of sick aboard were taken ashore with their luggage. After they had washed and been disinfected, they were taken directly to Montréal.

SHIPS ARRIVING AT GROSSE ÎLE

Name of ship	Captain	Port of departure	Crossing time (in days)	Passengers Steerage	Cabin	No. of sick on arrival	No. of deaths during crossing
Linden	H. Caithness	Limerick (Ireland)	42	179	0	1	1
New Zealand	J. Wilson	Newry (Ireland)	41	477	0	2	6
TOTAL				656	0	3	

SHIPS LEAVING GROSSE ÎLE FOR QUÉBEC CITY

Name of ship	Quarantine time (in days)	Deaths in Grosse Île hospitals	Deaths on quarantined ships
Ann	7	18	1
Elliotts	6	3	0
John Bell	2	0	0
New York Packet	2	1	0
Panope	2	1	0
Solway	2	1	0

WEDNESDAY,
JUNE 30, 1847

According to the *Canadien*, Father Roy, parish priest of Charlesbourg, and Father Montminy, curate at Saint-Gervais, had come back sick from Grosse Île. The priests who had returned previously in ill health were no longer in danger.

Based on the latest statistics in the *Quebec Mercury*, the *Quebec Gazette* corrected its report to the effect that 140 people had died at Grosse Île on June 25. The newspaper attributed the error to the fact that it was unable to obtain official statistics from the quarantine station despite repeated requests. Such information was needed to prevent the circulation of exaggerated rumours about the situation on the island.

In late June, the *Quebec Mercury*, the *Quebec Morning Chronicle*, the *Quebec Gazette* and the *Montreal Gazette* listed the personnel of the Grosse Île quarantine station. The medical staff included Dr. Douglas, the medical superintendent, and his assistant, Dr. Jacques. Other physicians, namely, Drs. Fenwick, Dickinson, Malhiot, Larocque, Jameson Jr., Damours and Dease were in charge of the tents, while Drs. Pinet, Watt, Robillard and Sauvé worked in the hospitals. Each physician was in charge of a certain number of patients and could count on the assistance of 77 support staff: 10 hospital stewards, 15 cooks and assistant cooks and 52 nurses and orderlies. Grosse Île's medical personnel also included Mr. Cullingford, the apothecary, Mr. McKay, the chief hospital steward, and Mrs. Fisher, the matron, or head nurse. In addition, the *Quebec Mercury* mentioned the presence of Dr. Jameson Sr.

According to Dr. Douglas, an average of 1 508 people were in hospital per day from June 1 to 30.

Thirty-eight burials were recorded in the register of the Catholic chapel and two in that of the Protestant chapel.

SHIPS ARRIVING AT GROSSE ÎLE

Name of ship	Captain	Port of departure	Crossing time (in days)	Passengers Steerage	Cabin	No. of sick on arrival	No. of deaths during crossing
Agnes and Ann	E. Bowie	Newry (Ireland)	47	297	0	0	7
Ellen Forristal	C. Bumbarry	Limerick (Ireland)	32	127	3	2	1
Margrette	J. Hardcastle	New Ross (Ireland)	59	399	0	14	21
TOTAL				823	3	16	

1847

JULY

S	M	T	W	T	F	S
				1	2	3
4	5	6	7	8	9	10
11	12	13	14	15	16	17
18	19	20	21	22	23	24
25	26	27	28	29	30	31

THURSDAY,
JULY 1, 1847

According to the *Quebec Mercury*, the Reverend George Mackie, a Protestant clergyman from the diocese of Québec, returned to Québec City after spending a week at Grosse Île. He was replaced by the Reverend Richard Lonsdell, minister of St. Paul's chapel. The Reverend John Torrance, Anglican rector of Pointe-Lévy, had worked on the island prior to Mackie. The Reverend Edward G. Sutton was still stationed at the quarantine facility.

The *Quebec Mercury* reported that a third hospital was finished and that some of the sick from the quarantined ships and small tents had been transferred there. The newspaper also mentioned that two other hospitals would be erected that week. Workers were coming from Québec City to build cooking facilities.

The *Quebec Mercury* also reported that the medical superintendent was taking steps to ensure that the operation of the quarantine station would be controlled more effectively. The small tents were being removed and the upper berths in the sheds dismantled. The author of the article mentioned that there was a steady improvement in the general state of health of passengers arriving at the time. All healthy emigrants from the *Progress*, the *Junior* and the *W. S. Hamilton* were housed at the east end of the island.

The *Quebec Mercury* indicated that Drs. Dease, Dickinson, Malhiot, Fenwick and Jameson had returned sick from the quarantine station. In addition, it reported that Father Robson, a member of the Catholic clergy, had died on July 1 from typhus, contracted while kindly attending the sick at Grosse Île. All the other priests who had come down with the disease while working on the island were doing well, including Father Montminy and Father Roy. As for Mr. Symes and Dr. McGrath, they were both on the road to recovery, and the latter would return to work in a few days. The Reverend G. Mackie left Grosse Île after spending a week there helping the Reverend E. G. Sutton, the only Protestant minister at the quarantine station.

THE MEDICAL INSPECTOR'S OFFICE AT THE PORT OF LIVERPOOL. (*ILLUSTRATED LONDON NEWS*, JULY 6, 1850, McGILL UNIVERSITY, McLELLAN LIBRARY.)

The *Montreal Gazette* published an official report from Grosse Île. According to the document, there was a substantial decline in the number of sick emigrants arriving at the quarantine station as well as in the number of deaths during the journey overseas. In general, emigrants arrived in much better health than at the beginning of the season; the improvement was particularly marked among those from Liverpool, who used to be in the worst condition. These improvements were attributed to the new regulations in force in the port of Liverpool, which required that steamers carrying emigrants from Ireland be inspected by a medical officer. If people had died or fallen ill on board, the steamers were immediately placed in quarantine in Liverpool. As a result of these measures, Irish emigrants underwent a selection process: all sick or doubtful-looking passengers were rejected unless they could produce a medical certificate attesting that they did not have typhus. The steamers also doubled the price of a ticket across the Irish Sea.

The *Quebec Morning Chronicle* reported that all sick emigrants who had arrived at Grosse Île since June 26 had been taken ashore because there was now enough room on the island. The fine weather of the past few days had promoted the convalescence of the sick people housed in tents.

Death of nurse Elizabeth Maxwell at age 30.

SHIPS ARRIVING AT GROSSE ÎLE

Name of ship	Captain	Port of departure	Crossing time (in days)	Passengers Steerage	Cabin	No. of sick on arrival	No. of deaths during crossing
Eleonora and Henrietta	L. Deneken	Bremen (Germany)	44	125	0	0	3
W.S. Hamilton	W. Joyce	New Ross (Ireland)	42	207	0	30	4
Woodbine	R. [Skeoch]	Londonderry (Ireland)	35	243	0	0	0
TOTAL				575	0	30	

SHIPS LEAVING GROSSE ÎLE FOR QUÉBEC CITY

Name of ship	Quarantine time (in days)	Deaths in Grosse Île hospitals	Deaths on quarantined ships
Agent	4	4	1
Coromandel	4	15	2
Ellen Forristal	2	0	0
Linden	2	1	0
Rose	21	40	47

SHIPS ARRIVING IN QUÉBEC CITY WITHOUT A STOP-OVER AT GROSSE ÎLE

Name of ship	Port of departure	Passengers Steerage	Cabin
Québec	Glasgow (Scotland)	10	0

FRIDAY, JULY 2, 1847

The *Saint-Roch*, commanded by Captain J. Blais, brought 20 steerage passengers to Grosse Île from Gaspé. Since no deaths or cases of illness were reported, the ship left the quarantine station that same day.

The *Tadoussac*, commanded by Captain Bernier, arrived in Québec City from Newfoundland with five steerage passengers. Once again, no deaths or cases of illness were reported.

Pierre Laurencel, an agent of the Board of Works, said that five new sheds and hospitals would be finished the following week. Together, these buildings would cover an area 590 feet long by 25 feet wide. Good workmen had been brought in from Québec City to replace those who refused to work for the wages offered. The number employed, i.e. 12 carpenters, 6 sawyers and 10 labourers, was quite sufficient.

On behalf of the Governor General, the provincial secretary explained to the Archbishop of Québec that the authorities at Grosse Île were

A shed for healthy emigrants, built in 1847 in the eastern part of the island. Better known nowadays as the Lazaretto, this building is the only survivor of a dozen sheds that were put up on this spot in August and September of 1847. (Louise McNicoll, Parks Canada, 1984).

AN AERIAL VIEW OF GROSSE ÎLE. TODAY, AS IN 1847, ONLY A NARROW BAND ALONG THE SOUTH SHORE IS INHABITED. (LOUISE MCNICOLL, PARKS CANADA, 1984).

A VIEW OF THE HOSPITAL SECTOR ON GROSSE ÎLE BEFORE THE CONSTRUCTION OF NEW SHEDS IN 1847. (BERNARD DUCHESNE, PARKS CANADA, 1996).

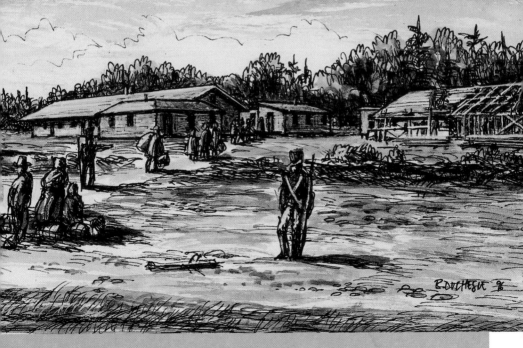

C3

THE MONUMENT TO PHYSICIANS IN THE IRISH CEMETERY IN THE WESTERN PART OF THE ISLAND. IT HONOURS IN PARTICULAR THE MEMORY OF DRS. BENSON, PINET, MALHIOT AND JAMESON, FOUR PHYSICIANS WHO DIED IN 1847 AFTER CONTRACTING TYPHUS ON GROSSE ÎLE. THE MONUMENT WAS PUT UP IN THE MID-19TH CENTURY BY MEDICAL SUPERINTENDENT GEORGE DOUGLAS AND 18 PHYSICIANS WHO HAD ASSISTED HIM IN 1847. (X. BONACORSI, PARKS CANADA, 1996).

authorized to build as many hospitals and sheds as necessary for the emigrants. If the number erected thus far was insufficient, it was due to a lack of workmen or to other circumstances beyond the authorities' control. Dr. Douglas had informed the provincial secretary on June 27 that sanitary conditions on board the vessels arriving at the time were totally satisfactory, owing apparently to the new regulations in force in the port of Liverpool and applicable to passenger ships.

The *Canadien* reported that Father Robson, who had died on July 1 at age 39, had been buried in Québec City. "A victim of his own devotion," the newspaper added, "he was one of those who returned sick from Grosse Île after attending to the spiritual needs of the emigrants in the most assiduous and moving manner. The lives of other sick priests are still in grave danger." [*Translation*]

The *Canadien* also reported that the situation at the quarantine station had improved. All the sick had been taken ashore and were receiving more care than those treated earlier in the season. A steamer arriving from Rivière-du-Loup had passed 12 ships along the way, eight of which were loaded with emigrants. Because of the strong wind blowing at the time, a large number of vessels were expected to arrive. Four or five captains were said to have died of typhus contracted from passengers.

According to the *Quebec Mercury*, the Reverend C. Forest, Protestant chaplain at the quarantine station, had been under medical observation in Trois-Rivières since he left Grosse Île two weeks earlier.

Twenty burials were recorded in the register of the Catholic chapel and three in that of the Protestant chapel.

SHIPS ARRIVING AT GROSSE ÎLE

Name of ship	Captain	Port of departure	Crossing time (in days)	Passengers Steerage	Cabin	No. of sick on arrival	No. of deaths during crossing
Aberfoyle	J. William	Waterford (Ireland)	37	327	1	0	7
Charles	G. Skinner	Limerick (Ireland)	36	116	9	0	1
City of Derry	W. Maurice	London (England)	40	293	2	0	8
Clansman	D. Peek	Greenock (Scotland)	37	217	1	3	0
Ebenezer	C. Belhoche	Saint Helier (Jersey)	37	19	0	0	0
Emily	J. Coombs	Cork (Ireland)	51	157	0	16	9
Yorkshire Lass	J. Price	Killala (Ireland)	40	282	0	62	5
TOTAL				1411	13	81	

SHIPS LEAVING GROSSE ÎLE FOR QUÉBEC CITY

Name of ship	Quarantine time (in days)	Deaths in Grosse Île hospitals	Deaths on quarantined ships
Agnes and Ann	2	0	0
Charles	A few hours	0	0
Margaret	4	11	5
New Zealand	3	0	1
Woodbine	1	1	0

SATURDAY,
JULY 3, 1847

The *Quebec Mercury* reported that 16 ships, 8 of which had passengers aboard, were sailing up the St. Lawrence; 12 others were anchored off Grosse Île.

Three burials were recorded in the register of the Protestant chapel.

By July 3, 32 622 emigrants had arrived in the port of Québec.

According to a list published in the *Quebec Morning Chronicle*, 144 people had died at Grosse Île during the week of June 27 to July 3.

SHIPS ARRIVING AT GROSSE ÎLE

Name of ship	Captain	Port of departure	Crossing time (in days)	Passengers Steerage	Cabin	No. of sick on arrival	No. of deaths during crossing
Agnes	H. Ernesfelot	Bremen (Germany)	49	331	3	0	8
Durham	J. Davidson	Liverpool (England)	46	269	0	0	7
Elizabeth	T. Richards	Limerick (Ireland)	35	111	1	0	0
Energy	M. Warren	Limerick (Ireland)	37	209	0	0	6
Graham	T. C. Beach	Southampton (England)	49	240	10	0	0
John Smith	W. Schmidt	Bremen (Germany)	51	404	0	0	8
Kate Robinson	J. Watt	Youghal (Ireland)	36	25	0	0	0
Lively	W. Checkley	Cork (Ireland)	39	189	0	14	31
Lord Panmure	P. Clarke	Glasgow (Scotland)	38	175	0	0	0
Tamarac	Cooper	Liverpool (England)	39	497	0	42	20
Triumph	P. O'Brien	Donegal (Ireland)	37	111	4	0	0
Venilia	P. Marshall	Limerick (Ireland)	37	380	11	6	13
Wakefield	J. Broomheaud	Cork (Ireland)	37	393	5	46	26
TOTAL				3334	34	108	

SHIPS LEAVING GROSSE ÎLE FOR QUÉBEC CITY

Name of ship	Quarantine time (in days)	Deaths in Grosse Île hospitals	Deaths on quarantined ships
Aberfoyle	1	0	0
Agnes	A few hours	0	0
City of Derry	1	0	0
Ebenezer	A few hours	0	0
Eliza Morrison	5	10	0
Elizabeth	A few hours	0	0
Graham	A few hours	0	0
John Smith	A few hours	0	0
Junior	5	21	0
Kate Robinson	A few hours	0	0
Lord Panmure	A few hours	0	0
Triumph	A few hours	0	0

NUMBER OF PEOPLE IN HOSPITAL ON GROSSE ÎLE DURING THE WEEK OF JUNE 27 TO JULY 3

Emigrants	Patients discharged (-)	Deaths (-)	New total
Men	134	51	922
Women	101	52	444
Children	96	41	451
TOTAL	331	144	1817

Forty-two other people, mainly children, died on board ship and were buried on Grosse Île.

SUNDAY, JULY 4, 1847

The *Quebec Morning Chronicle* reported that emigrants had died aboard the *Redwing* during the week of July 4 to 10, 1847. This vessel is not mentioned in the list of ships that were inspected at Grosse Île or the list of those that arrived in Québec City.

Death of Samuel Long, a sailor aboard the *Rankin*, during the week of July 4 to 10.

Four burials were recorded in the register of the Catholic chapel and two in that of the Protestant chapel.

SHIPS ARRIVING AT GROSSE ÎLE

Name of ship	Captain	Port of departure	Crossing time (in days)	Passengers		No. of sick on arrival	No. of deaths during crossing
				Steerage	Cabin		
Independance	J. Harper	Belfast (Ireland)	43	432	0	15	5
Rodeng	J. H. Ashton	Cork (Ireland)	45	92	2	7	2
Sophia	M. Addicks	Bremen (Germany)	60	105	0	0	0
TOTAL				629	2	22	

SHIPS LEAVING GROSSE ÎLE FOR QUÉBEC CITY

Name of ship	Quarantine time (in days)	Deaths in Grosse Île hospitals	Deaths on quarantined ships
Clansman	2	1	0
Durham	1	1	0
Eleonora and Henrietta	2	0	0
Energy	1	0	0
Sophia	A few hours	0	0

MONDAY, JULY 5, 1847

The Commissariat invited tenders for supplying Grosse Île with various articles on a regular or daily basis. The supplies listed in the announcement included foodstuffs such as fresh pork, bread, milk, tea, sugar, oatmeal, rice, salt, arrowroot and lime juice; alcoholic beverages like port wine, brandy and London porter; and, lastly, fire wood and spruce planks to make coffins. Bids were to be made before July 12.

Death of a relative of Murdoch McKay, the chief hospital steward.

Death of William Bonney, a sailor on the *James Moran*, at age 20.

One hundred and sixteen burials were recorded in the register of the Catholic chapel and eleven in that of the Protestant chapel.

SHIPS ARRIVING AT GROSSE ÎLE

Name of ship	Captain	Port of departure	Crossing time (in days)	Passengers		No. of sick on arrival	No. of deaths during crossing
				Steerage	Cabin		
Admiral	R. Buchanan	Waterford (Ireland)	34	479	1	4	6
Bolton	J. Stone	Dublin (Ireland)	40	208	0	13	2
Free Briton	W. Sanderson	Cork (Ireland)	39	185	0	11	6
James Moran	G. Morrison	Liverpool (England)	44	353	0	41	9
TOTAL				1225	1	69	

SHIPS LEAVING GROSSE ÎLE FOR QUÉBEC CITY

Name of ship	Quarantine time (in days)	Deaths in Grosse Île hospitals	Deaths on quarantined ships
Yorkshire	3	40	0

TUESDAY,
JULY 6, 1847

The *Apollo*, a ship commanded by Commodore Radcliffe which was transporting soldiers from Halifax, stopped at Grosse Île because some of its passengers had smallpox.

The *Journal de Québec* reported that a domestic at the Québec Seminary, by the name of Giroux, had died on the previous Saturday, July 3; this man had returned sick from Grosse Île after accompanying several priests to the quarantine station. Father Pierre-Télesphore Sax, who had come back from the island with no apparent symptoms of illness, was now sick with typhus.

Twenty-seven burials were recorded in the register of the Catholic chapel and four in that of the Protestant chapel.

SHIPS ARRIVING AT GROSSE ÎLE

Name of ship	Captain	Port of departure	Crossing time (in days)	Passengers Steerage	Cabin	No. of sick on arrival	No. of deaths during crossing
Unicorn	J. Boyd	Londonderry (Ireland)	45	178	0	15	4

SHIPS LEAVING GROSSE ÎLE FOR QUÉBEC CITY

Name of ship	Quarantine time (in days)	Deaths in Grosse Île hospitals	Deaths on quarantined ships
Emily	4	6	0

WEDNESDAY,
JULY 7, 1847

Dr. Douglas asked for permission to charter a "large bateau with sails" for 25s. a day to take the sick ashore with their baggage and transport healthy emigrants to the encampment set up for them on the farm at the east end of the island. This boat would replace the small steamer that had been hired previously. Douglas also asked the government to authorize expenses incurred since June 1 for hiring men and carts to bury the dead (at 15s. a day) and to carry wood and water to the kitchens and the hospitals (at 10s. a day).

The secretary of the archdiocese, Father Charles-Félix Cazeau, wrote a letter on behalf of Archbishop Signay, requesting that the government defray the extra expenses related to the unprecedented influx of emigrants. In all likelihood, the expenses incurred in providing spiritual comfort to the sick on Grosse Île and at the Marine Hospital in Québec City would exceed £ 500. So far, 11 of the priests who had been working at Grosse Île had fallen ill. The medical treatment which they required accounted for a significant proportion of the extra expenses. Several of these missionaries lived in the country and it was necessary to provide them with Québec City doctors with experience in treating their disease, since it was almost unknown outside urban areas.

Death of Father Édouard Montminy, of the parish of Saint-Gervais, from an illness he had come down with during his eight-day stay on Grosse Île.

The *Canadien* reported that Father Jean Harper, parish priest of Saint-Grégoire, Father Bernard O'Reilly, parish priest of Sherbrooke, and Father Étienne Hallé, curate at Saint-André, had recently left for Grosse Île.

Thirty-three burials were recorded in the register of the Catholic chapel.

SHIPS ARRIVING AT GROSSE ÎLE

Name of ship	Captain	Port of departure	Crossing time (in days)	Passengers Steerage	Cabin	No. of sick on arrival	No. of deaths during crossing
Camillia	J. Laughton	Sligo (Ireland)	49	138	0	0	4

SHIPS LEAVING GROSSE ÎLE FOR QUÉBEC CITY

Name of ship	Quarantine time (in days)	Deaths in Grosse Île hospitals	Deaths on quarantined ships
Admiral	2	0	0
Apollo	1 1/2	1	0
Bolton	2	1	1
Camillia	A few hours	0	0
Independance	3	12	2
Margrette	6	0	5
Rodeng	3	0	0
Wm S. Hamilton	6	18	2

THURSDAY,
JULY 8, 1847

The *Maria Julia* arrived at Grosse Île from Gaspé with 21 steerage passengers who had been rescued from the *Carricks*, after it was shipwrecked off Cap-des-Rosiers on its way from Sligo, Ireland. No deaths or cases of illness were reported among its passengers or crew.

The *Quebec Mercury* mentioned that Mr. Robert Symes, the emigration agent on Grosse Île, was convalescing from an attack of typhus. He was to return to work at the quarantine station the next day. The steamer *Queen* had arrived at Québec City on June 8, bringing about 600 passengers from Grosse Île. Only 12 ships were anchored off the station at that time.

Twenty-five burials were recorded in the register of the Catholic chapel and six in that of the Protestant chapel.

SHIPS ARRIVING AT GROSSE ÎLE

Name of ship	Captain	Port of departure	Crossing time (in days)	Passengers Steerage	Cabin	No. of sick on arrival	No. of deaths during crossing
Huron	H. Eavans	Belfast (Ireland)	43	329	0	0	9
Royal Albert	W. Balderson	London (England)	55	171	7	0	0
TOTAL				500	7	0	

SHIPS LEAVING GROSSE ÎLE FOR QUÉBEC CITY

Name of ship	Quarantine time (in days)	Deaths in Grosse Île hospitals	Deaths on quarantined ships
Royal Albert	A few hours	0	0
Unicorn	2	8	0

FRIDAY,
JULY 9, 1847

Pierre Laurencel, the Board of Works agent on Grosse Île, stated that five new sheds were finished and that two others were planned. Negotiations were under way for the construction of another hospital measuring 130 feet long by 25 feet wide and a two-storey house measuring 30 feet by 20 feet, to be used for office and storage space and for lodging the apothecaries. One of the contractors was seriously ill.

The *Canadien* suggested various measures to alleviate the problems caused by the current influx of emigrants. The newspaper's proposals included establishing new quarantine areas, particularly in Québec City and Boucherville, and opening another hospital in Québec City or Pointe-Lévy.

Catholic baptism of William Baldwin, aged five weeks, son of Matthew Baldwin and Mary Hanlon, from County Waterford, Ireland. Father Étienne Hallé drew up the baptismal certificate.

Thirty-three burials were recorded in the register of the Catholic chapel and two in that of the Protestant chapel.

SHIPS ARRIVING AT GROSSE ÎLE

Name of ship	Captain	Port of departure	Crossing time (in days)	Passengers Steerage	Cabin	No. of sick on arrival	No. of deaths during crossing
Ellen	T. Hood	Sligo (Ireland)	43	248	0	11	6

SATURDAY, JULY 10, 1847

According to the *Quebec Mercury* and the *Quebec Gazette*, the *Unicorn* of Londonderry and the *Ellen* of Sligo had arrived in Québec City with cases of typhus on board and had therefore been placed in quarantine at the mouth of the Saint-Charles River. Nine passengers were sick on board the *Unicorn*, while six emigrants and two crew members were ill on the *Ellen*. Dr. Parant immediately requested authorization to send ships back to Grosse Île if they came to Québec City with cases of typhus on board.

> The Archbishop of Québec, Joseph Signay, wrote to Governor General Elgin, describing the lamentable situation on Grosse Île. The local authorities laboured in vain to check this flood of misery. Only the day before, the sick were still languishing in the ships' holds because there was no room for them on the island. Many of the patients were placed in tents, where they had to breathe infected air, which also threatened the health of those responsible for caring for them. In two of the temporary sheds there were still two tiers of beds, and the poor patients, crowded together without regard for their sex, communicated their diseases to one another, as might easily be imagined.

The *Quebec Mercury* reported that the Reverend J. Torrance, a minister of the Church of England and curate at Pointe-Lévy, was suffering from typhus, which he had caught during his stay on Grosse Île. The newspaper also stated that the Reverend R. Lonsdell, minister of St. Paul's chapel, had not been feeling well since he returned from the quarantine station.

Thirty-five burials were recorded in the register of the Catholic chapel and three in that of the Protestant chapel.

According to a list published in the *Quebec Morning Chronicle*, 165 people had died at Grosse Île during the week of July 4 to 10.

SHIPS ARRIVING AT GROSSE ÎLE

Name of ship	Captain	Port of departure	Crossing time (in days)	Passengers Steerage	Passengers Cabin	No. of sick on arrival	No. of deaths during crossing
Charles Richard	S. Angus	Sligo (Ireland)	44	178	0	8	9
Tom	W. Courthard	Dublin (Ireland)	46	115	0	0	4
TOTAL				293	0	8	

SHIPS LEAVING GROSSE ÎLE FOR QUÉBEC CITY

Name of ship	Quarantine time (in days)	Deaths in Grosse Île hospitals	Deaths on quarantined ships
Ellen	1	2	0
Free Briton	5	3	0
Tamarac	7	9	13
Venilia	7	1	0

EMIGRANTS ARRIVING IN THE PORT OF QUÉBEC DURING THE WEEK OF JULY 4 TO 10

Country of origin	Number
England	3898
Ireland	9782
Scotland	436
Germany	956
Canadian ports downstream from Québec City	42
Total	15114
Previous total (as at July 3)	32622
GRAND TOTAL	47736*

* This represents an increase of 25815 emigrants compared with the total reported by Buchanan up to the same period in 1846, i.e. 21921.

SUNDAY, JULY 11, 1847

The *Quebec Morning Chronicle* reported that emigrants had died on board the *Britain* and the *Johana* during the week of July 11 to 17, 1847. Neither of these vessels is mentioned in the list of ships that were inspected at Grosse Île or in the list of those that arrived in Québec City.

The *Quebec Gazette* announced that there were 21 vessels anchored at Grosse Île.

Catholic baptism of Catherine McLaughlin, aged three years nine months, and of Eliza McLaughlin, aged six years six months, daughters of Walter McLaughlin and Mary Murphy, from County Monaghan, Ireland. Father Célestin-Zéphirin Rousseau drew up the baptismal certificate.

Fifty-eight burials were recorded in the register of the Catholic chapel and four in that of the Protestant chapel.

SHIPS ARRIVING AT GROSSE ÎLE

Name of ship	Captain	Port of departure	Crossing time (in days)	Passengers Steerage	Cabin	No. of sick on arrival	No. of deaths during crossing
Alert	J. Laughlan	Waterford (Ireland)	37	234	0	9	4
Ceylon	J. Custard	New York (United States) *		0	0	2	1
Charlotte	R. Drewrey	Plymouth (England)	40	330	6	0	2
Collingwood	W. McClintock	Londonderry (Ireland)	46	202	0	1	4
Erin's Queen	J. Davidson	Liverpool (England)	40	517	1	130	45
Golden Spring	H. Poole	London (England)	46	149	0	0	3
Jessie	W. Oliver	Cork (Ireland)	38	437	4	85	36
John Jardine	J. Samson	Liverpool (England)	38	389	0	12	12
Manchester	P. Browne	Liverpool (England)	37	512	0	9	11
TOTAL				2770	11	248	

* This ship left the port of New York on June 16. The sick and dead consisted of crew members, since there were no emigrants aboard.

SHIPS LEAVING GROSSE ÎLE FOR QUÉBEC CITY

Name of ship	Quarantine time (in days)	Deaths in Grosse Île hospitals	Deaths on quarantined ships
Huron	3	6	5
James Moran	6	43	4
Tom	1	0	0
Wakefield	8	37	9

MONDAY,
JULY 12, 1847

Dr. Parant was given authority to turn ships back to Grosse Île if they arrived in the port of Québec with cases of typhus on board.

The provincial secretary informed Douglas and Buchanan of the various resolutions passed by the emigration commissioners concerning the transportation of emigrants to Montréal, so that the two men might act accordingly:

1. Strict measures should be taken to ensure that emigrants arriving at Grosse Île were clean. All passengers and their clothing should be washed; feather beds should be emptied, aired and cleaned, and mattress covers should be thoroughly washed.

2. Emigrants should not be overcrowded on the steamers; for example, no more than 600 passengers should be embarked on the largest boats.

3. Steamers without an upper deck should not be used to transport emigrants on the St. Lawrence River.

4. The embarking of emigrants should be supervised by a qualified medical officer to prevent sick people or doubtful cases from boarding unnoticed.

5. Emigrants should be separated into three groups that should be isolated from one another both on Grosse Île and on the steamers going to Montréal:

   a) healthy emigrants from ships without any cases of illness;

   b) healthy emigrants from ships on which disease had broken out; and

   c) convalescent emigrants.

6. Steamers transporting emigrants should be scheduled so that only one boat reached Montréal per day.

The Executive Council committee approved the request made by Dr. Douglas on July 7 that funds be provided to hire a new sailboat and pay for expenses related to burying the dead and transporting wood and water on the island.

According to the *Canadien*, the recent arrival of fine weather had helped to relieve the suffering of the sick emigrants in the sheds on Grosse Île: «The death rate, which had suddenly shot up, has now abated somewhat.» [*Translation*]

The *Quebec Mercury* announced that 16 ships were anchored at Grosse Île. Three others had left the quarantine station for the port of Québec.

Six burials were recorded in the register of the Protestant chapel.

SHIPS ARRIVING AT GROSSE ÎLE

Name of ship	Captain	Port of departure	Crossing time (in days)	Passengers Steerage	Cabin	No. of sick on arrival	No. of deaths during crossing
Avon	M. Johnston	Cork (Ireland)	54	550	2	140	137
Lloyds	W. Matthewson	London (England)	42	207	8	0	2
Sarah	G. Fletcher	Liverpool (England)	44	249	6	31	31
TOTAL				1006	16	171	

SHIPS LEAVING GROSSE ÎLE FOR QUÉBEC CITY

Name of ship	Quarantine time (in days)	Deaths in Grosse Île hospitals	Deaths on quarantined ships
Charlotte	1	0	0
Collingwood	1	0	0
Golden Spring	1	0	0

TUESDAY, JULY 13, 1847

Father Antoine Campeau, parish priest of Saint-Georges, and Father Joseph-Hercule Dorion, parish priest of Drummondville, arrived to take up their duties at Grosse Île. Father C.-Z. Rousseau, curate at Saint-Henri, had preceded them.

In response to the request made by the Archbishop of Québec on July 7, the Executive Council committee recommended that the sum of £ 250 be allocated to help pay for expenses incurred by priests providing spiritual comfort to emigrants on Grosse Île and at the Marine Hospital. The committee also proposed that similar assistance be offered to other religious denominations, in proportion to the services they rendered.

Testimony by the Reverend William Moylan, a Catholic priest, before the committee inquiring into the management of Grosse Île:

Father Moylan had stayed on Grosse Île on two occasions, at the beginning of May and the end of June. At the time of his first stay, there were 6 or 7 doctors at the quarantine station, while at the end of June, there were 10. In May, no additional accommodations had been put up to shelter the emigrants, apart from 300 to 400 tents. More tents were eventually erected for healthy emigrants at the east end of the island.

During the priest's first stay, there were over 1 100 sick people on the island and as many more on the ships. The sick were placed in the old hospital, in tents, in the sheds previously used by healthy emigrants and in the Catholic and Protestant chapels.

A NURSE AT WORK IN ONE OF THE HOSPITALS OF THE QUARANTINE STATION. IN THE SUMMER OF 1847, THE PITIFUL STATE OF THE PATIENTS IN THE HOSPITALS AND SHEDS WAS PARTLY DUE TO THE LACK OF TRAINED NURSES AT GROSSE ÎLE. (DANIEL RAINVILLE, PARKS CANADA, 1997.)

They had a roof over their head, but their living conditions were extremely crowded. Father Moylan did not know how many nurses were working on the island, but it was evident that there were far too few. The sick received little attention; the priest recalled, for example, that on one occasion, sick people had had to wait 18 hours before receiving assistance.

There was sufficient bedding but many tents had been put up without floors, and when it rained, the beds became soaked with water; the buildings, on the other hand, generally did not leak. In the older sheds, there was a double tier of beds with only three or four feet between the upper and lower levels. Since the planks of the upper berths were widely spaced, filth from the patients above would fall onto the beds below, making it impossible for their occupants to breathe clean air, confined as they were to such a tiny space. It was very difficult for patients in the upper tier of berths to leave or enter their beds. Father Moylan had noticed, however, that these shortcomings were being corrected when he returned to Grosse Île at the end of June.

In contrast to the situation on the ships, there seemed to be sufficient food on the island, but it was poorly distributed; the priest mentioned that he had been obliged to take meat away from a typhus patient, to whom it was not supposed to be served. Some effort was made to keep the new buildings and the hospital clean, but this was hardly the case in the old sheds and the tents, where the air was foul with the smell of excrement left in unemptied chamber pots.

Sick people lay for a long time one beside the other, often two or three to a bed. Apparently, the corpses of those who died were not removed until morning, even when it meant that the body was left overnight in a bed shared by another patient. As well, men and women were often placed in the same quarters, without regard for their sex. In the old hospital, patients were given plenty of liquids to drink; elsewhere, however, and especially in the tents and old sheds, this service was greatly neglected and very often the priests took it upon themselves to give patients something to drink.

At the time of Father Moylan's first visit, in May, sick people on the ships were given almost no medical attention. On some vessels, the sick had to wait four or five days before seeing a doctor. These people could have at least been allowed to disembark and stay in tents, which were not lacking at the time. Because these sick people were not taken ashore, the mortality rate on the ships was twice as high as that on the island. It was only at the end of June that all sick passengers were systematically given permission to land.

Father Moylan was of the opinion that, in general, the emigrants had not been given suitable care by the ships' captains and crews. Insufficient food and poor hygienic conditions had aggravated the risk of disease breaking out on the vessels. Most of those he had visited were in a disgusting state: filth had accumulated on the floor of the holds and, in some cases, chamber pots had not been emptied for several days. He also noticed that beds were extremely dirty and full of vermin.

Burials were performed without delay on Grosse Île. Father Moylan recalled that, at the time of his first visit, the graves were not deep enough; coffins were piled one on top of the other and the uppermost ones were covered with scarcely a foot and a half of earth. By the end of June, there had been some improvement in this respect. The cemetery was only about two hundred yards away from the hospital and it was simply a matter of luck so far that the infection had not spread.

There was a sutler selling provisions on the island, and his prices for the emigrants were much higher than those charged in Québec City. Milk supplies came in part from the parish of Saint-Thomas-de-Montmagny on the south shore and in part from Dr. Douglas' farm, which covered most of the level land on the island. However, Father Moylan did not know the price of milk sold to the emigrants. He commented that Dr. Douglas had shouldered such enormous responsibilities that it was impossible for him to carry them out satisfactorily. Furthermore, several of the abuses observed during the season could have been avoided if the medical superintendent had been responsible solely for managing the hospital.

Father Moylan ended his testimony with various remarks and suggestions:

1. The new hospitals had been built much too close to one another and to the buildings already standing; the farm would have been a much more suitable site.

2. There should be a return to the earlier system in which one doctor was in charge of the hospitals and an inspecting physician was responsible for visiting the ships and each of these doctors had distinct, clearly defined duties.

3. There should always be a detachment of troops on the island to maintain order; the six policemen who had been stationed on the island for the past two years had not been up to the task, especially since several of them set poor examples with regard to drunkenness and immorality.

4. A major source of discontent among those working on the island was the fact that Dr. Douglas had been granted the privilege of operating the farm as a private enterprise. Several boatmen receiving government pay were employed by Dr. Douglas on his farm when they had no work to do, without being paid by him. The other employees wanted to obtain similar privileges and be allowed to use government boats to go to the mainland for their personal affairs.

5. According to all the priests and pastors who had worked on the island, unscrupulous nurses and orderlies took money from the sick and dying. In fact, convalescent patients sometimes stole from fellow sufferers.

Testimony by Dr. George M. Douglas, medical superintendent of the quarantine station, before the committee inquiring into the management of Grosse Île:

Dr. Douglas replied to certain comments made by Father Moylan before the committee. He stated that the number of sick people on quarantined ships had never surpassed 494, i.e. the total recorded on 19 ships on June 11. As for the lack of nurses, Douglas stated that he had told Father Hugh McGuirk that he was free to hire as many nurses as possible from among the healthy passengers; high salaries had been promised. The priest's attempts to recruit new employees had been unsuccessful; even next of kin abandoned one another as soon as they could. Douglas admitted that keeping the sick in tents, especially in those without floors, was not an appropriate solution. However, now that iron beds were being used, the situation was much better. As for the upper tier of beds in the sheds for healthy passengers, they had been removed.

The medical superintendent of Grosse Île asserted that food supplies were properly distributed on the island and that the doctors in charge of the hospitals were capable of providing diets that were appropriate for the sick. According to Douglas, the case cited by Father Moylan, in which a sick person had been served meat even though it was not allowed in his diet, had been misinterpreted: an inquiry among his staff had revealed that the sick man had stolen the meat from a convalescent patient. Douglas added that this situation occurred frequently, especially among the poorer Irish, who were unaccustomed to meat and believed that such food would give them strength.

At the beginning of the navigation season, the sick were overcrowded in the old sheds, and there was a lack of order and cleanliness. Members of the same family were put in the same bed owing to the limited amount of room and the need to remove the sick from the ships as quickly as possible. Douglas had given strict orders that the bodies of the dead were to be taken to the morgue as rapidly as could be managed. It was possible, however, that this rule had not always been respected in the tents where children had died.

In the old hospital, patients had never been placed two in a bed, except in the case of very young children, and persons of the opposite sex were always placed in separate rooms. Because of the shortage of nurses, it had been decided to keep families together, either in the tents or in the new hospitals, in the hope that this would encourage the stronger emigrants to help the weaker.

Douglas did not doubt that certain patients may have suffered from thirst on occasion, but he added that, as a general rule, the patients were given plenty of barley water and lime juice by the nurses. The doctors in charge of the hospitals had been told to provide the sick with cooling drinks and to keep them clean, since these measures were more effective than medicine against the diseases encountered at the quarantine station.

No ship with sick passengers on board had ever had to wait for more than five days before being visited by a doctor. Except when the weather was exceptionally bad, Douglas himself had visited each vessel at least once a day. Dr. Jacques, Dr. Fenwick and Dr. Allen, as well as other physicians, had also taken turns making daily visits to the ships in another boat. The lack of facilities on land (accommodations other than tents were needed) meant that the sick were better off on board the vessels than in the tents, contrary to the assertions of Father Moylan. On the ships, sick people had a chance of being cared for by their friends, who could not desert them; they were protected from bad weather and had access to cooking areas. It is true that the bodies of the dead were left for a while in their bunks, since the passengers and crew members sometimes refused to carry them away. The captains were then obliged to remove them on their own. Douglas had been told that in certain cases, boat hooks had to be used to pull out the bodies, since even close relatives refused to touch them.

The present site of the cemetery, a six-acre field, was the only place on the west end of the island where the soil was deep enough for coffins to be buried. At first, the corpses carried off the ships were buried by those who transported them. But the graves dug on these occasions had proven to be too shallow and now six men were regularly assigned to the task of burying the coffins in five- to six-foot-deep graves. It had been demonstrated that even six inches of soil over a body was sufficient to prevent any emanations from escaping. Since the beginning of the season, Douglas had made it quite clear to the Catholic priests and Protestant clergymen that responsibility for proper, decent burials lay entirely with them; they could refuse any burial that did not meet their requirements without having to check with the medical superintendent.

The sutler selling provisions on the island had the right to ask passengers for 15 percent more than what was charged in Québec City. This had been in the terms of his contract since 1832, and the price lists were approved by the chief emigration agent every spring. All supplies were sold to the hospitals and island employees at Québec City prices. Up to that time, all the milk produced on Grosse Île's farm had been provided to the patients in the hospitals at a cost of 3s. per quart. In June, a contract for additional milk supplies at 4.5s. per quart had been signed with a farmer at Saint-Thomas-de-Montmagny. Since then, the Commissariat Department had taken charge of expenditures for provisions and had negotiated contracts for all hospital supplies, including milk. At no time had milk from the farm been sold to the emigrants, except during September and October of the previous year. It was given only to the sick, apart from a small amount provided to the clergy in the morning and the evening.

A small area at the west end of the island was being used for farming; it was a piece of swampy land that had been cleared and drained by Dr. Douglas at his own expense over a six-year period. Marquees and ordinary tents had been set up there for the use of captains and cabin passengers suffering from typhus; the new storekeeper had also set up his storehouses and ovens there. At the east end of the island, the land had been cleared, fenced and drained over the past six years and was used for farming. The dry area in this sector was now completely occupied by the tents for healthy emigrants.

The year's problems were caused by a lack of medical personnel. Staff members often fell ill about two or three weeks after arriving, just when they were beginning to understand what their work entailed. This meant that Douglas had been unable to confine his duties to supervising the hospitals, since he had been required to visit and inspect the ships himself. Within the space of only five weeks, 12 physicians — Drs. McGrath, Johnstone, Fenwick, Allen, Malhiot, Dickinson, Damours, Jameson Jr., Dease, Sauvé, Jameson Sr. and Pinet — had come down with typhus, and two others, Dr. Robillard and Dr. Larocque, had left their duties for different reasons. Except in the case of Dr. Jacques, Douglas had been obliged to make do with new workers who were unfamiliar with the routine. He mentioned that he had just hired Mr. Aylwin, a senior medical student, and stressed the remarkable contribution made under difficult circumstances by Mr. Cullingford, the apothecary who had been working at the quarantine station for the past four years. The latter's vast experience had proved invaluable.

The police force of six men had been sufficient for the past five years. Douglas stated that there was less drunkenness and more order with six policemen than with 50 soldiers. In five years, he had fired only two for alcoholism. For the past five weeks, a detachment of troops had been stationed on Grosse Île along with the policemen, and anyone who wanted could easily compare the sobriety and moral behaviour of the two groups.

According to the medical superintendent, the «unremunerated» work done by boatmen on his farm was a matter between the men and himself. For the past two years, this work had taken very little of their time. The four boatmen had been working with him for 10 years and seemed to be content with their lot. Commenting on their «apparent lack of remuneration,» Douglas pointed out that at least two of them received more for the work they did at the farm than from their government jobs.

As for the theft of money from the sick and dying in the hospitals, it was no doubt true that, on occasion, some nurses and medical attendants were guilty of such acts. It was known that the same thing happened at the Marine and Emigrant Hospital in Québec City and at the emigrant sheds in Montréal. However, Dr. Douglas stressed that the only people who could be persuaded to care for the sick in times of pestilence were very often the most unprincipled members of both sexes.

When sick passengers arrived on the island, they were questioned by the chief hospital steward about the amount of money they had in their possession. When possible, the steward took this money into his keeping and noted the amount in a special book. If the person died, the money and any personal effects were sent to Mr. Buchanan, the emigration agent in Québec City. During the season, sums of money may also have been entrusted by patients to priests and pastors who had then fallen ill and left the island; in such instances, it was difficult to trace where the money had gone. Douglas concluded his testimony by saying that cases had been reported in which the sick were robbed by convalescing patients.

According to the *Canadien*, 13 vessels were anchored at Grosse Île. They had set out with a total of 4950 passengers, but 434 had perished during the crossing. On one ship that originally carried 550 passengers, 136 had died and the others were sick or weak.

The *Quebec Mercury* and the *Quebec Gazette* reported that, by June 30, 821 deaths had been recorded at Grosse Île; by July 13, the bodies of 715 individuals who had died aboard ship had been buried on Grosse Île, and 2559 people had perished at sea.

The *Quebec Gazette* reported that the steamer *St. George* had arrived at Québec City from Grosse Île with Captain Seaman and the entire crew of the cargo ship *Emma*, which had been shipwrecked on June 30 after colliding with the *John Jardine*, now in quarantine at Grosse Île.

Death of Nurse Garneau.

Two burials were recorded in the register of the Protestant chapel.

SHIPS ARRIVING AT GROSSE ÎLE

Name of ship	Captain	Port of departure	Crossing time (in days)	Passengers Steerage	Cabin	No. of sick on arrival	No. of deaths during crossing
Medusa	J. Woodworth	Cork (Ireland)	40	199	6	4	2
Perseverance	H. Briggs	Hamburg (Germany)	56	165	0	0	4
Royal Adelaide	A. Smith	Waterford (Ireland)	45	198	0	0	0
Triton	J. Smith	Liverpool (England)	61	483	10	108	93
Wonder	T. Hunter	Sligo (Ireland)	41	176	2	1	2
TOTAL				1221	18	113	

SHIPS LEAVING GROSSE ÎLE FOR QUÉBEC CITY

Name of ship	Quarantine time (in days)	Deaths in Grosse Île hospitals	Deaths on quarantined ships
Lively	10	14	0
Lloyds	1	0	0
Royal Adelaide	A few hours	0	0

WEDNESDAY,
JULY 14, 1847

The *Emarance*, commanded by Captain J.-B. Thibault, arrived at Grosse Île from Richibucto, New Brunswick, with 15 steerage passengers who had been rescued from the *Carricks*, after it had been shipwrecked off Cap-des-Rosiers. Since no deaths or cases of illness were reported among its passengers or crew, the ship left for Québec City the next day.

Dr. Douglas announced that the 463 beds in the five newly built hospitals were occupied by the sick. Mr. Fréchette, the contractor for two of these buildings, was suffering from typhus. Mr. Laurencel, the Board of Works agent, had concluded a contract for another 132- by 25-foot building and a small 30- by 25-foot house to lodge a medical assistant.

Governor General Elgin promised Archbishop Signay that he would, as far as possible, provide financial compensation for expenses incurred by the priests who brought spiritual comfort to the emigrants at Grosse Île. Since it was difficult to assess exactly how much money was needed, he was advancing the sum of £ 250. The Governor General expected to receive a report on how the funds were used.

In response to a petition sent to the Montréal Board of Health on July 13, denouncing the inefficiency of the Grosse Île quarantine station, the Executive Council committee recommended that the Solicitor General, John H. Cameron, be sent to Grosse Île to decide on a new location where healthy passengers from boats with sickness aboard might be placed in quarantine. The committee also declared that quarantine regulations should be enforced much more strictly so that no vessel could leave the quarantine area without the authorization of a health officer; the committee suggested that the battery on Grosse Île be armed so that it could be used to ensure that ships complied with the regulations.

The *Canadien* announced the death of Father Pierre Roy, parish priest of Charlesbourg, who had returned from Grosse Île about ten days earlier.

The *Quebec Gazette* told its readers that Dr. Damours had come back sick from Grosse Île.

Catholic baptism of Mary Morrison, aged 10, and of James Morrison, aged 4, children of Theresa Mooney and the late John Morrison, from County Down, Ireland. Father A. Campeau drew up the baptismal certificate.

Act of profession of the Catholic faith by Thomas Collins, in the presence of his wife, Johanna Gahaghan, and his son, Thomas. Father J.-H. Dorion drew up the act of abjuration.

Seventy-seven burials were recorded in the register of the Catholic chapel and two in that of the Protestant chapel.

SHIPS ARRIVING AT GROSSE ÎLE

Name of ship	Captain	Port of departure	Crossing time (in days)	Passengers Steerage	Cabin	No. of sick on arrival	No. of deaths during crossing
Goliah	Slater	Liverpool (England)	54	600	3	66	41
Thistle	J. Turner	Liverpool (England)	44	382	0	13	4
TOTAL				982	3	79	

SHIPS LEAVING GROSSE ÎLE FOR QUÉBEC CITY

Name of ship	Quarantine time (in days)	Deaths in Grosse Île hospitals	Deaths on quarantined ships
Ceylon	3	1	0
Perseverance	1	0	0
Progress	18	31	5
Wonder	1	1	0

SHIPS ARRIVING IN QUÉBEC CITY WITHOUT A STOP-OVER AT GROSSE ÎLE			
Name of ship	Port of departure	Passengers	
		Steerage	Cabin
Duchess of Beaufort	Benicaló (Spain)	0	3

THURSDAY, JULY 15, 1847

The Governor General announced that Solicitor General Cameron was being sent to Grosse Île to determine what measures might make the quarantine station more efficient. A military force consisting of a lieutenant and 25 men would be put at his service to enforce quarantine regulations more strictly and to help set up tents.

According to the *Quebec Gazette*, 10 ships were anchored at Grosse Île.

Catholic baptism of James Maher, born July 15, son of Eliza Waters and the late James Maher, from County Kilkenny, Ireland. Father A. Campeau drew up the baptismal certificate.

Three burials were recorded in the register of the Protestant chapel.

SHIPS ARRIVING AT GROSSE ÎLE

Name of ship	Captain	Port of departure	Crossing time (in days)	Passengers		No. of sick on arrival	No. of deaths during crossing
				Steerage	Cabin		
Pallas	R. Perris	Bremen (Germany)	57	153	0	1	2
Roseanna	W. Wilkinson	Cork (Ireland)	44	270	2	19	3
TOTAL				423	2	20	

SHIPS LEAVING GROSSE ÎLE FOR QUÉBEC CITY

Name of ship	Quarantine time (in days)	Deaths in Grosse Ile hospitals	Deaths on quarantined ships
Alert	3	1	1

FRIDAY, JULY 16, 1847

Father Léon Provencher, curate at Sainte-Marie-de-Beauce, arrived at Grosse Île.

The *Canadien* reported that the Reverend Richard Lonsdell and the Reverend Edward Cullen Parkin, two Protestant ministers, had come back sick from the quarantine facility.

The *Quebec Mercury* reported that Dr. Jameson Sr. had fallen ill and left the island.

Seventy-six burials were recorded in the register of the Catholic chapel.

SHIPS ARRIVING AT GROSSE ÎLE

Name of ship	Captain	Port of departure	Crossing time (in days)	Passengers Steerage	Cabin	No. of sick on arrival	No. of deaths during crossing
Princess	B. Murphys	Bremen (Germany)	55	320	0	1	1

SHIPS LEAVING GROSSE ÎLE FOR QUÉBEC CITY

Name of ship	Quarantine time (in days)	Deaths in Grosse Île hospitals	Deaths on quarantined ships
Charles Richards	6	8	0
John Jardine	4	6	0
Manchester	5	17	0
Medusa	3	0	0
Pallas	1	0	0
Princess	A few hours	0	0

SATURDAY, JULY 17, 1847

The military authorities informed the Governor General that they had no more tents for the emigrants on Grosse Île.

In an affidavit signed before notary Archibald Campbell of Québec City, Michael McGrath, captain of the *Aberdeen*, which had arrived at Grosse Île on May 23 and left on June 12, declared that disease had broken out on his ship even before it sailed from Liverpool. The charterer had allowed passengers to embark without inquiring into their state of health; some of the people who had boarded were suffering from typhus. McGrath had told the owner about the situation and requested that a doctor be sent on board to examine the passengers. He had asked the owner's agent several times to take the sick people off the vessel, but this man took no action until the morning that the *Aberdeen* was to set sail, when he sent a steamboat alongside. The sick did not disembark because their friends on board prevented them from leaving. Previous to this, McGrath had obliged four passengers suffering from dysentery and typhus to go ashore.

When the ship left Liverpool, there were six or seven cases of typhus on board; subsequently, the number increased every day. Since it did not take very long to make the crossing, only nine people died during the voyage. While the ship was in quarantine, 30 passengers died, as well as a mate and an apprentice. McGrath himself came down with typhus during this period. Captain McGrath said that he had taken great care of his passengers' well-being during the voyage, ensuring that the hatches were left open and taking other measures for their comfort and health. He said that during such a short trip, none of the passengers would have fallen ill if people with typhus had not embarked at Liverpool.

The Governor General asked Douglas, Buchanan and Parant to keep a record of all the emigrants who died during the journey overseas or after they arrived in the colony, so that lists might be published for relatives and friends seeking news of the deceased.

The *Quebec Mercury* reported that the *Erin's Queen*, which had arrived at Grosse Île the previous Sunday, had been abandoned by its captain and crew.

Catholic baptism of Patrick Sullivan, born July 17 to Michael Sullivan and Mary Foley, from County Kerry, Ireland. Father A. Campeau drew up the baptismal certificate.

According to a list published in the *Quebec Morning Chronicle*, 171 people had died at Grosse Île during the week of July 11 to 17.

SHIPS ARRIVING AT GROSSE ÎLE

Name of ship	Captain	Port of departure	Crossing time (in days)	Passengers Steerage	Cabin	No. of sick on arrival	No. of deaths during crossing
Mary	W. Copton	Sligo (Ireland)	54	154	0	5	9

SHIPS LEAVING GROSSE ÎLE FOR QUÉBEC CITY

Name of ship	Quarantine time (in days)	Deaths in Grosse Île hospitals	Deaths on quarantined ships
Thistle	3	6	3

EMIGRANTS ARRIVING IN THE PORT OF QUÉBEC DURING THE WEEK OF JULY 11 TO 17

Country of origin	Number
England	1 530
Ireland	2 170
Scotland	600*
Germany	168*
Canadian ports downstream from Québec City	10
Total	4 478
Previous total (as at July 10)	47 736
GRAND TOTAL	52 214**

* These figures may have been inverted.

** This represents an increase of 29 181 emigrants compared with the total reported by Buchanan up to the same period in 1846, i.e. 23 033.

NUMBER OF PEOPLE IN HOSPITAL ON GROSSE ÎLE DURING THE WEEK OF JULY 11 TO 17

Emigrants	Deaths (-)	New total
Men	76	863
Women	58	421
Children	37	389
TOTAL	171	1 673

Thirty-six other people who died on board ship were buried on Grosse Île.

SUNDAY,
JULY 18, 1847

The *Febulon*, commanded by Captain R. McKay, arrived at Grosse Île from Prince Edward Island with 52 steerage passengers. Since no deaths or cases of illness were reported, the ship left the quarantine station that same day.

According to the *Quebec Mercury* and the *Quebec Gazette*, 100 patients were admitted to hospital on Grosse Île on July 18. It was also reported that Dr. Pinet was seriously ill.

The *Quebec Gazette* mentioned that the captain of the *Erin's Queen* had returned to his ship, which he and his crew had abandoned on July 17.

Catholic baptism of John Kelly, born June 21 to Thomas Kelly and Ann McCabe, from County Roscommon, Ireland. Father A. Campeau drew up the baptismal certificate.

Catholic baptism of John Gaffney, born June 12 to James Gaffney and Mary Lynskey, from County Roscommon, Ireland. Father A. Campeau drew up the baptismal certificate.

Seventy-seven burials were recorded in the register of the Catholic chapel.

SHIPS LEAVING GROSSE ÎLE FOR QUÉBEC CITY

Name of ship	Quarantine time (in days)	Deaths in Grosse Île hospitals	Deaths on quarantined ships
Goliah	4	28	20
Roseanna	3	7	0

MONDAY,
JULY 19, 1847

The provincial secretary, in the name of the Governor General, authorized Douglas to build additional sheds to house 2 500 people in the area for healthy emigrants at the east end of the island, as well as accommodations for 1 000 convalescent patients. He instructed the medical superintendent to ensure that healthy passengers disembarking from ships with contagious or infectious diseases aboard were detained either for 20 days or for 7 days after the last case of illness was reported. Douglas was also to see that sick, convalescent and healthy emigrants were kept in separate areas.

A debate was held in the Legislative Assembly on the question of lodging the emigrants in sheds, especially in Montréal. Solicitor General Cameron stated that he had been to Grosse Île on Friday, July 16, and that at the time, there were 3 500 people on the island, 2 000 of whom were in the hospitals and 1 500 at the east end. He had given the medical superintendent orders to space the intervals at which emigrants were sent on to Montréal so as to prevent congestion at the point of arrival in that city.

Cameron also announced that stricter quarantine measures had been decided upon; from now on, emigrants would be kept at Grosse Île either for 20 days or for 7 days after the last case of fever was reported on their ship, whichever happened first. Clothing, mattresses and bedding were to be washed in boiling water. According to Cameron, the risk of contagion on Grosse Île was not that serious; this was proven by the fact that only one of the 50 soldiers billeted on the island had fallen ill, and he had been on guard near the hospital.

Another member of the Legislative Assembly, Mr. Aylwin, wanted to know why stricter quarantine regulations had not been applied earlier and, as well, what purpose Grosse Île served if, in the end, it was incapable of preventing disease from entering the country. He added that if the quarantine station had been properly managed, Québec City would not be trying to cope with 600 cases of typhus, as was now the case.

Mr. Aylwin went on to say that a committee inquiring into the emigration situation had reported that there were still emigrant lodgings on Grosse Île with beds built one over the other, that the bodies of the dead were left overnight in these beds and that the filth was horrible. According to him, if the disease was to be prevented from spreading to the whole country, there should be no hesitation about keeping emigrants in quarantine for two or even four months! Mr. Cameron replied that there were no longer any upper tiers of beds at the station and that people were no longer placed three to a bed. As for the more stringent quarantine measures requested, he reminded Mr. Aylwin that the government had just adopted them.

The Solicitor General added that the number of deaths on Grosse Île had been greatly exaggerated and that, at the time of his visit, the total stood at only 850 for the whole season. The editors of the *Quebec Gazette* questioned this figure in reporting the debate: had a member of the clergy not stated three weeks earlier that the number of deaths on Grosse Île was 1 300? They suggested that perhaps the figure given by Cameron referred strictly to deaths on land, while the larger figure included both those on the island and those on board the ships.

The newspaper wondered why the deaths at the quarantine station had not been recorded in regular reports that were signed and authenticated by the medical superintendent. This was the procedure followed at the St. John quarantine station in New Brunswick, where not only were such reports written up, but lists were published giving the names of the deceased, their age and place of origin. The clergymen working at Grosse Île, both Catholic and Protestant, were very sceptical about the mortality figures put forward by the island authorities. (See Dr. Douglas' reply on this subject on July 25.)

Father C.-F. Cazeau, secretary of the archdiocese, told Dr. Joseph Parant, the medical superintendent for the port of Québec, that a rowboat should be placed at the disposal of the Catholic priests to make it easier for them to visit the sick on quarantined ships at the station. The week before, the lack of transportation had prevented them from visiting the vessels for three or four days. As a result, on one ship alone, no less than 20 people had died without the last rites. Apparently, the men paid by the government to handle these boats were employed elsewhere.

Dr. Douglas' assistant had made it clear to the missionaries that their task would be much simpler if they had their own boat. In the end, the priests had been able to reach the vessels, but only through the goodwill of a captain who had come to deliver the bodies of typhus victims from his ship and who had agreed to lend them his rowboat.

A. C. Buchanan informed Governor General Elgin that several vessels had arrived at Grosse Île during the week with many sick people on board. These ships included the *Avon*, the *Jessie*, the *Triton*, the *Erin's Queen*, and the *Sarah*, which were still being kept in quarantine. He predicted that within the next two weeks 40 more ships carrying 11 000 to 12 000 passengers would arrive, and that 12 to 15 of them would come from Bremen, Germany. Emigrants on vessels from that port generally arrived in good health and had sufficient means to reach their destination.

The *Quebec Gazette* announced the death of Captain Harper, commander of the *Independance*, following an attack of typhus. The newspaper also reported that Dr. Sauvé had returned sick from Grosse Île. According to the *Quebec Mercury*, 40 patients were admitted to hospital on Grosse Île on July 19.

The *Canadien* reported that Father Harper, parish priest of Saint-Grégoire, had left on Friday to return to his parish, bringing back 12 orphans, who were eagerly awaited by his parishioners. Father O'Reilly, who had left on the same day, brought back three others. When they arrived at Trois-Rivières, they were besieged by charitable citizens who wanted to take the orphans into their homes, and the two gentlemen had great difficulty holding on to the children in their charge. None of the priests leaving the quarantine station had fallen ill since the return of Father Sax.

The *Quebec Gazette* published a long letter to the editor written under the pseudonym of Lower Town. In it, the author complained that the British government had not done enough to help find places for the sick, destitute emigrants arriving in Québec City. He wondered why they were not isolated from the rest of the population as they were in Montréal. In Québec City, the risk of contagion was exacerbated by the location of the emigration agent's office on Sault-au-Matelot Street and of the emigrant sheds on the India Wharf; these places were full of both sick and healthy emigrants and their contaminated luggage. A more suitable place to accommodate them should have been found.

The author of the letter also complained that the authorities allowed vessels to leave Grosse Île before they were properly washed and decontaminated; the cases of typhus at the Marine Hospital were eloquent proof of this. He wrote that in English ports, any ship on which contagious disease had been detected was sent to the Standgate Creek quarantine station for 40 days. There, the passengers, crew and cargo were taken off to be fumigated and disinfected. According to the author, shipowners would be less inclined to cram sick, impoverished emigrants onto their vessels if the latter were detained for longer periods at Grosse Île and, more importantly, if it was announced that Canadian quarantine regulations would be applied more strictly.

In closing, the anonymous letter writer asked why Canada did not adopt a law like the one in the United States, under which shipowners had to pledge that their passengers would not be a burden to the state for six months following their arrival.

Catholic baptism of Maria O'Melia, born July 18 to John O'Melia and Bridget Newcome, from County Mayo, Ireland. Father A. Campeau drew up the baptismal certificate.

SHIPS ARRIVING AT GROSSE ÎLE

Name of ship	Captain	Port of departure	Crossing time (in days)	Passengers		No. of sick on arrival	No. of deaths during crossing
				Steerage	Cabin		
Asia	J. Hanah	Cork (Ireland)	48	409	0	49	11

SHIPS LEAVING GROSSE ÎLE FOR QUÉBEC CITY

Name of ship	Quarantine time (in days)	Deaths in Grosse Île hospitals	Deaths on quarantined ships
Sarah	7	39	0

SHIPS ARRIVING IN QUÉBEC CITY WITHOUT A STOP-OVER AT GROSSE ÎLE

Name of ship	Port of departure	Passengers	
		Steerage	Cabin
Annette Gilbert	Chepstow (England)	1	0

TUESDAY, JULY 20, 1847

Testimony by Captain Edward Boxer, harbour master for the port of Québec, before the committee inquiring into the management of Grosse Île:

Captain Boxer had visited and inspected Grosse Île on May 31, 1847. He had been welcomed by an exhausted Dr. Douglas, who asked him to inspect the station and make a report to the Governor General in Montréal offering suggestions for improving the quarantine establishment. Boxer was also to report to the civil secretary on the situation of sick emigrants at the quarantine station. At the time, there were about 500 sick people on land and around the same number on board the ships. The hospitals were full, as were the sheds and the few tents. Eight men were employed by the Board of Works to put up tents for the emigrants. There were four or five doctors working on the island and Dr. Douglas complained about the lack of assistance.

The hospitals seemed to be well run and the patients clean and properly cared for. In the sheds, however, conditions were horrible: there were two tiers of beds and most of the patients suffered from dysentery. The buildings were poorly ventilated and the stench was unbearable. Dr. Douglas could do nothing about it, since he was obliged to take in the sick people forced off the ships; however, according to the witness, the disembarking of passengers was now better controlled.

Boxer stressed that additional assistance for sick people in the sheds was urgently needed. Douglas' attempts to recruit more doctors and medical attendants had been unsuccessful, apparently because the salaries offered were too low. Dr. Fenwick received only 17s. 6d. per day, and nurses were offered only about 3s. a day, which was less than they were paid in Québec City. Problems were also encountered when it came to hiring cooks and orderlies.

Following Captain Boxer's recommendations, Buchanan and the Governor General ordered the construction of more sheds to accommodate 2000 sick people. Healthy passengers were not brought ashore while the captain was at the quarantine station; therefore, the question of isolating the sick from the healthy had not yet arisen.

Boxer concluded his testimony with some recommendations for improving the organization of the quarantine station. For example, a superintendent should be put in charge of inspecting the vessels. Accompanied by a doctor, he could visit the ships twice a day and ensure that they were clean and well ventilated. This would enable the chief medical officer to devote his time to supervising the hospital. A civil officer could also be appointed as governor of the station, as was done in England.

Written testimony of Bishop George Mountain of the Anglican Church presented to the committee inquiring into the management of Grosse Île:

The testimony began with a lengthy eulogy to Dr. Douglas and his work on Grosse Île. Douglas had been the object of rumours and suspicion about his private interests on the island. There had been gossip about his selling milk to the quarantine station, but the Anglican Bishop knew nothing about the affair. However, he did know that Douglas had charitably donated milk to a ship so that it could be given to babies whose mothers had died before they were weaned.

The lack of nurses was the worst problem plaguing Grosse Île at the time of Mountain's visit. It was very difficult to recruit them at the quarantine station, as at the Marine Hospital in Québec City. The Anglican Bishop spoke of the joy with which Dr. Douglas had received a list from Dr. Parant giving the names of 16 nurses who were being sent to him from Québec City. However, 10 of them refused to work and returned to the city, after witnessing the scenes that transpired in the hospitals. Even when nurses agreed to stay at Grosse Île, the station authorities had to cope with the problem that many fell ill and died. Mountain concluded his testimony by praising Mr. Symes, the deputy emigration agent, for the amazing energy and selflessness with which he devoted himself to the cause. He also praised the work of the apothecary, Mr. Cullingford, a remarkable man, who was both attentive and humane.

Father Charles Tardif, curate at Baie-du-Febvre, and Father Adolphe Dupuis, missionary at Saint-Ferdinand d'Halifax, arrived at Grosse Île.

The *Quebec Mercury* reported that 376 more people had been admitted to hospital on Grosse Île since the newspaper's July 17 report, bringing the total number of patients to 2049. The *Canadien*, on the other hand, mentioned a total of 2069 patients.

Catholic baptism of Peter Hegarty, born June 29 to Moris Hegarty and Mary Corrigan, from Ireland. Father A. Dupuis drew up the baptismal certificate.

Twenty-eight burials were recorded in the register of the Catholic chapel.

SHIPS ARRIVING AT GROSSE ÎLE

Name of ship	Captain	Port of departure	Crossing time (in days)	Passengers Steerage	Cabin	No. of sick on arrival	No. of deaths during crossing
Greenock	A. Walker	Liverpool (England)	32	816	0	70	12
Henrietta Sophia	J. Watson	Hamburg (Germany)	69	186	0	2	8
John Campbell	A. Cornish	Bremen (Germany)	37	371	0	0	0
Numa	T. Miller	Sligo (Ireland)	48	256	1	39	10
TOTAL				1629	1	111	

SHIPS LEAVING GROSSE ÎLE FOR QUÉBEC CITY

Name of ship	Quarantine time (in days)	Deaths in Grosse Île hospitals	Deaths on quarantined ships
John Campbell	A few hours	0	0

WEDNESDAY, JULY 21, 1847

Testimony by A. C. Buchanan, the emigration agent in Québec City, before the committee inquiring into the management of Grosse Île:

At the time of his first visit to Grosse Île, at the end of May, there were 4 or 5 extra doctors and about 500 to 600 sick people on the island. The sick were placed in the hospital, in the sheds previously occupied by healthy emigrants and in tents. Buchanan had noticed a serious lack of nurses and beds, although the need for the latter was soon resolved by the arrival of beds from Québec City. In one or two of the buildings there were two tiers of beds.

The emigration agent provided a few new statistics in his testimony. The number of emigrants who had arrived at Québec City since the beginning of the navigation season stood at 56 000. By July 17, 1 269 people had died in hospital on Grosse Île. Eight hundred deaths had occurred on ships just before they arrived or while they were in quarantine, and the remains of these victims had been taken to the island and buried there. As well, 3 000 other people had perished during the crossing, bringing the total number of deaths so far to 5 069. Buchanan had expected that the incidence of disease among emigrants in 1847 would be much higher than usual, but he had not informed the government of his fears since the problem was not his responsibility.

Buchanan remarked that the quarantine station would be able to carry out its role more efficiently if extra sheds for healthy emigrants were built at the east end of the island to replace the tents standing there. It might be necessary to build another wharf in that sector to make it easier for healthy passengers to come ashore and to return to their ships. At the time, these operations were complicated by the fact that small boats had to be used. Before the navigation season began, Buchanan had believed that existing quarantine regulations would be sufficient, but that the number of doctors would have to be increased.

Catholic baptism of Helen Connor, born July 21 to Bryan Connor and Catherine Sullivan, from County Kerry, Ireland. Father C. Tardif drew up the baptismal certificate.

Catholic baptism of William Ryan, born the same day to Patrick Ryan and Mary Dwyer, from Ireland. Father C. Tardif drew up the baptismal certificate.

Thirty-seven burials were recorded in the register of the Catholic chapel and two in that of the Protestant chapel.

SHIPS ARRIVING AT GROSSE ÎLE

Name of ship	Captain	Port of departure	Crossing time (in days)	Passengers Steerage	Cabin	No. of sick on arrival	No. of deaths during crossing
Alexander Stewart	D. William	Limerick (Ireland)	48	103	0	13	3

A VIEW OF THE LAZARETTO.
(HÉLÈNE BOUCHER, PARKS CANADA, 1990).

SHIPS WAITING IN QUARANTINE OFF GROSSE ÎLE.
(BERNARD DUCHESNE, PARKS CANADA, 1996).

THE CELTIC CROSS PUT UP IN 1909
BY THE *ANCIENT ORDER OF HIBERNIANS*
TO COMMEMORATE THE TRAGEDY OF 1847.
(JEAN AUDET, PARKS CANADA, 1995).

DETAIL OF THE WESTERN CEMETERY.
(LOUIS JACOB, PARKS CANADA, 1989).

SHIPS LEAVING GROSSE ÎLE FOR QUÉBEC CITY			
Name of ship	Quarantine time (in days)	Deaths in Grosse Île hospitals	Deaths on quarantined ships
Henrietta Sophia	1	1	0

THURSDAY,
JULY 22, 1847

Dr. Douglas sent a letter to the civil secretary requesting that the salaries of medical assistants on Grosse Île be raised.

The Governor General approved the construction of a bakery on Grosse Île to be run by a contractor who would be responsible for making bread but under the control of the commissary general.

The *Quebec Mercury* and the *Quebec Gazette* reported that a total of 1 860 people (915 men, 540 women and 405 children) were hospitalized on Grosse Île at the time. Another 160 patients had also been taken ashore and placed in a temporary camp on the farm. This meant that there were 2 020 patients in all at the quarantine station. It was further observed that the death rate was influenced by the weather. A cold wind from the east on the previous Sunday (July 18) had led to the death of several old and weak people whose health had seemed somewhat uncertain a few days before. Similarly, the heavy rain and muggy weather on Wednesday, July 21, had been fatal for some of the emigrants in the tents.

The *Quebec Mercury* also mistakenly reported that Dr. Pinet had returned to live with friends since he had fallen ill. The newspaper told its readers that the *Greenoch* had arrived with 816 passengers on board; 12 people, including seven children, had died during the ocean voyage. It was said that the low incidence of disease on the ship was due not only to a relatively short crossing of around 30 days but also to the vessel's cleanness and good order.

Act of profession of the Catholic faith by Ann Kelly. Father A. Dupuis drew up the act of abjuration.

Thirty-six burials were recorded in the register of the Catholic chapel and five in that of the Protestant chapel.

SHIPS ARRIVING AT GROSSE ÎLE

Name of ship	Captain	Port of departure	Crossing time (in days)	Passengers Steerage	Cabin	No. of sick on arrival	No. of deaths during crossing
Friendship	J. Allen	Dublin (Ireland)	60	202	0	1	1
Rega	W. Patrick	Cork (Ireland)	33	132	0	2	3
TOTAL				334	0	3	

FRIDAY,
JULY 23, 1847

Dr. Parant informed the Executive Council committee that he had invited tenders for steamers to make extra trips between Québec City and Grosse Île, but that he had not received any bids. He also reported that Mr. Stevenson had raised the price of renting his boat from £ 45 to £ 50 per trip (a prohibitive rate, according to Dr. Parant) when his steamer service contract came to an end. The Executive Council committee was therefore obliged to recommend that the new rate be approved, at least until Dr. Parant was able to obtain a more reasonable deal, either from Mr. Stevenson or from another steamboat owner.

Father Joseph Bailey, a curate from Trois-Rivières, arrived at Grosse Île.

Testimony by Father Bernard O'Reilly, a Catholic priest, before the committee inquiring into the management of Grosse Île:

Father O'Reilly had been on Grosse Île from about Tuesday, July 6, to Wednesday, July 14. There was a lack of beds and furniture for the sick. In the sheds and tents, he had seen emigrants lying on the floor or even on the ground for days at a time. It seemed that straw was unobtainable. Often two or three people shared the same bed, without regard for sex, age or type of illness. In one of the old sheds, there were two tiers of beds.

There seemed to be a lack of food, and the nurses paid little attention to how it was distributed to the patients. The bread was underbaked. Considering the lack of nurses, an acceptable effort was made to keep things clean, but the place was far from immaculate. Father O'Reilly believed that the sick were given liquids, such as tea, gruel and broth, three times a day. The dead were buried without delay. Father Harper, who generally carried out the burials, had told O'Reilly that the graves were only four feet deep and contained three coffins one on top of the other; consequently, there was not enough soil mounded over them. The cemetery and the hospital were separated by about two acres, and there were tents all around the cemetery.

Coffins being buried in a mass grave in the western cemetery on Grosse Île. All witnesses agree that, despite the terrible circumstances, burials were always conducted with dignity and according to Christian ritual. The missionaries were solely responsible for burials. (Daniel Rainville, Parks Canada, 1997.)

Father O'Reilly had not heard any complaints on the island about the management of the station. On the morning of his testimony, he had visited the emigrant sheds near the Lachine Canal and had noticed that they were much more comfortable and well serviced than the tents and sheds on Grosse Île. When he left the island on July 14, there was a dearth of straw, spring water and lime juice. Although a steamer should have been available to make daily trips between Québec City and the quarantine station, Father O'Reilly had been obliged to wait for a week before the *St. George* arrived. The priests had to rely on the goodwill of some kind-hearted person for transportation to visit the sick on the vessels.

Dr. Douglas was making a superhuman effort to fulfil his duties. It would be difficult even for three doctors to do all that he accomplished without becoming exhausted. Tasks had to be redistributed. Douglas could not visit every boat that arrived and at the same time see to all his other responsibilities on the island.

O'Reilly observed that there were too few policemen at the quarantine station and that the sick emigrants' possessions were not properly safeguarded; there were not enough funds available to pay doctors sufficient wages and thus encourage them to come to the quarantine station to work. He protested that it was inacceptable that thousands of his fellow countrymen should be sacrificed through neglect and lack of foresight. He hoped that more hospitals (about six) would be built on Grosse Île and that they would be placed in a more suitable location. He also said that healthy emigrants should be isolated from the sick and given better lodgings.

O'Reilly had visited the tent area set up for healthy passengers at the east end of the island. During the few hours he spent in this encampment, he had administered the last rites to over 50 people. These sick people did not have beds since they had been classified as healthy and were expected to fend for themselves. They could not be transported to the hospitals directly, since the regulations in force required that they be returned to their respective ships first and then transferred to the hospitals.

It took two days from the time of O'Reilly's visit to the east end of the quarantine station for the sick people housed in the tents to be moved to the ships and then taken ashore to the new hospital. There, they were left to lie on the floor for a night and a day, without beds or blankets, groaning with fever and suffering from dysentery. After finishing their day of work, the priests had brought them something to drink and used rotten straw found around the hospital to fashion makeshift beds.

Father O'Reilly ended his testimony by observing that the sick were not allowed to disembark from the vessels for several days after their arrival and this had fatal consequences for many of them.

Testimony by Father Jean-Baptiste-Antoine Ferland, director of studies at the College of Nicolet, before the committee inquiring into the management of Grosse Île:

Father Ferland had stayed for one week at the quarantine station, beginning on June 29. At the time of his arrival, there were 1 800 to 2 000 sick people on the island. They were housed in tents, old sheds, two newly constructed buildings and the Catholic and Protestant chapels. In the tents, the sick were very close to one another and, in the old sheds, there were two tiers of beds. The upper tier had since been removed in all but one or two buildings. According to Father Ferland, the upper tiers of beds should be taken away entirely, given that they were very difficult for sick people to get in and out of and allowed excrement from patients with dysentery to fall onto the lower beds.

The priest also stated that the tents should be eliminated because they were poorly ventilated and because the straw floors became soaked with water when it rained. As well, the tents were scattered widely and it was easy for a doctor to forget some of them on his rounds. Ferland had come across such a tent, in which the sick had been left on their own for two days. They had been visited by neither a doctor nor an assistant, and had received no food, medicine or water. At Father Ferland's request, Dr. Damours had been kind enough to have these sick people transferred to a neighbouring shed.

At the time of Ferland's visit, there were only 7 or 8 doctors in a condition to visit the sick. Some of them had 400 to 500 patients on their hands, when 150 would have kept them working full time. As well, the number of assistants was insufficient; there were scarcely 1 or 2 for 150 patients, when normally there should be 1 for every 20 to 25 patients. The lack of assistants meant that the sick lay in their own excrement for days at a time and that they sometimes went without drinking for 10 or 12 hours.

When the assistants were reproached for this, they replied that even with the best intentions in the world they would be incapable of hauling all the river water needed for so many people and still have time to give the sick the care they needed. The station was understaffed because it was nearly impossible to hire assistants, despite the high salaries offered. Often those working there were not really qualified for the important work they had to do.

Few respectable women would agree to be a nurse in some of the sheds on Grosse Île. They had to sleep in the middle of the sickbeds, and had no separate room to which they could retire to change their clothes. They were given the same food as the emigrants and had to eat in haste amid the foul smells of the shed. They often fell ill and then had difficulty finding assistance.

This is what had happened to Mrs. Garneau, a Québec City nurse. She had come down with typhus and remained in a shed for three days, without any aid except for that provided by Father Harper, one of the missionaries. The poor woman, like many others, paid with her life for the service she had rendered to the emigrants. Facts like these were known in Québec City and had a very negative effect on hiring. In Father Ferland's opinion, the quarantine station's nurses played an indispensable role and should therefore be offered better conditions, with more privacy in their sleeping quarters and more nourishing food.

The priest proposed that men and women be placed in separate sheds and that patients suffering from contagious diseases be isolated from other patients. Additional sheds were needed, but in a better location. Privies should be built near the sheds so that sick people would stop defecating in the bushes beside the Catholic chapel and the missionaries' residence.

The dead were buried in coffins piled two or three deep in trenches, so that there was not enough earth to mound over the top coffins. A long ditch dug in the middle of the cemetery extended a considerable distance into the midst of an encampment. Decaying matter seeped from the graves into the ditch and when the sun burned down on this unwholesome muck, the resulting stench was quite sickening. The new sheds were kept clean to some degree and the old ones a bit more so, but everywhere else it was filthy.

Dr. Douglas was faced with an almost impossible task. His duties should have been divided among three people: the medical superintendent could have visited the ships, another doctor could have been in charge of medical matters in the sheds and a third person could have been responsible for the general organization of the sheds. This person could have supervised the hospital stewards and nurses, as well as the food services. He could have also been put in charge of an office where lists of the sick, the convalescing and the dead were drawn up and kept.

Such an office was sorely missed in 1847. The missionaries received letters almost every day requesting information about people who had landed at Grosse Île. According to Ferland, the priests should have been authorized to go on board the ships as soon as they arrived. Irish Catholics who arrived in ill health desired the comfort of a priest above all else. Their greatest sorrow was to die without the consolation of religion.

When asked where responsibility lay for the year's events on Grosse Île, Father Ferland replied that the previous winter, when there were signs that a great influx of emigrants was imminent, representations should have been made to the British government to prevent this migration. To put it bluntly, the government should have stopped the hospitals and poorhouses of Ireland and England from turning out their occupants and casting them onto the shores of the St. Lawrence.

Father C. Tardif wrote to Bishop Turgeon, coadjutor of Québec, about the difficulty of getting workers to stay on the island. For example, Mr. Armand Vincent, the layman serving the missionaries on Grosse Île, had not heard from his workman and was having difficulty hiring others. Mr. Vincent himself wanted to leave the following week, in spite of all the proposals made by Father Joseph Bailey to persuade him to stay on. A man by the name of Boucher, from Rivière-Ouelle, had offered to replace him for a salary of 3 louis a month. He was recommended by Vincent, who could train him for a day or two.

Father Tardif also wrote that about thirty-five to forty people were dying each day. He believed that the situation on Grosse Île would improve rapidly if the sick were kept in better ventilated places and if more staff were hired. In the tents, patients often passed whole days breathing the thick and pestilential air around them, without anyone going to the trouble of providing them with fresh air.

The *Canadien* of July 23 reported that the members of the clergy who had come down with typhus were better for the most part and considered out of danger, but that Father P.-T. Sax had suffered a relapse. It added that Dr. Damours had returned to Grosse Île. The number of people in the quarantine hospital on Tuesday, July 20, totalled 2069.

The *Canadien* had scathing criticism for Solicitor General Cameron's observations concerning Grosse Île. Cameron was accused of having painted a rosy picture of the situation at the quarantine station rather than presenting the true story. He had toured the island without entering any of the buildings. The colonial government and the medical superintendent were guilty of serious lack of foresight. Just before spring, despite warnings in the press of unprecedented emigration during the coming season, the government had done no more than buy 50 beds and 50 blankets.

Death of Vincent Andrews, a member of the quarantine station's nursing staff, at age 34.

Twenty-nine burials were recorded in the register of the Catholic chapel and one in that of the Protestant chapel.

SHIPS ARRIVING AT GROSSE ÎLE

Name of ship	Captain	Port of departure	Crossing time (in days)	Passengers		No. of sick on arrival	No. of deaths during crossing
				Steerage	Cabin		
Ann	J. Nicholson	Donegal (Ireland)	55	107	2	1	1

SHIPS LEAVING GROSSE ÎLE FOR QUÉBEC CITY

Name of ship	Quarantine time (in days)	Deaths in Grosse Île hospitals	Deaths on quarantined ships
Erin's Queen	12	71	20
Triton	10	83	10

SATURDAY,
JULY 24, 1847

The civil secretary informed commissary general Filder and Dr. Douglas that a sutler would sell certain articles to the emigrants at Grosse Île.

Stevenson's offer regarding extra steamer trips between Québec City and Grosse Île was accepted.

The civil secretary told Dr. Douglas that the person who had been given the contract for supplying the hospitals should be allowed to sell his goods to the ships' crews and people who could afford to pay for such items.

Archbishop Joseph Signay informed the Governor General, Lord Elgin, about the situation of emigrant orphans. So far, over 100 of them had

IRISH ORPHANS TAKEN IN BY A FRENCH-CANADIAN FAMILY IN 1847. MANY COUNTRY PRIESTS BROUGHT CHILDREN BACK TO THEIR PARISHES AND ENTRUSTED THEM TO "RESPECTABLE FAMILIES." (DANIEL RAINVILLE, PARKS CANADA, 1997.)

been taken in by respectable families. He believed that more of them could have been placed, but people had begun to fear that these children would bring infectious germs with them into their adoptive homes. Certain newspapers were already sounding the alarm. As a result, his parishioners' enthusiasm for adopting orphans had been dampened.

According to the *Quebec Mercury* and the *Quebec Gazette*, healthy passengers had been taken ashore at the quarantine station from a number of boats: 437 passengers from the *Jessie* (Cork), 517 from the *Erin's Queen* (Liverpool), 248 from the *Sarah* (Liverpool), 483 from the *Triton* (Liverpool) and 550 from the *Avon* (Cork). It was reported that these emigrants were among the weakest and most wretched-looking that had ever landed at the quarantine station. One eyewitness declared that, of the 2 235 people who had left Europe on board these vessels, only 500 at the very most would survive to settle in America.

The *Quebec Mercury* published a call for tenders, issued by the Commissariat Office, for supplying bread on Grosse Île for the duration of the navigation season. The bread was to be made with approved fine flour and each loaf was to weigh four pounds. The contractor would have to keep a week's supply of flour in the Grosse Île storehouses at all times, and this flour would have to be inspected and approved by the Commissariat. In the event that the contractor was unable to provide bread of the desired quality, it might be replaced by biscuits, at the rate of three quarters of a pound of biscuits for one pound of bread. A bakery would be put at the service of the contractor on Grosse Île. It was to be located far enough away from the hospitals to prevent the sick from approaching it.

Death of Dr. Alexis-Albert Pinet at age 22.

Forty-four burials were recorded in the register of the Catholic chapel and three in that of the Protestant chapel.

The *Quebec Mercury* reported on the number of dead between May 10 and July 24. A total of 1 458 deaths had been recorded in the hospitals on Grosse Île; the deceased comprised 575 men, 416 women and 467 children. In the tents at the east end of the island, where healthy passengers were brought ashore, 27 people had died. All told, 2 366 people had perished during the crossing, while 721 more had passed away on ships in quarantine or shortly before reaching Grosse Île. The latter had been buried on the island. This gave a grand total of 4 572 deaths.

Douglas reported that, from May 28 to July 24, 1847, 721 bodies had been removed from the ships and buried on land. Many of these passengers had died during the trip up the St. Lawrence and had been kept on board for burial on Grosse Île.

According to a list published in the *Quebec Morning Chronicle*, 162 people had died at Grosse Île during the week of July 18 to 24.

SHIPS LEAVING GROSSE ÎLE FOR QUÉBEC CITY

Name of ship	Quarantine time (in days)	Deaths in Grosse Île hospitals	Deaths on quarantined ships
Friendship	2	0	0
Jessie	13	40	7

EMIGRANTS ARRIVING IN THE PORT OF QUÉBEC DURING THE WEEK OF JULY 18 TO 24

Country of origin	Number
England	2 564*
Ireland	974*
Scotland	0
Germany	1 030
Canadian ports downstream from Québec City	73
Total	4 641
Previous total (as at July 17)	52 214
GRAND TOTAL	56 855**

* These figures may have been inverted.

** This represents an increase of 32 279 emigrants compared with the total reported by Buchanan up to the same period in 1846, i.e. 24 576.

NUMBER OF PEOPLE IN HOSPITAL ON GROSSE ÎLE DURING THE WEEK OF JULY 18 TO 24

Emigrants	Patients hospitalized as at last report	Patients admitted (+)	Patients discharged (-)	Deaths (-)	New total
Men	863	340	67	92	1 044
Women	421	198	85	57	477
Children	389	114	32	48	423
TOTAL	1 673	652	184	197	1 944*

* Of this number, 1904 (1036 men, 465 women and 403 children) had typhus and dysentery and 40 (8 men, 12 women and 20 children) had smallpox.

SUNDAY,
JULY 25, 1847

In a letter to the editor of the *Quebec Gazette*, Dr. Douglas denounced certain rumours, according to which some thirty to forty deaths went unregistered each day and that they did not figure in the official records. The doctor affirmed that complete lists of every death in the hospitals, giving the emigrant's name, age, ship and date of death, were sent each week to Dr. Parant, inspecting physician for the port of Québec. Similarly, the emigration agent, A. C. Buchanan, received a list of everyone who died on the ships, whether during the crossing or while in quarantine. Furthermore, the Governor General had ordered that these lists be made public.

The medical superintendent was incensed by the facile criticisms made by some. He stressed that 14 young doctors had fallen ill with typhus since July 1 and that Dr. Malhiot and Dr. Pinet had succumbed to the disease. Other staff members had also died, including several hospital stewards, nurses and even a policeman.

Anglican baptism of William John Piton, born July 20 to Nicolas Piton, a clerk employed on Grosse Île, and Elizabeth Arless. The Reverend Charles Rollit drew up the baptismal certificate.

Thirty-three burials were recorded in the register of the Catholic chapel.

SHIPS ARRIVING AT GROSSE ÎLE

Name of ship	Captain	Port of departure	Crossing time (in days)	Passengers Steerage	Cabin	No. of sick on arrival	No. of deaths during crossing
Agamemnon	J. McKenly	Liverpool (England)	31	646	0	10	23
Euclid	G. Bainbridge	Glasgow (Scotland)	53	327	3	16	3
TOTAL				973	3	26	

SHIPS LEAVING GROSSE ÎLE FOR QUÉBEC CITY

Name of ship	Quarantine time (in days)	Deaths in Grosse Île hospitals	Deaths on quarantined ships
Avon	13	84	26
Rega	3	0	0

MONDAY,
JULY 26, 1847

Public Works commissioners signed contracts with a number of Québec City contractors for the rapid construction of six emigrant sheds on Grosse Île. The buildings were to be prefabricated in Québec City and assembled at the quarantine station. Five of them were to measure 408 feet by 25 feet and stand 10 feet high. The sixth was to be 204 feet long. The buildings were all supposed to have shingled roofs and rough plank clapboarding on the outer walls. For every 100 feet of length, there were to be six casement windows, two double doors and eight ventilators measuring 6 feet by 15 feet.

EMIGRANTS' SHEDS PREFABRICATED IN QUÉBEC CITY BEING PUT UP ON GROSSE ÎLE. UNFORTUNATELY, THE NUMBER OF SHEDS AND HOSPITALS REMAINED INSUFFICIENT UNTIL LATE SUMMER. (DANIEL RAINVILLE, PARKS CANADA, 1997.)

There would be a 6-foot double door with a central jamb in each gable wall. Every building was to contain a row of beds along each wall and a double tier of beds in the centre. The buildings would also be furnished with 6-foot by 4-foot tables at every 100 feet, and two 13- to 14-foot ladders would be placed at either end. A ventilator would be installed at every 25 feet along the rooftop. The contractors were Basile Monier; Edouard Dorion; Pierre Laberge and Joseph Hélie *dit* Breton; Pierre Lapointe; and Jean Trudel and Zacharie Chabot. Each of the 408-foot sheds could be divided to make two buildings 204 feet in length.

Douglas requested an extra boat to make the trip between Grosse Île and Québec City. He also asked that the policemen's salaries be raised.

Archbishop Signay complained of the difficulties encountered by the priests in visiting the sick at Grosse Île and asked that a boat be placed at their disposal.

The Archbishop of Québec wrote to Father Pouliot, parish priest of Saint-André, saying that the missionaries' work at Grosse Île now involved less risk of infection and that their daily work schedule gave them some time off during the day and allowed them to rest from supper time to the following morning.

The *Canadien* reported that several contracts had been concluded for the construction of emigrant sheds on Grosse Île and announced that a Public Works commissioner, Mr. C.-E. Casgrain, would soon visit the quarantine station.

The *Canadien* scoffed at the report made by Solicitor General Cameron before the Legislative Assembly on the situation at Grosse Île. The newspaper said that he had not even entered the hospitals when he visited the island and that he had relied solely on the opinion of the station's medical superintendent.

The *Quebec Gazette* warned the public about a sudden, fatal form of typhus, with symptoms somewhat different from those usually associated with the disease. To support its assertions, it reported that a healthy emigrant on Grosse Île had fixed his dinner without showing any signs of illness and then suddenly rolled out of his tent and died.

Taking up a news item published by the *Quebec Mercury*, the *Quebec Gazette* reported on the inadequacies of the quarantine system in the port of Liverpool. Sick or doubtful-looking emigrants leaving Irish ports by way of Liverpool were placed in 15 or 16 old hulks at anchor and, after a short quarantine period, they were allowed to embark on vessels sailing for Canada. Many of the emigrants were not fit to make the voyage, and disease broke out as soon as the ships left the port of Liverpool. A pointed example of this was the *Triton*, which had recently arrived at Grosse Île. During the crossing, it had lost 88 sick people, including all the officers and several crew members.

The *Quebec Gazette* also published the news that an asylum for emigrant orphans had been set up by the Archbishop and the Roman Catholic clergy in Saint-Roch, in Québec City. The newspaper hoped that the government would come to the aid of these clergymen, since many other demands were made of them by charitable and educational institutions.

Catholic baptism of Rose Miskelly, born July 4 to Patrick Miskelly and Rose McVey, from Ireland. Father J. Bailey drew up the baptismal certificate.

Fifteen burials were recorded in the register of the Catholic chapel and two in that of the Protestant chapel.

SHIPS ARRIVING AT GROSSE ÎLE

Name of ship	Captain	Port of departure	Crossing time (in days)	Passengers Steerage	Cabin	No. of sick on arrival	No. of deaths during crossing
Jamaica	T. Martin	Greenock (Scotland)	46	209	3	33	0
Leontine	C. Fecter	Bremen (Germany)	60	326	0	0	6
Tamerlane	R. James	Aberyswith (Wales)	55	243	0	0	1
TOTAL				778	3	33	

SHIPS LEAVING GROSSE ÎLE FOR QUÉBEC CITY

Name of ship	Quarantine time (in days)	Deaths in Grosse Île hospitals	Deaths on quarantined ships
Ann	3	0	0
Asia	7	20	5
Mary	9	1	2
Numa	7	27	0

TUESDAY, JULY 27, 1847

The Governor General gave instructions that a boat should be placed at the disposal of the priests visiting the sick on board the ships.

The Governor General announced that religious communities would be granted the sum of £ 1 per month for each emigrant orphan taken in and kept until either a good home was found with a respectable family or the child was claimed by family or friends. In addition, the government was prepared to pay some of the cost of clothing these children.

Having visited and inspected Grosse Île, the Public Works commissioner, Mr. C.-E. Casgrain, reported on the progress of construction activities on the island and made some suggestions. The sector for convalescent patients should be moved to the east end of the quarantine station, since it was situated too close to the hospital zone. The hospitals were overcrowded, and tents for the sick had been erected just beside the cemetery. These tents and those for convalescing patients would soon be replaced by a 132-foot hospital, now under construction, and three new hospitals measuring 204 feet each.

The east end of the island offered the best location for new buildings. It would be necessary to build a small wharf there to enable healthy passengers to land without having to pass through the hospital sector and walk with their baggage for over a mile to reach the area reserved for them. Casgrain had invited tenders for the construction of 204-foot buildings, but he was having difficulty finding materials and workmen. He had found good contractors, who were all Canadian-born.

Casgrain added that, at the time, 13 ships were being held in quarantine, with 2000 passengers waiting to disembark. He said that by July 4, 15005 emigrants had left British ports on ships sailing for Canada. Buchanan expected that as many more would emigrate in July and August. On the island, there were 700 sick people in the tents, 1400 in the hospitals and 60 in the churches. A total of 120 healthy emigrants were also housed in the tents.

Father Jean-Baptiste Perras of Saint-Vallier and Father Félix-Séverin Bardy of Cacouna arrived at Grosse Île.

The steamer *Neptune* transported 40 emigrant orphans accompanied by two Roman Catholic priests to Québec City.

The *Quebec Gazette* reported that Father A. Campeau had fallen ill with typhus.

The *Quebec Mercury* announced the death of Dr. Alexis-Albert Pinet on Grosse Île. He had been buried on the island, since it had been impossible to take him to his friends near Montréal.

Thirty-seven burials were recorded in the register of the Catholic chapel.

SHIPS ARRIVING AT GROSSE ÎLE

Name of ship	Captain	Port of departure	Crossing time (in days)	Passengers Steerage	Passengers Cabin	No. of sick on arrival	No. of deaths during crossing
Abbeyland	C. Arken	Liverpool (England)	43	398	0	1	4
Argo	P. Fearson	Sligo (Ireland)	47	127	0	2	3
Charles Walton	J. Baker	Killala (Ireland)	34	272	0	10	5
Heroine	J. Baker	Aberdeen (Scotland)	59	75	6	0	0
Leander	B. Sheridan	Londonderry (Ireland)	45	427	0	2	4
Marchioness of Breadalbane	J. Reid	Sligo (Ireland)	46	187	0	23	10
Marchioness of Bute	J. Renning	Belfast (Ireland)	48	493	4	9	15
Oregon	T. Robertson	Killala (Ireland)	49	228	3	3	8
Panama	J. H. Turner	Loch Saxford (Scotland?)	36	279	0	0	0
TOTAL				2486	13	50	

SHIPS LEAVING GROSSE ÎLE FOR QUÉBEC CITY

Name of ship	Quarantine time (in days)	Deaths in Grosse Île hospitals	Deaths on quarantined ships
Alexander Stewart	6	2	3
Leontine	1	0	2

WEDNESDAY, JULY 28, 1847

Public Works commissioners signed contracts with Basile Monier and Charles Touchette, carpentry contractors in Québec City, to construct two wooden buildings rapidly on Grosse Île. The buildings were to be prefabricated in Québec City and assembled at the quarantine station. One was to measure 612 feet long by 25 feet wide and stand 10 feet high. The other would be only 204 feet long.

Pierre Dassilva, a Québec City roofer, hired Pierre Ferland, Alphé Gamache and Joseph Gamache of Saint-Roch to shingle 900 feet of roofing at Grosse Île. These workers also agreed to be available for any other contracts that Dassilva might have at Grosse Île over the summer.

The Public Works commissioner, C.-E. Casgrain, suggested that hospitals be built in the southwest part of the island and that the sick people in the tents be transferred there.

> Eyewitness account by Robert Whyte, an Irish emigrant who left the port of Dublin on May 30 and arrived at Grosse Île in the evening of July 27. He was a cabin passenger, probably on the *George*, a ship commanded by Captain Sheridan whose arrival at the quarantine station was registered on July 28. Whyte stayed at Grosse Île until August 2. His diary was published in 1848 under the title *The Ocean Plague: The Diary of a Cabin Passenger.*[1]
>
> At the end of the day on July 27, Robert Whyte wrote: "A few miles further sail brought us among a number of beautiful islets — so beautiful that they seemed like a fairy scene; their verdant turf was almost level with the blue water that wound amongst them, submerging not a few, so that the first that grew upon them appeared to rise from the river. A vast fleet of vessels lying at anchor told that we had arrived at Grosse Isle; and after wending our way amongst isles and ships, we dropped anchor in the ground allotted for vessels upon arrival, and hoisted our ensign at the peak, as a signal for the inspecting physician to board us."
>
> Whyte continued his account on July 28: "By 6 A. M., we were settled in our new position before the quarantine station. The

---

1. To make it easier to read, this original text was divided in shorter paragraphs.

passengers that were able to be up were all busy cleaning and washing, some clearing the hold of filth, others assisting the sailors in swabbing the deck. The mistress herself washed out the cabin last evening, and put everything in order. The captain commenced shaving himself at 7, and completed the operation in about an hour and a half. The mate was unable to do anything, but kept repeatedly calling to the mistress for brandy, and requested that his illness should be kept from the doctor, as he was sure he had not fever. Breakfast was speedily despatched, and anxiety was depicted on every countenance.

"At 9 o'clock a boat was perceived pulling towards us, with four oars and a steersman with a broad leafed straw hat and leather coat, who the pilot told us was the inspecting physician. In a few minutes the boat was alongside, and the doctor on deck. He hastily enquired for the captain, and before he could be answered was down in the cabin where the mistress was finishing her toilet. Having introduced himself, he enquired if we had sickness aboard? —Its nature? —How many deaths? —How many patients at present? These questions being answered, and the replies noted upon his tablet, he snatched up his hat,—ran up the ladder, — along the deck, — and down into the hold. Arrived there, 'ha!' said he, sagaciously, 'there is fever here.'

"He stopped beside the first berth in which a patient was lying, — felt his pulse, — examined his tongue, — and ran up the ladder again. As he passed by me he handed me some papers to be filled up by the captain, and to have ready 'tomorrow or the next day.' In an instant he was in his boat, from which, while the men were taking up the oars, he shouted out to me that I was not obliged to remain in quarantine, and might go up to Quebec when I pleased.

"I brought the papers to the captain, who remained in the cabin, supposing that the doctor would return thither, in order to give directions for our guidance; and when he learned that that gentleman had gone, he was desperately enraged. The mistress endeavoured to pacify him by suggesting that it was likely he would visit us again in the course of the day, or at least that he would send a message to us. When I acquainted the mistress that I was at liberty to leave the brig, she looked at me most pitifully, as if she would say, 'Are you too going to desert us.' But I had no such intention, and was determined to remain with them, at all events until they reached Quebec.

"The poor passengers expecting that they would all be reviewed, were dressed in their best clothes, and were clean, though haggard and weak. They were greatly disappointed in their expectations, as they were under the impression that the sick would be immediately admitted to the hospital, and the healthy landed upon the island, there to remain until taken to Quebec by a steamer. Indeed, such was the procedure to be inferred from the book or directions given to the captain by the pilot, when he came aboard.

"When the mistress appeared on deck, I scarcely knew her. She usually wore a black stuff gown, a red worsted 'bosom friend,' which she told me (at least once a day,) was knit for her by her neice [sic]; — with a cap having three full borders, which projected beyond the leaf of the little straw bonnet, covered with the accumulated stains and smoke of many a voyage. Now, she had on a new fancy striped calico dress, as showy as deep reds, yellows, blues and greens could make it, — a black satin bonnet, with no lack of red ribands, and a little conservatory of artificials around her good natured face, — not forgetting her silver spectacles.

"All day long we kept watching out for a message from shore, and in watching the doctor's boat, going from vessel to vessel; his visit to each occupying about the same time as to us, which was exactly five minutes. We sometimes fancied that he was making for us, but the boat the next moment would be concealed by some large ship; then we were sure we would be the next; but no, the rowers pulled for shore. The day wore away before we gave up hope. I could not believe it possible, that here within reach of help we could be left as neglected as when upon the ocean; — that after a voyage of two months' duration, we were to be left still enveloped by reeking pestilence, the sick without medicine, medical skill, nourishment, or so much as a drop of pure water; for the river although not saline here, was polluted by the most disgusting objects, thrown overboard from the several vessels. In short, it was a floating mass of filthy straw, the refuse of foul beds, barrels containing the vilest matter, old rags, and tattered clothes, &c., &c. The Head committee was greatly grieved for his wife, whose death he momentarily expected. He had looked anxiously forward to the time when we should arrive here, hoping that at least the doctor would see her; but his hopes, as well as those of others, were suddenly blasted.

"The brig that arrived with us sailed for Quebec immediately after the doctor's visit, possibly not having had any sickness: five other vessels also were discharged. How long they were detained, we could not tell; but the captain was so provoked, that he vowed he would sail without permission. The pilot, who did not well understand his hasty disposition, ventured to remonstrate with him, and fell in for a hurricane of curses and abuse; to which, though ignorant of many of the expressions, he replied in French, not finding himself sufficiently eloquent in the English tongue.

"Four vessels arrived with the evening tide, and hoisted their signals, but were not visited. Several sailed by us without stopping, not having passengers, and a vast number went down the river during the day. Two huge steamers also arrived, and in the afternoon brought off hundreds of human beings from the island."

Seven burials were recorded in the register of the Catholic chapel and one in that of the Protestant chapel.

SHIPS ARRIVING AT GROSSE ÎLE

Name of ship	Captain	Port of departure	Crossing time (in days)	Passengers Steerage	Cabin	No. of sick on arrival	No. of deaths during crossing
Blenheim*	A. Morrison	Cork (Ireland)	42	378	6	6	10
Broom	W. White	Liverpool (England)	46	515	0	62	16
Delta	M. Mutter	Bremen (Germany)	66	143	0	0	2
George	W. Sheridan	Dublin (Ireland)	60	104	0	2	7
Sir Henry Pottinger	M. Crowel	Cork (Ireland)	60	399	1	100	101
TOTAL				1 539	7	170	

* This ship was transporting retired military personnel and their families.

SHIPS LEAVING GROSSE ÎLE FOR QUÉBEC CITY

Name of ship	Quarantine time (in days)	Deaths in Grosse Île hospitals	Deaths on quarantined ships
Delta	A few hours	0	0
Euclid	3	9	4
Greenock	8	42	26
Heroine	A few hours	0	0
Panama	1/2	0	0

THURSDAY,
JULY 29, 1847

Dr. Douglas requested authorization to charter another boat for the sum of £ 14 10s.; the Executive Council agreed.

The Executive Council authorized an increase in the salary of medical assistants from $5 to $10 per day; rations for the assistants and their domestics were included.

Jean-Baptiste Martel died in Saint-Roch, Québec City, at age 22. According to the *Canadien*, this young man had returned from Grosse Île in apparent good health and was preparing to go back to the island when he came down with typhus. He succumbed to the disease within eight days.

Eyewitness account by Robert Whyte (cont'd):

"This morning a boat was perceived making towards us, which at first was thought to be the doctor's; but when it approached nearer there appeared but two persons in it, both of whom were rowing. In a few minutes more the boat was alongside, and from the cassocks and bands of the two gentlemen we learned that they were Canadian priests. They came on deck, each carrying a large black bag. They inquired for the captain, who received them courteously, and introduced them to the mistress and to me, after which they conversed awhile in French with the pilot, whom they knew; when, having put on their vestments, they descended into the hold. They there spent a few minutes with each of the sick, and administered the last rites to the dying woman and an old man, terminating their duties by baptizing the infant.

"They remained in the hold for about an hour, and when they returned complimented the captain on the cleanliness of the vessel. They staid a short time talking to us upon deck, and the account they gave of the horrid condition of many of the ships in quarantine was frightful. In the holds of some of them they said, that they were up to their ankles in filth. The wretched emigrants crowded together like cattle, and corpses remaining long unburied, the sailors being ill, and the passengers unwilling to touch them.

"They also told us of the vast numbers of sick in the hospitals, and in tents upon the island, and that many nuns, clergymen and doctors, were lying in typhus fever, taken from the patients. [*Authors' note: this is the only historical reference to the presence of nuns at Grosse Île during the season of 1847.*] They were exceedingly intelligent and gentlemanly men, and telling us that we had great cause of thankfulness in having escaped much better that so many others, they politely bowed, and got into their little boat, amid the blessings of the passengers, who watched them until they arrived beside a distant ship.

"The Head committee expressed himself satisfied that his wife saw a priest before her death, which occurred about an hour after; and as the pilot said that the remains should not be thrown into the river, there being a burial ground upon the island, the corpse lay in the hold until the next day. The mate continued to grow worse, and the mistress was unceasing in her attention to him. The day was exceedingly hot and sultry, and I could not have remained on deck, but the captain spread an awning over it, which kept the cabin cool.

"We lay at some distance from the island, the distant view of which was exceedingly beautiful. At the far end were rows of white tents and marquees, resembling the encampment of an army; somewhat nearer was the little fort, and residence of the superintendent physician, and nearer still the chapel, seaman's hospital, and little village, with its wharf and a few sail boats [sic]; the most adjacent extremity being rugged rocks, among which grew beautiful fir trees. At high water this portion was detached from the main island, and formed a most picturesque islet. But this scene of natural beauty was sadly deformed by the dismal display of human suffering that it presented; — helpless creatures being carried by sailors over the rocks, on their way to the hospital, — boats arriving with patients, some of whom had died in their transmission from their ships.

"Another and still more awful sight, was a continuous line of boats, each carrying its freight of dead to the burial-ground, and forming an endless funeral procession. Some had several corpses, so tied up in canvass that the stiff, sharp outline of death was easily traceable; others had rude coffins, constructed by the sailors, from the boards of their berths, or I should rather say, cribs. In a few, a solitary mourner attended the remains; but the majority contained no living beings save the rowers. I could not remove my eyes until boat after boat was hid by the projecting point of the island, round which they steered their gloomy way. From one ship, a boat proceeded four times during the day; each time laden with a cargo of dead. I ventured to count the number of boats that passed, but had to give up the sickening task. The inspecting doctor went about from vessel to vessel, six of which came in each tide, and as many sailed. We expected him to visit us every moment; but he did not come near us. In the afternoon a boat made for our brig, and the mistress, who was on deck, was greatly delighted to find that it contained two 'captains,' one of whom was her nephew. One arrived the day before we came; the other a day previous. They were as ignorant of the course of proceeding as we; and before they went away it was agreed on, that they, our captain, and I, should wait on the superintendent physician the next day."

Thirty-eight burials were recorded in the register of the Catholic chapel.

SHIPS ARRIVING AT GROSSE ÎLE

Name of ship	Captain	Port of departure	Crossing time (in days)	Passengers Steerage	Cabin	No. of sick on arrival	No. of deaths during crossing
Cumberland	T. W. Lewis	Bremerhaven (Germany)	52	365	0	0	0
Diamond	T. Irvine	Bremerhaven (Germany)	52	166	0	2	5
Kilblain	H. Curry	London (England)	54	253	5	0	0
Lady Campbell	J. Hodge	Dublin (Ireland)	55	241	1	50	13
Yorkshire	T. Tripp	Liverpool (England)	50	416	0	0	47
TOTAL				1441	6	52	

SHIPS LEAVING GROSSE ÎLE FOR QUÉBEC CITY

Name of ship	Quarantine time (in days)	Deaths in Grosse Île hospitals	Deaths on quarantined ships
Blenheim	1*	4	2
Cumberland	A few hours	0	0
Jamaica	3	2	0
Tamerlane	3	0	0

* It is hard to understand why this ship was not quarantined for a longer period since six of its passengers were sick when it arrived at Grosse Île and 10 others had died during the crossing.

SHIPS ARRIVING IN QUÉBEC CITY WITHOUT A STOP-OVER AT GROSSE ÎLE

Name of ship	Port of departure	Passengers Steerage	Cabin
Leo	Liverpool (England)	8	12

FRIDAY,
JULY 30, 1847

Father Moïse Duguay, curate at Yamachiche, and the Reverend George Mackie arrived at Grosse Île.

According to the *Canadien*, Dr. Stewart and Dr. Vivian had fallen ill at the quarantine station. Father Campeau, who had recently returned from the island, was very sick with typhus; it was hoped, however, that appropriate care would prevent his condition from deteriorating.

The *Quebec Gazette* reported that the Reverend C. Rollit, of the Church of England, had returned to Québec City after staying on Grosse Île.

Catholic baptism of Helen Leddy, born July 15 to Peter Leddy and Margaret Shandon. Father J. Bailey drew up the baptismal certificate.

Eyewitness account by Robert Whyte (cont'd):

"This morning, when I came on deck, a sailor was busily employed constructing a coffin for the remains of the Head committee's wife; and it was afflicting to hear the husband's groans and sobs accompanying each sound of the saw and hammer, while with his motherless infant in his arms he looked on. About an hour after, the boat was lowered, and the bereaved husband, with four rowers, proceeded to the burial ground to inter the corpse; and they were followed by many a tearful eye, until the boat disappeared behind the rocky point.

"At 10 A. M., we descried the doctor making for us, his boatmen pulling lustily through the heavy sea; a few minutes brought him alongside and on board, when he ran down to the cabin and demanded if the papers were filled up with a return of the number of deaths at sea? how many cases of sickness? &c. He was handed them by the captain; when he enquired, — how many patients we then had; he was told there were twelve; when he wrote an order to admit six to hospital; saying that the rest should be admitted when there was room; there being 2 500 at that time upon the island, and hundreds lying in the various vessels before it. The order written, he returned to his boat, and then boarded a ship lying close to us, which lowered her signal when he approached. Several other vessels that arrived in the morning, had their ensigns flying at the peak, until each was visited in turn.

"Immediately after the doctor left us, the captain gave orders to have the patients in readiness. Shortly after, our second boat was launched, and four of the passengers volunteered to row; the sailors that were able to work, being with the other. O God! may I never again witness such a scene as that which followed; — the husband, — the only support of an emaciated wife and helpless family, — torn away forcibly from them, in a strange land; the mother dragged from her orphan children, that clung to her until she was lifted over the bulwarks, rending the air with their shrieks; children snatched from their bereaved parents, who were perhaps ever to remain ignorant of their recovery, or death. The screams pierced my brain; and the excessive agony so rent my heart, that I was obliged to retire to the cabin, where the mistress sat weeping bitterly.

"The captain went in the boat, and returned in about an hour; giving us a frightful account of what he witnessed upon the island. The steamers returned, and all the afternoon were engaged, taking the *healthy* passengers out of some of the vessels; they went alongside several until their cargo was complete, when they sailed for Montreal, their decks thickly crowded with human beings; and most extraordinary to relate, each of them had a fiddler, and a dancing party in the prow.

"Early in the evening the captain's nephew came to take us in his boat, on shore. After a long pull through a heavy swell, we landed upon the Isle of Pestilence; and climbing over the rocks passed through the little town, and by the hospitals, behind which were piles upon piles of unsightly coffins. A little further on, at the edge of a beautiful sandy beach, were several tents, into one of which I looked, but had no desire to see the interior of any others.

"We pursued our way, by a road cut through a romantic grove of firs, birch, beech, and ash, beneath the shade of which grew and blossomed charming wild flowers, while the most curious fungi vegetated upon odd, decayed stumps. The path led us into a cleared lawn, passing through which, we arrived in front of the superintendent physician's cottage, placed upon a sloping bank at the river's side, on which were mounted two pieces of ordnance guarded by a sentinel. The view from this spot was exquisitely beautiful; — upon the distant bank of the broad river were the smiling, happy-looking Canadian villages, backed by deep, blue hills, while the agitated water in front tossed the noble vessels that lay at anchor, and which were being swung round by the turning tide.

The doctor not being within, we walked about until his return; when he invited us into his cottage and heard what the captains had to say; after which he promised to discharge our friend the next day, and that he would send a steamer to take our passengers. He also gave the captain an order for the admission of the mate to the seaman's hospital. Our mission having been so successful, we thanked the doctor and departed.

"Upon our return, we called at the store licensed to sell provisions upon the island. It was well stocked with various commodities, among which were carrion beef, and cattish mutton, bread, flour, cheese, &c. Although the captain wished to treat the mistress to fresh meat, he declined purchasing what we saw, and merely bought some flour. The storekeeper did not lack better customers, however, for there was a vast concourse of mates, stewards, seamen, and boys, buying his different articles, and stowing them away in their boats. The demand for bread was very great; and several batches were yielded from a large oven, while we remained.

"Hearing the music of a fiddle accompanied by the stamping of feet in time with the tune, I walked up to the shed from which it issued. There were two men dancing a jig; one of them a Canadian, the other a sailor, — both fine fellows, who were evidently pitted against each other, in a trial of skill. The former wore huge boots coming above the knees, and drawn over his gray trowsers composed of 'etoffe du pays,' — a light blue flannel shirt confined at the waist by a scarlet scarf, whose parti colored ends hung at one side. On his head was a woolen 'bonnet rouge,' whose tassel jumped about with the wearer's movements. His brilliant black eyes lighted up his sallow visage, and his arms were as busily engaged as his legs.

"The sailor was rigged out in pumps, white trowsers, blue jacket, and straw hat with streaming black ribands; his ruddy face glowing with the exercise. The fiddler's costume was similar to that of his brother Canadian, except that his 'bonnet' was blue; he stood upon a barrel; and around the dancers was a circle of 'habitans' and sailors, who encouraged them by repeated 'bravos.' I did not remain long, nor could I enjoy the amusement in such a place; and therefore joined my companions in the boat where we were detained a few moments, while one of the men returned for lime, which the captain had forgotten to procure.

"He soon returned, and again ploughing through the waves, we shortly arrived beneath the 'Leander'; after examining which noble ship, the captain and I returned to the brig, and acquainted the mistress with the issue of our adventure. Our boat returned, just at the same time; the men having been away all the day. It appeared that they could not find the burial ground, and consequently dug a grave upon an island, when as they were depositing the remains they were discovered, and obliged to decamp. They were returning to the brig, when they perceived several boats proceeding in another direction, and having joined them, were conducted to the right place.

"The wretched husband was a very picture of desperation and misery, that increased the ugliness of his countenance; — for he was sadly disfigured by the marks of small pox, and was blind of an eye. He walked moodily along the deck, snatched his child from a woman's arms, and went down into the hold without speaking a word. Shortly after, one of the sailors who was with the boat told me, that after the grave was filled up, he took the shovels and placing them crosswise upon it, calling heaven to witness said, 'By that cross, Mary, I swear to revenge your death; as soon as I earn the price of my passage home, I'll go

back, and shoot the man that murdered you, and that's the landlord."

Thirty-one burials were recorded in the register of the Catholic chapel.

SHIPS ARRIVING AT GROSSE ÎLE

Name of ship	Captain	Port of departure	Crossing time (in days)	Passengers Steerage	Cabin	No. of sick on arrival	No. of deaths during crossing
Cygnet	W. Thompson	Londonderry (Ireland)	53	208	2	0	0
Martengale	E. Browne	Hamburg (Germany)	35	168	0	0	0
Naomi	J. Wilson	Liverpool (England)	45	334	0	100	78
Pandora	W. White	New Ross (Ireland)	50	401	0	59	12
Virginius	W. Austin	Liverpool (England)	63	476	0	106	159
X.L.	W. Owen	Galway (Ireland)	51	130	0	3	2
TOTAL				1717	2	268	

SHIPS LEAVING GROSSE ÎLE FOR QUÉBEC CITY

Name of ship	Quarantine time (in days)	Deaths in Grosse Île hospitals	Deaths on quarantined ships
Abbeylands	3	1	0
Agamemnon	5	3	19
Argo	3	0	0
Diamond	1	0	0
Kilblain	A few hours	0	0
Leander	3	2	0

SATURDAY, JULY 31, 1847

According to the *Quebec Mercury*, several of the Catholic and Protestant
clergymen who had come down with typhus while attending the emigrants on Grosse Île were doing well. The Reverend C. Rollit, of the
Church of England, had returned sick from the island. The Reverend
G. Mackie had spent a few hours there the day before, when the steamer
that travelled between Québec City and the quarantine station was
detained at the facility. Mackie described the improvements that had
been made since his last visit, especially in the sheds, which were now
cleaner and more comfortable.

The same edition of the *Quebec Mercury* published alarming news about
Grosse Île. The ships that had arrived recently were in a deplorable
state, rife with disease, death, squalor and misery. The *Lady Campbell*,
a barque from Dublin, had lost 13 passengers during the crossing and
had 50 sick people aboard when it reached the island. The barque

Naomi, which carried 334 passengers from Liverpool, reported 78 deaths and 100 cases of illness. Lastly, the captain of the *Virginius* was dying or dead, and only three of the ship's sailors were fit to work.

The newspaper added that the number of sick was increasing daily at Grosse Île, not only because of the fresh cases disembarking from the vessels that had just arrived but also because of disease breaking out among healthy emigrants. With colder weather approaching, the newspaper was seriously concerned about the situation; the sheds and tents on Grosse Île could not be heated, and the Marine Hospital in Québec City was crowded with patients. The government had to find solutions.

Eyewitness account by Robert Whyte (cont'd):

"It was with great reluctance the mate consented to go to hospital, and as he went into the boat he charged the captain, the mistress and me with cruelty. The captain went with him, and gave him in charge of a doctor. In consequence of the superintendent's promise to send a steamer to take our passengers, and to give us clean bills if the vessel were well whitewashed between decks, that passengers' births [sic] were all knocked away, and the filthy boards thrown into the river; after which four men worked away cleaning and whitening all the day; but no steamer arrived that day. One which lay over night, took 250 passengers from the captain's nephew, who sailed not long after.

"Vessels were arriving with every tide; two ships from Bremen came in the morning and were discharged at once, having no sickness; some others sailed up with the evening tide, after which there were more than thirty in quarantine. Boats were plying all day long, between the several vessels and the island; and the sea being high the miserable patients were drenched by the spray; after which they had to clamber over the slimy rocks, or were carried by sailors. There was also an almost unbroken line of boats carrying the dead for interment; then there was the doctor's boat unceasingly shooting about; besides several others containing captains of ships, many of whom had handsome gigs with six oars and uniformly dressed rowers. It was indeed a busy scene of life and death.

"To complete the picture, the rigging of the vessels was covered over with the passengers' linen, hanging out to dry; by the character of which as they fluttered in the breeze, I could tell with accuracy from what country they came; alas! the wretched rags of the majority told but too plainly that they were Irish."

Twenty-five burials were recorded in the register of the Catholic chapel.

A total of 1704 patients were in hospital on Grosse Île during the week of July 24 to 31.

According to a list published in the *Quebec Morning Chronicle*, 188 people had died at Grosse Île during the week of July 24 to 31.

Dr. Douglas reported that an average of 1454 people were in hospital per day from July 1 to 31 inclusively.

SHIPS ARRIVING AT GROSSE ÎLE

Name of ship	Captain	Port of departure	Crossing time (in days)	Passengers Steerage	Cabin	No. of sick on arrival	No. of deaths during crossing
Augusta Melina	G. Von Lubby	Bremen (Germany)	54	150	0	0	1
Covenanter	J. Patterson	Cork (Ireland)	44	389	11	80	43
Eliza Ann	J. Ferguson	Limerick (Ireland)	32	112	0	1	0
Globe	W. Smith	Bremen (Germany)	69	159	0	0	0
John and Robert	A. McKeckny	Liverpool (England)	53	346	0	45	7
Ophelia and Mary	J. Klut	Hamburg (Germany)	73	183	0	0	3
Union	D. Francis	Limerick (Ireland)	57	54	0	0	0
TOTAL				1393	11	126	

SHIPS LEAVING GROSSE ÎLE FOR QUÉBEC CITY

Name of ship	Quarantine time (in days)	Deaths in Grosse Île hospitals	Deaths on quarantined ships
Augusta Melina	A few hours	0	1
Cygnet	1	0	0
Eliza Ann	A few hours	0	0
Globe	A few hours	0	0
Marchioness of Bute	4	5	6
Martengale	A few hours	0	0
Ophelia and Mary	A few hours	0	0
X.L.	1	2	0

EMIGRANTS ARRIVING IN THE PORT OF QUÉBEC DURING THE WEEK OF JULY 25 TO 31

Country of origin	Number
England	2 827
Ireland	2 268
Scotland	782
Germany	997
Canadian ports downstream from Québec City	0
Total	6 874
Previous total (as at July 24)	56 855
GRAND TOTAL	63 729*

* This represents an increase of 36 893 emigrants compared with the total reported by Buchanan up to the same period in 1846, i.e. 26 836.

1847

AUGUST

S	M	T	W	T	F	S
1	2	3	4	5	6	7
8	9	10	11	12	13	14
15	16	17	18	19	20	21
22	23	24	25	26	27	28
29	30	31				

SUNDAY,
AUGUST 1, 1847

The *Quebec Morning Chronicle* reported that emigrants had died on the *Harry Lorrequer* during the week of August 1 to 7, 1847. This vessel is not mentioned in either the list of ships that were inspected at Grosse Île or the list of those that arrived in Québec City.

Eyewitness account by Robert Whyte (cont'd):

"The passengers passed a miserable night, huddled up, as they were without room to stretch their weary limbs. I pitied them from my soul, and it was sickening to see them drink the filthy water. I could not refuse to give one or two of them a mouthful from the cask upon the quarter deck, which fortunately was filled lower down the river. They asked for it so pitifully, and were so thankful; but I could not satisfy all and regretted the disappointment of many. They had on their best clothes, and were all clean, with the exception of one incorrigible family.

"The doctor came on board in the forenoon, to inspect the passengers, who were all called on deck, but those who were unable. Placing himself at a barrier, he allowed each to pass, one by one; making those he suspected of being feverish, show their tongues. This proceeding lasted about a quarter of an hour; when the doctor went into the hold to examine those below, and to see if it were clean; he then wrote out the order to admit the six patients to hospital, and promised to send the steamer to take the remainder; after which we should have clean bills.

"When he had gone, the patients were lowered into the boat amid a renewal of the indescribable woe that followed the previous separations. Two of them were orphan sisters, who were sent for by a brother in Upper Canada. Another was a mother, who had tended all her family through illness, — now careworn, and heart-broken, she became herself a prey.

"In the early part of the voyage, I observed the unfilial conduct of a boy, who frequently abused, and even cursed his mother, following the example set by his wretched father. On one

BOAT USED TO TAKE EMIGRANTS TO THE HOSPITALS AND SHEDS ON GROSSE ÎLE. AT TIMES, OBSERVERS STATED, THE QUARANTINE PASS WAS CHOKED WITH THESE BOATS, SOME GOING TO THE HOSPITALS AND OTHERS TO THE TENTS AND SHEDS IN THE EASTERN PART OF THE ISLAND. MANY, HOWEVER, WERE HEADED FOR THE WESTERN CEMETERY. (DANIEL RAINVILLE, PARKS CANADA, 1997.)

occasion, his hand was raised to strike her, when his arm was arrested by a bystander; but the poor woman begged of the man not to punish him, and wept for the depravity of her son. It was she who was now being carried to the boat; while the boy who cursed and would have stricken her, clung to her, crying, and imploring her blessing and forgiveness; but she was unable to utter a word, and by an effort raised her arm feebly and looked sadly upon the afflicted boy, who seized her hand and bathed it with his tears, until he was torn away, and she dropped into the boat, which a moment after rowed off.

"I felt much for the poor fellow, who was conscious that he should never again see his mother; for there was no hope of her recovery; and I little thought that any one could be so heartless as to aggravate his sufferings, as did two or three women who surrounded him, one of them saying, 'Ha! you villain, there's the mother you abused, and cursed, you rascal! you may now take your last look at her.' He followed the boat with his eyes, until it reached the shore; when he beheld the inanimate figure borne to the hospital. It was evident from the poignancy of his sorrow, that his heart was not depraved, but that his misconduct arose from education.

"The morning was fine, clear and warm, and many of the vessels were decorated with their flags, giving a cheerful aspect to the scene, which alas, was marred by the ensigns of two ships (one on either side of us), which were hoisted half-mast high, the captain of one, and the chief mate of the other, being dead. While the captain was away with the boat the steamer came alongside of us to take our passengers. It did not take very long to transship them, as few of them had any luggage. Many of them were sadly disappointed when they learned that they were to be carried on to Montreal, as those who had left their relatives upon Grosse Isle, hoped, that as Quebec was not far distant, they would be enabled by some means to hear of them, by staying there. Each of them shook hands with the mistress, and all heaped blessings upon her head; and as to the captain, one of them remarked that 'though he was a divil [sic], he was a gintleman [sic].'

"The steamer pushed off, amid the cheers of her motley freight, and was soon out of sight. The mistress was quite overcome by the expressions of the poor creatures' gratitude for her unceasing, and otherwise unrequited attention, and benevolence. The captain returned, and after dinner he and I went ashore for our cleans bills of health. We saw Dr. Douglas, who informed us that the inspecting physician, Dr. Jacques, had them, and that he was going his rounds among the vessels; with the intention of calling at the brig. But as we considered that it would proba-bly be late before he would reach her, we pulled for a barque, beside which we descried the well known boat.

"Before we were half way, it was gone and making for a ship some distance off; however, we still followed, and again were dis-appointed. We determined not to give up the chase, and at length caught the doctor on board a German emigrant vessel. He was inspecting the passengers, of whom there were 500, — all of them (without a single exception) comfortably and neatly clad, clean, and happy. There was no sickness amongst them, and each comely fair haired girl laughed as she passed the doctor, to join the group of robust young men who had undergone the ordeal. Although it was pleasing to see so many joyous beings, it made me sad when I thought of the very, very different state of my unfortunate compatriots; and I had become so habituated to misery, disease, and death, that the happiness that now surrounded me was quite discordant with my feelings.

"The doctor having completed his task, countersigned our clean bills, and handed them to the captain; we therefore thanked him and took our leave. Before returning to the brig, we called to see the mate, who was lying with his clothes on, upon a bed; the next one to which contained a figure writhing in torture, and, as the face was turned towards me, I recognized to my great surprise and dismay, the sailor, who, but the evening but one before, was dancing with the Canadian. When the mate perceived us, he rose from the bed, and taking the captain by one arm, and me by the other, walked us both out of the hospital, to the porch; saying that we had no business there, as there was fever upon all sides of us.

"The hospital was a large chapel, transformed to its present use, and was exceedingly clean and well ventilated, the large windows were all open, causing a draught of air that was agreeable; the evening being very sultry. We did not remain long with the mate, who raved considerably in his conversation, though he said he was quite well; so, the captain giving him in charge of the attendant, with pressing injunctions to have every attention paid to him, and saying that he hoped he would be able to join the brig upon his return, we departed.

"As we got into the boat, we made a signal to the pilot (who was desired to be on the lookout,) to weigh anchor, so as not to lose the tide by any unnecessary delay. As we repassed the German ship, the deck was covered with emigrants, who were singing a charming hymn, in whose beautiful harmony all took part; spreading the music of their five hundred voices upon the calm, still air, that wafted it around. The vessel being discharged, began to move almost imperceptibly, so that we quickly passed her; but she gradually gained speed, and was ahead of us by the time we reached the brig, and as the distance between us increased, the anthem died away, until it became inaudible. It was the finest chorus I ever heard, — performed in a theatre of unrivalled magnificence.

"The mistress was delighted when she learned that we were free, and all were glad to leave behind the Isle of Death, though we regretted leaving the mate there. The sailors that had been ill, still continuing very weak, the captain induced two young men to remain, in order to assist in working the vessel. At 7 P. M. the anchor was weighed, the sails unreefed, and we glided slowly along."

The day after he left Grosse Île, Robert Whyte wrote: "It was indeed with gratefulness to the Almighty for having preserved me scathless [sic] in the midst of the dread pestilence, that I left Grosse Isle; and a more beautiful panorama I never beheld, than the country through which we passed, — the churches of St. Thomas' and St. Pierre's, surrounded by handsome cottages and beautiful fields...."

Catholic baptism of Mary Stonix, aged 2, daughter of Mary Ann Best and the late James Stonix. Father F.-S. Bardy drew up the baptismal certificate.

Twenty-seven burials were recorded in the register of the Catholic chapel.

SHIPS ARRIVING AT GROSSE ÎLE

Name of ship	Captain	Port of departure	Crossing time (in days)	Passengers Steerage	Cabin	No. of sick on arrival	No. of deaths during crossing
Edward Kenny	D. Cook	Belfast (Ireland)	51	245	0	0	0
Favourite	J. Horste	Bremen (Germany)	55	201	0	0	1
John Munn	J. Watt	Liverpool (England)	47	452	0	100	59
Liberia	T. Gibson	Hamburg (Germany)	62	153	0	0	0
Maria	M. O'Malley	Limerick (Ireland)	44	132	0	0	0
Odessa	C. Laverty	Dublin (Ireland)	53	235	7	20	22
Rockshire	P. McLeury	Liverpool (England)	49	44	4	0	0
Rosalinda	D. Hay	Belfast (Ireland)	40	506	2	7	17
Royal Adelaide	T. Potts	Killala (Ireland)	53	367	0	8	7
TOTAL				2335	13	135	

SHIPS LEAVING GROSSE ÎLE FOR QUÉBEC CITY

Name of ship	Quarantine time (in days)	Deaths in Grosse Île hospitals	Deaths on quarantined ships
Edward Kenny	A few hours	0	0
Favourite	A few hours	0	0
George	5	4	0
Liberia	A few hours	0	0
Oregon	5	2	1
Union	1	15*	0

* Since no cases of illness were reported when this ship arrived at Grosse Île, it seems odd that 15 of its passengers died while the vessel was in quarantine.

MONDAY,
AUGUST 2, 1847

The Board of Works was about to spend large sums of money in Québec City on the construction of emigrant sheds for Grosse Île. A contract worth £ 750 had already been awarded to a contractor for the supply of 3 300 feet of framework, ready to be erected at the quarantine station. In addition, 1 200 feet of framing had been shipped to the island along with basic materials, and 40 workmen had been sent to assemble the structures and do finishing work. The rest of the framing was to be delivered the following Friday, August 6. Both the wood and the workmanship were of good quality.

Captain Boxer, harbour master for the port of Québec, was asked to be on hand at Grosse Île to ensure that the sheds were placed in a location where they would benefit from the free circulation of the prevailing winds and to see that they were as near as possible to the shore so that it would be easier to embark and disembark emigrants and to fetch water supplies.

Charles-Félix Cazeau, the secretary of the archdiocese, informed Dr. Parant, the medical superintendent for the port of Québec, that the priests at Grosse Île still did not have access to a rowboat for visiting the sick on ships detained at the station, despite the fact that the Governor General had ordered that one be placed at their disposal. The failure to carry out these orders did not stem from a lack of goodwill on the part of the station's medical superintendent, but probably from the fact that there were not enough rowboats at the island for him to allot one every time a boat was needed.

A sufficient number of rowboats had to be available for providing the sick with spiritual and temporal assistance. These poor people could not be left to die without receiving the last rites. Occasionally, the priests had been able to use the inspecting physician's boat, but almost never when they actually needed it. Moreover, this boat, after letting them off at a ship, usually took the inspecting physician elsewhere and did not return to take the priests ashore or transport them to other vessels.

Emigration agent Buchanan wrote to the Governor General about the problem of housing sick or convalescent emigrants when colder weather set in. These people would have to be evacuated from Grosse Île since it was inaccessible in winter. In five or six weeks, both the tents and the sheds at the quarantine station would be uninhabitable, since it would be too cold at night. In Buchanan's opinion, the new sheds at Pointe-Saint-Charles, in Montréal, could be made inhabitable for the winter and would thus be suitable for lodging the emigrants from Grosse Île.

The *Canadien* informed its readers that a young carpenter, who had helped to build temporary hospitals at the quarantine station and at the Marine Hospital in Québec City, had died from typhus in Saint-Vallier on the previous Saturday, July 31.

Catholic baptism of Peter Breen, born July 30 to Daniel Breen and Ann Bryan. Father F.-S. Bardy drew up the baptismal certificate.

Thirty-one burials were recorded in the register of the Catholic chapel.

SHIPS ARRIVING AT GROSSE ÎLE

Name of ship	Captain	Port of departure	Crossing time (in days)	Passengers Steerage	Cabin	No. of sick on arrival	No. of deaths during crossing
Ann Kenny	W. Baldwin	Waterford (Ireland)	36	354	6	26	4
Curraghmore	W. Ball	Waterford (Ireland)	43	214	0	0	1
Egbert	T. Bell	Bremen (Germany)	73	164	0	0	0
Ocean Queen	J. McBride	Cork (Ireland)	34	497	1	3	2
TOTAL				1 229	7	29	

SHIPS LEAVING GROSSE ÎLE FOR QUÉBEC CITY

Name of ship	Quarantine time (in days)	Deaths in Grosse Île hospitals	Deaths on quarantined ships
Egbert	A few hours	0	0
Maria	A few hours	0	0

TUESDAY, AUGUST 3, 1847

After learning that the salary of medical assistants had been increased from $5 to $10 per day, Douglas asked that his salary be raised from $6.75 to $12 a day. His request was not motivated simply by monetary considerations since, in his opinion, no amount of money could ever compensate for the anxiety, workload and health risks he endured in fulfilling his duties. Douglas also justified his request by saying that offering medical assistants twice his salary for doing one tenth of what he did constituted an anomaly that would undermine his authority.

Pierre Laurencel, the Board of Works agent, reported that the construction of new sheds was going well. The day before, the framework of a 408-foot hospital had arrived at Grosse Île along with a large number of carpenters. The hospital was to be erected in the bay at the west end of the island. Another 132-foot hospital was finished, and preparations were under way to place the sick there. A building made by Pierre Laberge and Joseph Hélie *dit* Breton for the east end of the island was expected to arrive that morning; another, made by Pierre Lapointe and Basile Monier, was also supposed to be delivered soon. The framing of the domestics' quarters was progressing well. Lastly, work continued on the wharf, and 24 workers had been assigned to this task.

According to Mr. Patry of the Board of Works, the construction of the new sheds was progressing satisfactorily. Already, 1 224 feet of framing could be erected on Grosse Île, and all the necessary materials and workmen had arrived. Framework for other housing units being made in Québec City was going well and would be delivered to the island the following Saturday, August 7. All told, 3 060 feet of framing was available for new sheds. It was difficult to find men willing to work on Grosse Île. A Canadian workman had returned to Québec City in ill health and had died, arousing considerable concern among the workers there.

Father Michel Forgues, parish priest of Sainte-Marie, and Father Antoine Lebel, curate at Rimouski, arrived at Grosse Île.

The *Quebec Mercury* and the *Quebec Gazette* reported that the Anglican Bishop of Montréal, George J. Mountain, had left for the quarantine station on the morning boat. It was his third visit to the station and he intended to spend a week there providing spiritual comfort to the sick.

The *Quebec Mercury* also reported that the steamer *St. George* had arrived in Québec City at about two o'clock with 66 convalescent patients from Grosse Île. The sickness rate had not abated on the island and mortality was much the same, i.e. 30 to 40 deaths a day. The quarantine station's hospitals were full, owing to the recent arrival of a large number of emigrants.

The *Canadien* announced the death of Dr. Jameson, the son of Captain Jameson. A former resident of Sanguinet Street in Montréal, he had died at the age of 34 from an illness contracted on Grosse Île.

Fifteen burials were recorded in the register of the Catholic chapel and seven in that of the Protestant chapel.

SHIPS ARRIVING AT GROSSE ÎLE

Name of ship	Captain	Port of departure	Crossing time (in days)	Passengers Steerage	Cabin	No. of sick on arrival	No. of deaths during crossing
Allan Kerr	W. Gily	Sligo (Ireland)	41	414	2	11	9
Helen	W. Hasson	Belfast (Ireland)	63	210	2	0	0
Marchioness of Abercorn	J. Hagerty	Londonderry (Ireland)	49	416	0	4	10
Marinus	J. Dick	Dublin (Ireland)	60	202	0	62	6
Westmoreland	M. G. Walker	Sligo (Ireland)	52	207	0	10	5
TOTAL				1 449	4	87	

SHIPS LEAVING GROSSE ÎLE FOR QUÉBEC CITY

Name of ship	Quarantine time (in days)	Deaths in Grosse Île hospitals	Deaths on quarantined ships
Curraghmore	1	0	0
Ocean Queen	1	1	3
Pandora	5	9	3
Rockshire	2	0	0

WEDNESDAY, AUGUST 4, 1847

Act of profession of the Catholic faith by John Galloway and William Gibson. Father J.-A. Lebel drew up the act of abjuration.

Catholic marriage of John Galloway, a Scottish sailor on the *Marinus*, and Maria O'Neill, from County Longford, Ireland. Father J.-A. Lebel drew up the marriage certificate.

Catholic marriage of William Gibson, a Scottish sailor on the *Marinus*, and Mary Carty, from County Longford, Ireland. Father J.-A. Lebel drew up the marriage certificate.

Twenty burials were recorded in the register of the Catholic chapel and one in that of the Protestant chapel.

SHIPS ARRIVING AT GROSSE ÎLE

Name of ship	Captain	Port of departure	Crossing time (in days)	Passengers Steerage	Cabin	No. of sick on arrival	No. of deaths during crossing
John Christophe	P. Peterson	Bremen (Germany)	57	173	0	0	0

SHIPS LEAVING GROSSE ÎLE FOR QUÉBEC CITY

Name of ship	Quarantine time (in days)	Deaths in Grosse Île hospitals	Deaths on quarantined ships
Allan Kerr	1	1	5
Charles Walton	8	2	9
Helen	1	0	0
John Christophe	A few hours	0	0

THURSDAY,
AUGUST 5, 1847

Dr. Douglas asked the Board of Works to provide an additional £ 500 to pay for the buildings that were under construction at the quarantine station. Work on the various structures was progressing satisfactorily. A sixth hospital, with room for 125 patients, had been finished the day before and would be fully occupied that evening.

Mr. Finch and Mr. Doran, retail butchers in Québec City, requested permission to sell, under the supervision of the medical superintendent, meat, vegetables and other provisions to ships that stopped at Grosse Île. (See reply of August 20.)

According to the *Quebec Mercury*, 789 men, 755 women and 542 children were in hospital on Grosse Île, representing a total of 2086 patients.

Catholic baptism of Mary McCoy, aged 18 (after abjuration). Father M. Duguay drew up the baptismal certificate.

Death of William Staunton, a sailor aboard the *Marchioness of Breadalbane*.

Twenty-four burials were recorded in the register of the Catholic chapel and one in that of the Protestant chapel.

SHIPS ARRIVING AT GROSSE ÎLE

Name of ship	Captain	Port of departure	Crossing time (in days)	Passengers Steerage	Cabin	No. of sick on arrival	No. of deaths during crossing
Fenella	J. Hay	London (England)	58	16	3	0	2
Jessie	H. McAllister	Limerick (Ireland)	41	108	0	10	2
Zealous	J. Richards	London (England)	49	120	4	5	1
TOTAL				244	7	15	

SHIPS LEAVING GROSSE ÎLE FOR QUÉBEC CITY

Name of ship	Quarantine time (in days)	Deaths in Grosse Île hospitals	Deaths on quarantined ships
Ann Kenny	3	6	0
Broom	8	39	9
Fenella	A few hours	0	0
John and Robert	5	20	7
Lady Campbell	7	26	2
Marchioness of Abercorn	2	7	0

FRIDAY,
AUGUST 6, 1847

According to Pierre Laurencel, construction work at Grosse Île was going well; over 150 workers of all trades were at the quarantine station. Two new sheds were up at the farm, and their flooring, shingle roofs and exterior clapboarding were being installed. The construction of a 408-foot hospital at the west end of the island was proceeding rapidly. Work on the wharf was also going well; a gangway measuring about 4 feet wide was being built for the benefit of passengers.

The Executive Council committee recommended that Dr. Douglas should be free to decide how long healthy emigrants from ships where contagious disease had broken out during the ocean voyage would be detained in quarantine. In addition, the committee agreed with the medical superintendent that vessels should be considered insalubrious if 1.5 percent of their passengers (excluding children and the elderly) had died and over 2 percent were ill. In view of the situation in 1847, the committee considered that these figures were perfectly justified.

Father Prisque Gariépy, parish priest of Sainte-Claire, arrived at Grosse Île.

According to the *Quebec Mercury*, 2 148 patients (831 men, 745 women and 572 children) were in hospital on the island.

Death of John Reid, captain of the *Marchioness of Breadalbane*, at age 54.

Twenty-nine burials were recorded in the register of the Catholic chapel and four in that of the Protestant chapel.

SHIPS ARRIVING AT GROSSE ÎLE

Name of ship	Captain	Port of departure	Crossing time (in days)	Passengers Steerage	Cabin	No. of sick on arrival	No. of deaths during crossing
Canton	M. J. Mang	Bremen (Germany)	48	240	0	0	6
Frankfield	J. Robinson	Liverpool (England)	38	529	0	8	8
Free Trader	J. Thompson	Liverpool (England)	46	481	0	31	40
Grace	T. Bell	Westport (Ireland)	49	29	12	0	1
Minerva	G. Cobbitt	Galway (Ireland)	51	138	0	26	4
Saguenay	R. Trannack	Cork (Ireland)	62	466	10	160	104
TOTAL				1 883	22	225	

SHIPS LEAVING GROSSE ÎLE FOR QUÉBEC CITY

Name of ship	Quarantine time (in days)	Deaths in Grosse Île hospitals	Deaths on quarantined ships
Canton	A few hours	0	0
Grace	A few hours	0	0
Rosalinda	5	2	0

SATURDAY, AUGUST 7, 1847

The *Quebec Mercury* reported that more than 2000 healthy passengers had disembarked from nine vessels and were now staying in tents at the east end of the island. All the tents and hospitals at the quarantine station were full. The newspaper also mentioned that many of the supposedly healthy emigrants in the tent sector were falling ill.

The *Quebec Mercury* informed its readers that Drs. Dease, Allen and Johnston had returned to their duties at Grosse Île and that Dr. Newton was going there that evening. Dr. Wallace was suffering from typhus.

Death of Charles Boyd, a carpenter on the *Marchioness of Bute,* at about age 27.

Five burials were recorded in the register of the Protestant chapel.

According to a list published in the *Quebec Morning Chronicle*, 220 people had died at Grosse Île during the week of August 1 to 7.

SHIPS ARRIVING AT GROSSE ÎLE

Name of ship	Captain	Port of departure	Crossing time (in days)	Passengers Steerage	Cabin	No. of sick on arrival	No. of deaths during crossing
Ann Rankin	J. McArthur	Glasgow (Scotland)	41	332	4	3	2

SHIPS LEAVING GROSSE ÎLE FOR QUÉBEC CITY

Name of ship	Quarantine time (in days)	Deaths in Grosse Île hospitals	Deaths on quarantined ships
Sir Henry Pottinger	10	22	7

EMIGRANTS ARRIVING IN THE PORT OF QUÉBEC DURING THE WEEK OF AUGUST 1 TO 7

Country of origin	Number
England	918
Ireland	4021
Scotland	0
Germany	1328
Canadian ports downstream from Québec City	10
Total	6277
Previous total (as at July 31)	63729
GRAND TOTAL	70006*

* This represents an increase of 42863 emigrants compared with the total reported by Buchanan up to the same period in 1846, i.e. 27143.

NUMBER OF PEOPLE IN HOSPITAL ON GROSSE ÎLE DURING THE WEEK OF AUGUST 1 TO 7

Emigrants	Patients hospitalized as at last report	Patients admitted (+)	Patients discharged (-)	Deaths (-)	New total
TOTAL	1704	778	170	196*	2116

* During the same period, 24 healthy passengers died in the tents. In addition, the bodies of 40 adults and 47 children were taken ashore and buried on the island. The total number of burials over this period was 307.

SUNDAY, AUGUST 8, 1847

Three nurses died during the week of August 8 to 14. They were Catherine McConaty (32 years old), Ellen Stanley (30 years old), and Mrs. Hobbs, the wife of a sergeant.

Death of James Buchanan, a cook aboard the *Ajax*, at age 25.

Thirty-five burials were recorded in the register of the Catholic chapel and three in that of the Protestant chapel.

SHIPS ARRIVING AT GROSSE ÎLE

Name of ship	Captain	Port of departure	Crossing time (in days)	Passengers Steerage	Passengers Cabin	No. of sick on arrival	No. of deaths during crossing
Countess of Arran	J. Henderson	Donegal (Ireland)	40	205	2	0	2
Ellen Simpson	W. Newman	Limerick (Ireland)	59	186	6	9	4
Henry Volante	J. Collins	Ballyshannon (Ireland)	54	64	2	0	0
Vesta	A. Bagg	Limerick (Ireland)	48	118	0	0	1
TOTAL				573	10	9	

MONDAY,
AUGUST 9, 1847

The *Victoria*, commanded by Captain J. Blais, arrived at Grosse Île with 31 steerage passengers rescued from the *Loosthank*, a ship that had run into difficulty off Miramichi, New Brunswick. Since no deaths or cases of illness were reported among its passengers and crew, the ship left the quarantine station that same day.

The Governor General told Dr. Douglas that it was absolutely necessary to disembark all healthy passengers from any ship with cases of illness aboard as soon as it arrived at Grosse Île. Such passengers would have to be kept in quarantine long enough for them to bathe thoroughly and wash their clothing and personal effects. The medical superintendent should also ensure that sick people and suspicious cases were separated from healthy emigrants. Only those who were perfectly healthy should be allowed to board steamers heading for Montréal.

According to the *Canadien* of August 9, two scientists had been sent to Canada recently by the British government and were on their way to Grosse Île. There they planned to test a chemical agent which they claimed could purify the unwholesome air in hospitals where patients suffering from contagious diseases were confined.

The *Canadien* also published an article originally appearing in the *Minerve* on the alarming state of affairs at Grosse Île, where a number of disease- and death-ridden ships had arrived in a deplorable condition. The author of the article denounced the British government and the Irish lords for forcing the colony to accept the emigration of all the poorest, most degenerate and least desirable elements in the British Isles. These emigrants, he said, spread death wherever they went, in the towns and throughout the countryside, and they were supposed to be accepted without a murmur. This was what it meant to be a colony.

Seventeen burials were recorded in the register of the Catholic chapel and six in that of the Protestant chapel.

SHIPS ARRIVING AT GROSSE ÎLE

Name of ship	Captain	Port of departure	Crossing time (in days)	Passengers Steerage	Cabin	No. of sick on arrival	No. of deaths during crossing
Amy	W. White	Bremen (Germany)	45	291	1	0	1
Anna Maria	T. Dillon	Limerick (Ireland)	38	119	0	1	2
Britannia	R. Simpson	Greenock (Scotland)	28	388	0	25	7
Brothers	J. Craighill	Dublin (Ireland)	35	318	3	8	4
Corea	J. Finlay	Liverpool (England)	38	501	11	7	17
Corsair	J. McGreggor	Bristol (England)	44	39	6	0	0
Larch	A. Dove	Sligo (Ireland)	29	440	0	150	113
Lillias	T. Harrison	Dublin (Ireland)	41	214	0	6	6
Pomona	T. B. Culley	Bremen (Germany)	60	226	1	0	0
Tropic	J. J. Burgess	London (England)	38	76	10	0	0
Watchful	T. Timbles	Hamburg (Germany)	69	145	0	0	0
TOTAL				2 757	32	197	

SHIPS LEAVING GROSSE ÎLE FOR QUÉBEC CITY

Name of ship	Quarantine time (in days)	Deaths in Grosse Île hospitals	Deaths on quarantined ships
Ann Rankin	2	1	5
Corsair	A few hours	0	0
Countess of Arran	1	0	0
Covenanter	9	71	16
Frankfield	3	3	2
Henry Volante	A few hours	0	0
Jessie	4	0	0
Odessa	8	49	4
Pomona	A few hours	0	0
Royal Adelaide	8	10	4
Tropic	A few hours	0	0
Vesta	1	0	1
Zealous	4	3	0

SHIPS ARRIVING IN QUÉBEC CITY WITHOUT A STOP-OVER AT GROSSE ÎLE

Name of ship	Port of departure	Passengers Steerage	Cabin
Marchioness of Ailsa	Glasgow (Scotland)	1	0

TUESDAY,
AUGUST 10, 1847

The Executive Council committee rejected the request made by Dr. Douglas on August 3 respecting a raise in salary. The committee was of the opinion that the medical superintendent was an officer employed on a permanent basis, with an annual allowance as payment for services rendered during the year; the medical assistants, on the other hand, were employed by the day for a limited period and could be dismissed at any time. (The Governor General ratified this decision the following day.)

Father William Dunn, parish priest of Frampton, Father Thomas Caron, assistant director of the Seminary of Nicolet, and Father Maxime Tardif, curate at Lotbinière, arrived at Grosse Île. Father Michel Forgues, parish priest of Sainte-Marie-de-Beauce, and Father Antoine Lebel, curate at Rimouski, left the quarantine station in good health.

Father C.-F. Cazeau, the secretary of the archdiocese, wrote to the Governor General on behalf of Archbishop Signay to say that the Catholic priests working at Grosse Île were finding it difficult to serve the healthy emigrants who, after being taken ashore, were falling ill in increasing numbers. These passengers were kept at the east end of the island, about a mile away from the hospitals and the Catholic priests' lodgings. The missionaries who had to cover this distance on foot several times a day could not continue to do so without becoming exhausted and thus endangering their health.

Therefore, the Archbishop asked the Governor General to ensure that a horse and cart were placed at the priests' disposal, as had already been proposed by the medical superintendent. (See the Governor General's reply of August 21.) The Archbishop also informed the Governor General that two priests recently employed at the station had come down with typhus; 14 others had caught the disease previously.

The *Canadien* reported that the *Eliza and Sarah* was anchored at Grosse Île. The vessel had 276 passengers on board, even though it had room for only around 185. Twenty-two people had died during the crossing and 20 others were ill.

The *Quebec Mercury* published an article on the alarming situation at Grosse Île. The day before, on August 9, there were 2 240 patients in hospital. A number of ships had been placed in quarantine and they were rife with disease. The hospitals were more crowded than ever and the poor emigrants in tents were dying by the dozens. Eleven people had passed away during the night of August 8 and another on the way to hospital on the morning of August 10. The captain of the *Virginius* had died the day after his ship anchored at Grosse Île.

According to the *Quebec Mercury*, 2100 patients (856 men, 726 women and 518 children) were in hospital on Grosse Île.

Catholic baptism of Sean Sullivan, born August 9 to Jeremy Sullivan and Honora Buckley. Father M. Tardif drew up the baptismal certificate.

Twelve burials were recorded in the register of the Catholic chapel.

SHIPS ARRIVING AT GROSSE ÎLE

Name of ship	Captain	Port of departure	Crossing time (in days)	Passengers Steerage	Cabin	No. of sick on arrival	No. of deaths during crossing
Auguste	C. H. Von Puttle	Bremen (Germany)	57	170	0	0	0
Elza Ann	M. Lamb	Hamburg (Germany)	55	143	0	0	1
TOTAL				313	0	0	

SHIPS LEAVING GROSSE ÎLE FOR QUÉBEC CITY

Name of ship	Quarantine time (in days)	Deaths in Grosse Île hospitals	Deaths on quarantined ships
Amy	1	0	0
Anna Maria	1	0	0
Auguste	A few hours	0	0
Elza Ann	A few hours	0	0
Naomi	11	87	31
Watchful	A few hours	0	0
Westmoreland	7	6	4
Yorkshire	12	27	10

WEDNESDAY, AUGUST 11, 1847

Since it was difficult to find personnel to wash bedding at Grosse Île, commissary general Filder requested permission to make arrangements to have this work done by a Mr. Cobrick of Québec City. (The Executive Council committee approved this request on August 13.)

The *Canadien* published disturbing news from Grosse Île. On Monday, August 9, the sick numbered 2240 and the mortality rate was exceptionally high. On one of the ships that had arrived recently, conditions were truly shocking: 108 of the 440 passengers had already died and 150 more were ill. Furthermore, there was no more room in the hospitals for the 300 sick emigrants who had reached the quarantine station on August 8 and 9.

According to the *Canadien*, Father J. Bailey, Father F.-S. Bardy and Father C. Tardif had come back from Grosse Île a little while earlier and were now in hospital.

The *Quebec Gazette* reported that the mortality rate among emigrants as a whole was about one eighth. This proportion included deaths that occurred during the crossing, at Grosse Île and in Canadian towns and cities to which the emigrants travelled. The newspaper added that it was evident that the quarantine station could not halt the spread of disease if emigrants continued to be crowded into the ships.

Catholic baptism of Jean Smith, born August 10 to John Smith and Catherine Swift. Father W. Dunn drew up the baptismal certificate.

Forty-five burials were recorded in the register of the Catholic chapel and six in that of the Protestant chapel.

SHIPS ARRIVING AT GROSSE ÎLE

Name of ship	Captain	Port of departure	Crossing time (in days)	Passengers Steerage	Cabin	No. of sick on arrival	No. of deaths during crossing
Trinity	T. Boler	Limerick (Ireland)	53	86	3	0	0

SHIPS LEAVING GROSSE ÎLE FOR QUÉBEC CITY

Name of ship	Quarantine time (in days)	Deaths in Grosse Île hospitals	Deaths on quarantined ships
Marchioness of Breadalbane	15	8	9
Trinity	A few hours	0	0

THURSDAY, AUGUST 12, 1847

The Governor General announced that arrangements were being made to have a new disinfectant used at Grosse Île. The inventor would go to the island to supervise its application in person.

The *Quebec Mercury* reported that the passengers aboard the *Freetrader*, the *Larch*, the *Saguenay* and the *Ganges* were waiting to disembark at Grosse Île. Since the 2000 places in the tents were already occupied, these emigrants had to remain on board ship.

According to the *Quebec Mercury*, the prefabricated framework for new sheds had been delivered to Grosse Île. Mr. Casgrain, the Public Works commissioner, had gone to the island to select the site where they would be erected and had returned to Montréal in the evening of August 11.

The *Quebec Mercury* also mentioned that Dr. Dease had come back from the quarantine station, since the medical staff was considered too large. Dr. Wallace was still sick with typhus. Besides Dr. George Douglas, the following physicians were employed on the island at the time: Drs. Jacques, McGrath, Johnston, Allen, Damours, Watt, Stewart, Beardon, Vivian, Fortin and Eastaff. Mr. Barter and Mr. Cullingford worked as apothecaries. The newspaper had just learned that Dr. Fortin was seriously ill with typhus and that Dr. Beardon was showing symptoms of the disease.

The *Quebec Mercury* reported that a strange and fatal illness had broken out among the cattle on Grosse Île.

With colder weather approaching, the *Quebec Morning Chronicle* wondered what would happen to the emigrants at Grosse Île and publicly asked the Québec Board of Health a series of questions: Was it really necessary to evacuate the sick emigrants at Grosse Île when winter came? Could temporary wooden buildings not be heated just as well and just as easily at Grosse Île as elsewhere? Would it not be possible to install stoves? Would it be any more difficult to heat a temporary wooden building in that disease-ridden spot than it had been to heat similar structures built on Saint-Louis Road for those left homeless by the great fire of 1845? Was it very much colder in Québec City than it was at Grosse Île? Would all communication with the island be cut off during the winter?

Catholic baptism of two children whose parents were unknown; both of them were given the first name Thomas. Father W. Dunn drew up the baptismal certificates.

Fifty-two burials were recorded in the register of the Catholic chapel.

SHIPS ARRIVING AT GROSSE ÎLE

Name of ship	Captain	Port of departure	Crossing time (in days)	Passengers Steerage	Cabin	No. of sick on arrival	No. of deaths during crossing
Ganges	G. Smith	Liverpool (England)	58	393	0	80	45
Naparina	J. Birely*	Dublin (Ireland)	57	226	3	34	24
TOTAL				619	3	114	

* The captain of this ship died aboard his vessel off Île du Bic on August 3.

SHIPS LEAVING GROSSE ÎLE FOR QUÉBEC CITY

Name of ship	Quarantine time (in days)	Deaths in Grosse Île hospitals	Deaths on quarantined ships
John Munn	10	118	11
Marinus	9	38	2
Virginius	13	90	19

FRIDAY, AUGUST 13, 1847

Dr. Fortin, who was extremely ill, left Grosse Île for Québec City.

Father Michael Kerrigan, a young Irish priest who had come to the colony earlier in the year, arrived at the quarantine station.

The *Canadien* reported that the cows on the island were suffering from a fatal disease.

According to the *Quebec Mercury*, 2200 patients (903 men, 746 women and 551 children) were in hospital on Grosse Île. The newspaper said that this was probably the highest number yet. In addition, there were 250 sick people on board ship or in tents, waiting to be hospitalized.

Thirty-one burials were recorded in the register of the Catholic chapel and seven in that of the Protestant chapel.

SHIPS LEAVING GROSSE ÎLE FOR QUÉBEC CITY

Name of ship	Quarantine time (in days)	Deaths in Grosse Île hospitals	Deaths on quarantined ships
Ellen Simpson	5	2	0
Free Trader	7	85	13
Minerva	7	13	5

SATURDAY, AUGUST 14, 1847

The deaths of emigrants from the *Brougham* were recorded in the burial register of the Protestant chapel. This vessel is not mentioned in either the list of ships that were inspected at Grosse Île or the list of those that arrived in Québec City.

Dr. Douglas was informed that a complaint had been lodged on August 12 by James Stansfield, a medical officer in Montréal, concerning 35 sick emigrants who had arrived in the city recently and who had been ill before leaving Grosse Île. Douglas was ordered to see that no emigrants left the island in poor health. (See Dr. Douglas' reply of August 16.)

Letters were sent by the Executive Council to leading clergymen of various denominations in Québec City, informing them that the government was prepared to reimburse expenses arising from the reception and care of orphans from the quarantine station.

According to the *Quebec Mercury*, the situation was deteriorating at Grosse Île. More and more so-called healthy people were dying. Over the past four days, up to August 13, there had been 67 deaths in the sector for healthy emigrants. These people were all sick to some extent. In the space of one day, Thursday, August 12, Roman Catholic priests had administered the last rites to no less than 150 of these poor creatures living in the tents. The day after that, 31 people had passed away before 10 o'clock in the morning. The newspaper found the situation truly appalling.

The *Quebec Mercury* reported that Father P. Roy was still sick and that Father Hudon, vicar general, who had contracted typhus at the quarantine station, was dead.

The *Quebec Mercury* joined other newspapers in wondering what lay in store for the emigrants detained at Grosse Île, now that summer was coming to an end. It seemed certain that at least 1000 people, and perhaps twice that number, would require care at the station. Québec City would no doubt be the place they would be transported to. If the government took no steps, scenes of horror would surely ensue.

Catholic baptism of Anne Daly, born August 12 to James Daly and Alice Daly. Father M. Kerrigan drew up the baptismal certificate.

Twenty-eight burials were recorded in the register of the Catholic chapel and three in that of the Protestant chapel.

According to a list published in the *Quebec Morning Chronicle*, 322 people had died at Grosse Île during the week of August 8 to 14.

SHIPS LEAVING GROSSE ÎLE FOR QUÉBEC CITY

Name of ship	Quarantine time (in days)	Deaths in Grosse Île hospitals	Deaths on quarantined ships
Corea	5	8	0

SHIPS ARRIVING IN QUÉBEC CITY WITHOUT A STOP-OVER AT GROSSE ÎLE

Name of ship	Port of departure	Passengers Steerage	Cabin
Empress	Sunderland (England)	3	0

NUMBER OF PEOPLE IN HOSPITAL ON GROSSE ÎLE DURING THE WEEK OF AUGUST 8 TO 14

Emigrants	Patients hospitalized as at last report	Patients admitted (+)	Patients discharged (-)	Deaths (-)	New total
Men	843	286	152	108	869
Women	714	249	114	74	775
Children	559	159	159	52	507
TOTAL	2116	694	425	234*	2151**

* Eighty-eight supposedly healthy people died in addition to these 234 sickpeople, bringing the total number of deaths at Grosse Île during the week to 322. This does not include the deaths that occurred on quarantined ships. Two nurses from Québec City, namely, Ellen Stanley and Catherine McConaty, as well as sergeant Hobbs' wife, who was also a nurse, were among the 88 supposedly healthy people who died.

** Of this number, 2089 (861 men, 751 women and 477 children) had typhus and 62 (8 men, 24 women and 30 children) had smallpox.

SUNDAY, AUGUST 15, 1847

Dr. Fortin came back sick to Québec City aboard the steamer *Rowland Hill*. The boat also carried 152 convalescents, comprising 43 men, 32 women, 53 children and 24 orphans.

Death of Bartholemew Hare, a sailor on the *Saguenay*, at age 24, and of George Crowell, a sailor on the *Sir Henry Pottinger* and son of the ship's captain, at about age 18.

Twenty-four burials were recorded in the register of the Catholic chapel and seven in that of the Protestant chapel.

SHIPS LEAVING GROSSE ÎLE FOR QUÉBEC CITY

Name of ship	Quarantine time (in days)	Deaths in Grosse Île hospitals	Deaths on quarantined ships
Britannia	6	3	0
Brothers	6	11	0
Lillias	6	6	0

MONDAY, AUGUST 16, 1847

Given the high risk of fire in the tents and in the quarantine station's numerous wooden buildings, and considering that, with so many people unable to move around on their own, an accidental fire would claim many lives, Dr. Douglas requested permission to obtain a small fire engine with a hose. (See reply of August 25.)

Medical superintendent Douglas responded to the complaint made by James Stansfield, the medical officer in Montréal, concerning sick people who had apparently embarked on the steamer taking emigrants to that city:

The supposedly sick people who had embarked on the steamer *Queen* at Grosse Île had been examined regularly by Dr. Beardon and had been given a clean bill of health. In support of this diagnosis, Dr. Douglas asserted that these people had walked from the east end of the island to the wharf, a distance of 1.25 mile. He was surprised that Dr. Stansfield, who was well aware of the particular situation of emigrants in 1847, would presume to judge what state of health these people were in 24 hours before setting eyes on them. The fact was, he said, that every day, and even every hour, there were cases of apparently healthy emigrants who fell gravely ill within the space of a few hours and died in even less time.

The medical superintendent declared that the tents currently housed 1 840 healthy passengers from vessels on which disease had broken out. He did not think that a military medical officer would classify even 50 of these people as being in good health, although none of them suffered from any specific illness, apart from a certain lingering fatigue from being cooped up and breathing foul air during the crossing. Before these passengers disembarked at Grosse Île, they had been examined, and those showing any signs of illness had been sent to hospital. The rest, who appeared healthy, had been taken ashore and put in tents, but within four days, 180 of them had fallen ill and were admitted to hospital, while another 67 had died before they could be removed from their canvas shelters. There had been cases of emigrants going out of their tents, lying down in the grass, and dying there. One man had been found dead, sitting on a pile of shingles.

Dr. Douglas had foreseen that passengers would become more vulnerable when they left their ships for dry land and began to eat unaccustomed food; he had already warned that such emigrants would be subject to increased sickness and mortality. Similarly, a 24-hour trip on a steamer could trigger the symptoms of a disease that had remained latent in people who had withstood being transferred from their ship to a tent, but whose health had been undermined by the "miasmas," or unwholesome air, inhaled during the long ocean voyage and the months of undernourishment previously endured in Ireland.

Dr. Beardon, who had been responsible for examining passengers before they left the island, was fairly advanced in years and had perhaps not been as attentive as he should have been. He had offered his resignation of his own accord the previous Saturday. He had been replaced by Dr. Fenwick, who, Dr. Douglas hoped, would be more reliable. If, however, the emigration commissioners knew of any doctor who could predict the future well enough to know which emigrants could leave the island without falling ill before they reached Montréal, Douglas would be only too pleased to engage his services. What he knew of Dr. Stansfield did not convince him that the gentleman would be better than any other in the medical profession at making such a prediction.

The *Canadien*, like several other newspapers, wondered about what would happen at Grosse Île when winter set in. Instead of improving, the state of affairs at the quarantine station was actually growing worse, despite the stronger measures taken by the government. With colder weather on the way, people had begun to worry about what the government intended to do. Would the sick be left at the quarantine station? Would the government wait until Grosse Île was practically cut off from the rest of the world by ice before discussing what should be done?

A number of rumours were circulating. Some people said that the sick would be transported to Montréal, while others held that they would be left where they were. Still others said that they would be housed in public buildings in Québec City. The members of the medical profession were most anxious to know what to expect. The *Canadien* added that it was concerned about the following emigration season, since Grosse Île might very well be uninhabitable next summer, given the large number of dead buried on the island.

According to the *Canadien*, Father C. Tardif and Father F.-S. Bardy were ill at Hôtel-Dieu Hospital and Father A. Campeau was convalescing.

Thirteen burials were recorded in the register of the Catholic chapel and nine in that of the Protestant chapel.

SHIPS ARRIVING AT GROSSE ÎLE

Name of ship	Captain	Port of departure	Crossing time (in days)	Passengers Steerage	Cabin	No. of sick on arrival	No. of deaths during crossing
Ayrshire	N. G. Neil	Newry (Ireland)	43	431	3	14	3

TUESDAY, AUGUST 17, 1847

Dr. Douglas requested more medical assistance, given that an ever-growing number of emigrants were falling ill in the tent sector, where healthy passengers were sent. He wished to employ Mr. Aylwin, a young man who had recently finished medical school and who had already assisted Dr. Jacques at Grosse Île. His salary would be 25s. per day. (See reply of August 23.)

Dr. Douglas sought higher wages for the boatmen. He wanted their salary to be increased by 2s. 6d. per day, retroactive to July 1. According to him, they were the only employees who had not received a raise — since he had forgotten to include them when requesting a pay increase for the policemen — and they deserved one more than anybody. Douglas praised the unflagging efforts of the boatmen, who could always be depended on even though they were confronted with distressful scenes and often solicited by building contractors on the island who offered them two or three times the amount they were making. (See reply of August 23.)

The medical superintendent informed the Executive Council of an altercation that had occurred in public at Grosse Île between Dr. Beardon and Mr. Robert Symes, the deputy emigration agent at the quarantine station. Dr. Beardon had resigned from his duties and left the island as a result. Finding both parties at fault, the Executive Council committee demanded that Mr. Symes be dismissed. (See August 26.)

Father François Morin, parish priest of Saint-Joseph-de-Beauce, and Father Pierre-Grégoire Tremblay, a professor at Sainte-Anne-de-la-Pocatière College, arrived at Grosse Île.

According to the *Quebec Gazette*, the steamer *St. George* had brought 171 convalescent emigrants to Québec City and had put them ashore at the India Wharf. The group comprised 66 men, 57 women and 48 children, many of whom were orphans. A number of emigrants living in the sheds at the India Wharf had left the place, fearing infection. Some of them had sought refuge under the awnings covering the deck of the *St. George*, while others had spent the night outside in the rain.

The *Journal de Québec* raised questions about the way food was distributed at Grosse Île . According to a reliable source, who had communicated with the newspaper on August 16, the growing number of deaths among healthy emigrants at Grosse Île could be attributed to the fact that many of them were not getting enough to eat.

Food was distributed to these unfortunate people, numbering some 2000, by Mr. Robert Symes. This man worked very systematically: for example, before giving a bit of meat and a piece of bread to a woman, even if she were dying of hunger, he would ask her to give her name, her place of birth, the number of children she had, the name of the port at which she had embarked for North America and the length of the crossing. As a result, he was unable to feed more than 100 people a day, and the 1900 others were literally left to starve.

The *Journal de Québec* also reported that a large quantity of meat had been lost in hot weather because it had been cut up and divided into portions too far in advance. The newspaper asked whether a man like Mr. Symes should be entrusted with the fate of the poor souls at the quarantine station, who had left their desolate homeland only to perish on a foreign and inhospitable shore.

Thirty-four burials were recorded in the register of the Catholic chapel and two in that of the Protestant chapel.

WEDNESDAY,
AUGUST 18, 1847

The *Canadien* reported that the Governor General was having hospitals built on an island near Montréal and that the people at Grosse Île were to be transported there. The newspaper suggested that the coming winter would be a good time to erect additional buildings on Grosse Île, or somewhere near the quarantine station, so that the following year there would be sufficient accommodations to prevent people from being overcrowded. If disease had run rampant in 1847, it was because people had been confined to such cramped quarters.

Fifty burials were recorded in the register of the Catholic chapel and nine in that of the Protestant chapel.

THURSDAY,
AUGUST 19, 1847

The *Quebec Mercury* reported that Dr. Wallace was convalescing and that Dr. Beardon had returned to his home in Stanstead.

Death of Abraham Banks, a sailor aboard the *Sir Henry Pottinger*, at age 22.

Sixty-two burials were recorded in the register of the Catholic chapel and three in that of the Protestant chapel.

SHIPS LEAVING GROSSE ÎLE FOR QUÉBEC CITY

Name of ship	Quarantine time (in days)	Deaths in Grosse Île hospitals	Deaths on quarantined ships
Ayrshire	3	8	0

FRIDAY,
AUGUST 20, 1847

The Executive Council committee authorized a request made by Finch and Doran, retail butchers, on August 5, for permission to sell food supplies to the vessels anchored at Grosse Île. However, this authorization was subject to conditions set by Dr. Douglas and the customs officer on duty at Grosse Île. Douglas had no objections to the plan from the standpoint of public health, but permission should be granted only if Mr. Dinning, the present contractor on the island, was unable to supply the ships with what they needed at the same price as that proposed by Finch and Doran. The medical superintendent mentioned, as well, that Dinning kept live cattle, employed workers and had even gone to the expense of building a slaughterhouse on the island.

Dr. Douglas argued that if Finch and Doran came to sell their products when there were a great many ships at Grosse Île, but were not obliged to do so when there were few, the vessels might become dependent on unreliable supplies from the city, a situation that should be avoided at all costs. According to Douglas, the best way to do justice to all parties — the ships, the present contractor Dinning and the petitioners Finch and Doran — was to allow the petitioners to supply the vessels as long as they agreed that the meat they sold would come from cattle they kept on the island and had slaughtered when needed. The food would have to be sold to the ships from a boat, in the presence of the customs officer.

The *Quebec Mercury* reported that 2181 people (892 men, 775 women and 514 children) were in hospital on Grosse Île.

Eight burials were recorded in the register of the Protestant chapel.

SHIPS LEAVING GROSSE ÎLE FOR QUÉBEC CITY

Name of ship	Quarantine time (in days)	Deaths in Grosse Île hospitals	Deaths on quarantined ships
Ganges	8	44	9
Larch	11	62	24

SATURDAY,
AUGUST 21, 1847

The civil secretary wrote on behalf of the Governor General to inform the Archbishop of Québec that the Catholic clergymen on Grosse Île would not be granted permission to obtain a horse and cart to go about the island, as had been requested on August 10.

According to the *Quebec Mercury*, 21 deaths had been recorded in the hospitals on August 19. Now that cooler weather had arrived, there were fewer cases of disease in the tent sector. Since the beginning of the 1847 season, a total of 2126 people had died in the hospitals and the tents.

The *Quebec Morning Chronicle* reported that emigrants had died on board the *Yeoman* during the week of August 27. This vessel is not mentioned in either the list of ships that were inspected at Grosse Île or the list of those that arrived in Québec City.

Fifty burials were recorded in the register of the Catholic chapel and one in that of the Protestant chapel.

According to a list published in the *Quebec Morning Chronicle*, 288 people had died at Grosse Île during the week of August 15 to 21.

SHIPS LEAVING GROSSE ÎLE FOR QUÉBEC CITY

Name of ship	Quarantine time (in days)	Deaths in Grosse Île hospitals	Deaths on quarantined ships
Saguenay	16	47	16

NUMBER OF PEOPLE IN HOSPITAL ON GROSSE ÎLE DURING THE WEEK OF AUGUST 15 TO 21

Emigrants	Patients hospitalized as at last report	Patients admitted (+)	Patients discharged (-)	Deaths (-)	New total
Men	869	183	102	99	851
Women	775	69	80	69	695·
Children	507	136	85	56	502
TOTAL	2151	388	267	224*	2048

* Sixty-four supposedly healthy people died in addition to these 224 sickpeople, bringing the total number of deaths at Grosse Île during the week to 288. This does not include the deaths that occurred on quarantined ships.

SUNDAY, AUGUST 22, 1847

Anglican baptism of Mary Jane McBrien, born August 16 to Thomas McBrien, a farmer, and Catherine Carbray. Although Thomas McBrien now lived on Grosse Île, he was born in County Fermanagh, Ireland. The Reverend Richard Anderson drew up the baptismal certificate.

Fifty-one burials were recorded in the register of the Catholic chapel and eight in that of the Protestant chapel.

SHIPS ARRIVING AT GROSSE ÎLE

Name of ship	Captain	Port of departure	Crossing time (in days)	Passengers Steerage	Cabin	No. of sick on arrival	No. of deaths during crossing
Emma	E. Head	Limerick (Ireland)	49	118	0	3	2

MONDAY,
AUGUST 23, 1847

The Executive Council committee approved the request made by Dr. Douglas on August 17, concerning a new medical assistant and a pay increase for the boatmen. (Ratified by the Governor General on August 26.)

The *Canadien* told its readers that nearly 15 000 more emigrants were expected in 1847; the newspaper wondered what would happen to those who arrived only at the end of the navigation season. The authorities, who were taking no steps to halt this emigration, should be asked if they were prepared to feed and care for so many sick, destitute people.

Seven burials were recorded in the register of the Protestant chapel.

SHIPS ARRIVING AT GROSSE ÎLE

Name of ship	Captain	Port of departure	Crossing time (in days)	Passengers Steerage	Cabin	No. of sick on arrival	No. of deaths during crossing
Washington	J. Wilkie	Liverpool (England)	45	308	0	22	22

SHIPS LEAVING GROSSE ÎLE FOR QUÉBEC CITY

Name of ship	Quarantine time (in days)	Deaths in Grosse Île hospitals	Deaths on quarantined ships
Naparina	11	17	0

SHIPS ARRIVING IN QUÉBEC CITY WITHOUT A STOP-OVER AT GROSSE ÎLE

Name of ship	Port of departure	Passengers Steerage	Cabin
Chieftain	Liverpool (England)	0	6

TUESDAY,
AUGUST 24, 1847

The *Indépendance*, commanded by Captain A. Blais, brought 23 steerage passengers to Grosse Île from Miramichi, New Brunswick, where they had been rescued from the *Loosthank*, a vessel in distress. Since no deaths or cases of illness were reported among its passengers and crew, the ship left the quarantine station that same day.

Father Louis-Stanislas Malo, parish priest of Trois-Pistoles, Father Antoine Proulx, pastor of Rivière-du-Loup, and Father James Francis McDonnell, curate at Saint-Gilles, arrived at Grosse Île. Father McDonnell had been on the island in the spring and had come down with typhus after leaving; this time, he would stay on longer than his fellow clergymen.

According to the *Quebec Mercury*, the situation at Grosse Île had not been improved by the recent arrival of four vessels from Liverpool and Limerick, with the customary host of sick passengers.

The *Quebec Mercury* reported that Dr. Vivian had come back from Grosse Île seriously ill with typhus. Dr. Wallace had suffered a relapse and Dr. Damours was not feeling very well. Dr. McGrath had returned to the city, but he had not caught typhus. Dr. Dickinson had gone back to work at the quarantine station.

According to the *Canadien*, when the steamer left Grosse Île for Québec City on August 24, there were eight ships anchored off the island and three others approaching the quarantine station.

Death of William Sutherland, a sailor aboard the *Blenheim,* at age 17.

Forty burials were recorded in the register of the Catholic chapel and four in that of the Protestant chapel.

SHIPS ARRIVING AT GROSSE ÎLE

Name of ship	Captain	Port of departure	Crossing time (in days)	Passengers Steerage	Cabin	No. of sick on arrival	No. of deaths during crossing
Bridgetown	J. Wilson	Liverpool (England)	52	471	9	128	74
Champion	J. Cochrane	Liverpool (England)	42	422	0	60	29
Colonist	J. Sinott	New Ross (Ireland)	43	453	0	30	12
*Maria Somes**	H. Taylor	Cork (Ireland)	42	329	0	30	17
TOTAL				1675	9	248	

* This ship was transporting retired military personnel and their families.

SHIPS LEAVING GROSSE ÎLE FOR QUÉBEC CITY

Name of ship	Quarantine time (in days)	Deaths in Grosse Île hospitals	Deaths on quarantined ships
Emma	2	0	0

WEDNESDAY, AUGUST 25, 1847

The Executive Council committee approved the request made by Dr. Douglas for a small fire engine at Grosse Île. It specified, however, that if one could not be provided by the military stores in Québec City, emigration agent Buchanan would have to take the necessary steps to obtain one. (Ratified by the Governor General on August 26.)

Thirty-two burials were recorded in the register of the Catholic chapel and four in that of the Protestant chapel.

SHIPS ARRIVING AT GROSSE ÎLE

Name of ship	Captain	Port of departure	Crossing time (in days)	Passengers Steerage	Cabin	No. of sick on arrival	No. of deaths during crossing
Mecca	C. Hale	Dublin (Ireland)	48	74	0	2	1

THURSDAY, AUGUST 26, 1847

Pierre Laurencel reported on the progress of construction work on Grosse Île. At the time, 215 people of all trades were engaged in these activities. Six emigrant sheds were now ready on the farm. A few kitchens were also completed and could be used by the emigrants. At the west end of the island, near Green Bay (Cholera Bay), Jean Trudel and Zacharie Chabot were working on the last hospital, which would be 204 feet long. Workers were laying the deck of the wharf and putting up vertical planking along it. One hundred and eighty toises of stone were still needed to finish the wharf.

The Board of Works decided to delay paying the sum of £ 600 to the contractor W. Patton, who was in charge of constructing the Grosse Île wharf, because the superintendent's report on the progress of the work had not been favourable.

The Governor General ordered emigration agent Buchanan to dismiss Robert Symes, his deputy at Grosse Île, on account of his conduct in an altercation with Dr. Beardon. Buchanan was authorized to hire someone else to replace Mr. Symes. (See August 17.)

Anglican baptism of Hugh McDonald, born July 28 to Duncan McDonald and Christina McMullen. The Reverend Andrew Trew

Whitten drew up the baptismal certificate.

Thirty-one burials were recorded in the register of the Catholic chapel and one in that of the Protestant chapel.

SHIPS ARRIVING AT GROSSE ÎLE

Name of ship	Captain	Port of departure	Crossing time (in days)	Passengers Steerage	Passengers Cabin	No. of sick on arrival	No. of deaths during crossing
Industry	E. Vincent	Sligo (Ireland)	51	177	1	3	7
Juliet	T. Watson	London (England)	53	268	3	1	16
Minerva	A. Parker	Waterford (Ireland)	45	126	0	0	0
Royalist	J. Campbell	Limerick (Ireland)	45	167	1	2	1
TOTAL				738	5	6	

SHIPS LEAVING GROSSE ÎLE FOR QUÉBEC CITY

Name of ship	Quarantine time (in days)	Deaths in Grosse Île hospitals	Deaths on quarantined ships
Mecca	1	0	0
Washington	3	22	3

FRIDAY, AUGUST 27, 1847

The civil secretary mentioned that the quarantine station might be kept open longer than usual because some of the patients would be difficult to transport elsewhere.

Father Malo, Father Proulx and Father McDonnell wrote to Archbishop Signay that there were now about 3000 sick people at Grosse Île and that, in the "healthy camp", which was supposed to be for convalescents only, there were at least as many sick people in danger of dying as in the hospitals. To make it easier for the priests to visit this area regularly, Dr. Douglas had agreed to provide them with a cart each day. It was hoped that hospital beds would soon be found for the sick people in the tents. Many of these canvas shelters, which were hotbeds of infection, had already been removed and only about forty remained.

Mr. C.-E. Casgrain, the Public Works commissioner, wrote to the Archbishop of Québec to tell him that there were over 2000 patients at Grosse Île at the time. Unfortunately, 350 to 400 of them were still in tents. Casgrain said that a new 204-foot hospital would be ready in a few days, and that he had given instructions for another one to be built as quickly as possible if Dr. Douglas deemed it necessary.

According to the *Quebec Mercury* and the *Quebec Gazette*, 2054 people were in hospital at Grosse Île. Of this number, 859 were men, 702 were women and 493 were children. Eighty-eight patients (38 men, 27 women and 19 children) were discharged from hospital on August 27.

Twenty-eight burials were recorded in the register of the Catholic chapel and five in that of the Protestant chapel.

A. C. Buchanan presented a compilation of emigration statistics since the beginning of the navigation season and compared them with those for 1846:

COMPARISON OF EMIGRATION STATISTICS FOR THE PORT OF QUÉBEC IN 1846 AND 1847 (MAY 9 TO AUGUST 27)

Country of origin	1847	1846
England	26 568	7 334
Ireland	45 961	19 327
Scotland	2 699	1 253
Germany	6 212	887
TOTAL	81 440	28 801

According to A. C. Buchanan, the number of passengers had increased by 52 639 in comparison with the number reported for the same period in 1846. Since the beginning of the 1847 season, 4 647 people had died on ships and 2 503 in hospital at the quarantine station, resulting in a grand total of 7 150 deaths.

SHIPS ARRIVING AT GROSSE ÎLE

Name of ship	Captain	Port of departure	Crossing time (in days)	Passengers Steerage	Cabin	No. of sick on arrival	No. of deaths during crossing
Sir Henry Pottinger	A. Loss	Belfast (Ireland)	49	253	0	12	5

SATURDAY, AUGUST 28, 1847

The *Quebec Mercury* reported that Dr. Stratton of the Royal Navy was in Québec City on an official mission to try out two disinfecting fluids.

The *Quebec Mercury* also said that Dr. Newton, a zealous and active physician, was sick with typhus. Dr. Wallace and Dr. Vivian were better. The former would return to his duties within a day or two. The newspaper also reported that the *Maria Somes* had arrived from Cork, with pensioners and their families aboard in very ill health. There were 30 cases of typhus on the vessel and 17 people had already died.

The *Quebec Mercury* informed its readers that tents were no longer needed at Grosse Île. The new sheds at the east end of the island were almost completely finished and healthy people could move into them.

There were now enough hospitals to accommodate all the sick people, including those who had been in the regular tents. The marquees, however, were still being used.

Thirty-one burials were recorded in the register of the Catholic chapel and four in that of the Protestant chapel.

According to a list published in the *Quebec Morning Chronicle,* 256 people had died at Grosse Île during the week of August 22 to 28.

SHIPS LEAVING GROSSE ÎLE FOR QUÉBEC CITY

Name of ship	Quarantine time (in days)	Deaths in Grosse Île hospitals	Deaths on quarantined ships
Champion	4	65	0
Colonist	4	13	0
Juliet	2	0	0
Minerva*	2	0	0
Royalist	2	0	0

* It is hard to understand why this ship was placed in quarantine, since no deaths or cases of illness were reported among its passengers or crew.

NUMBER OF PEOPLE IN HOSPITAL ON GROSSE ÎLE DURING THE WEEK OF AUGUST 22 TO 28

Emigrants	Patients hospitalized as at last report	Patients admitted (+)	Patients discharged (-)	Deaths (-)	New total
TOTAL	2 048	466	284	236*	1 994

* In addition, 20 healthy passengers died in the tents, bringing the total number of deaths during the week to 256.

SUNDAY, AUGUST 29, 1847

Twenty-four burials were recorded in the register of the Catholic chapel and seven in that of the Protestant chapel.

SHIPS ARRIVING AT GROSSE ÎLE

Name of ship	Captain	Port of departure	Crossing time (in days)	Passengers Steerage	Cabin	No. of sick on arrival	No. of deaths during crossing
Ellen	G. Pittingall	Plymouth (England)	42	159	5	0	0
Robert Newton	W. Mosely	Limerick (Ireland)	42	204	2	3	1
TOTAL				363	7	3	

Name of ship	Quarantine time (in days)	Deaths in Grosse Île hospitals	Deaths on quarantined ships
Bridgetown	5	63	24
Ellen	A few hours	0	0
Industry	3	2	0
Robert Newton	A few hours	0	0
Sir Henry Pottinger	2	30	0

MONDAY, AUGUST 30, 1847

The *Canadien* reported that Father Narcisse Bélanger, a curate from Sainte-Croix who had recently come back from Grosse Île, was seriously ill at Hôtel-Dieu Hospital.

According to the *Quebec Gazette*, Dr. Newton had returned sick to Québec City.

The deaths of emigrants who had disembarked from the *Daniel Rankin* were recorded in the register of the Protestant chapel. This vessel is not mentioned in either the list of ships that were inspected at Grosse Île or the list of those that arrived in Québec City.

Death of John Edwards, a second mate aboard the *Ganges*, at age 26.

Thirty-one burials were recorded in the register of the Catholic chapel and eight in that of the Protestant chapel.

SHIPS ARRIVING AT GROSSE ÎLE

Name of ship	Captain	Port of departure	Crossing time (in days)	Passengers Steerage	Cabin	No. of sick on arrival	No. of deaths during crossing
Martha	T. L. Lamni	Bremen (Germany)	53	224	5	0	0

SHIPS LEAVING GROSSE ÎLE FOR QUÉBEC CITY

Name of ship	Quarantine time (in days)	Deaths in Grosse Île hospitals	Deaths on quarantined ships
Martha	A few hours	0	0

TUESDAY, AUGUST 31, 1847

Dr. Douglas asked the civil secretary to authorize an increase in the salaries of the nurses and other workers in the sheds.

Father Jean-Baptiste-Antoine Ferland, prefect of studies at the Seminary of Nicolet and Father Bernard McGauran, a curate from

Québec City, arrived at Grosse Île. For both clergymen, it was the second time they had come to care for the sick at the quarantine station.

Reporting on the progress of construction work on Grosse Île, Pierre Laurencel wrote that at the west end of the island, near Green Bay (Cholera Bay), two kitchens had been built and a 204-foot hospital completed by the contractor Mr. Trudel. At the east end, Mr. Dorion had erected another shed on the farm; the policemen's lodgings, the police superintendent's house and three kitchens had also been erected. The wash house, which was to hold four large boilers, was nearing completion and a well was being dug by four men. The decking on the wharf was finished and work continued on the upright planking. Quarry stone was supposed to be delivered that week to complete the wharf's foundations.

Because of the large number of patients still in tents, another hospital had been ordered. It was to measure 240 feet in length and be built on the rocks near the water's edge, in the same sector as the cemetery. This location was best suited to the station's needs, but it would entail extra construction costs because the ground was uneven and rocky. Mr. Trudel had agreed at once to build the hospital. Laurencel concluded his report by suggesting that a lantern be hung from a mast at the end of the wharf, in case lighting was needed on dark autumn nights.

Robert Symes, the former deputy emigration agent who had been dismissed because of a fight he had with Dr. Beardon at the quarantine station, asked to be reinstated. In his favour, he provided references by the chief emigration agent, Mr. Buchanan; the medical superintendent of Grosse Île, Dr. Douglas; several members of the clergy; and a number of physicians working at the station. He claimed to have been provoked by Dr. Beardon and expressed sincere regrets for what had happened. (See reply of September 3.)

According to the *Quebec Gazette*, Dr. Eastaff and Dr. Damours had returned to Québec City.

Fifteen burials were recorded in the register of the Catholic chapel and six in that of the Protestant chapel.

Dr. Douglas reported that an average of 2021 patients were in hospital per day between August 1 and 31 inclusively.

SHIPS ARRIVING AT GROSSE ÎLE

Name of ship	Captain	Port of departure	Crossing time (in days)	Passengers		No. of sick on arrival	No. of deaths during crossing
				Steerage	Cabin		
Haubet	Swenfoyn	Hamburg (Germany)	60	199	0	7	13
Horatio	A. Trason	Limerick (Ireland)	45	277	0	7	10
TOTAL				476	0	14	

1847

SEPTEMBER

S	M	T	W	T	F	S
			1	2	3	4
5	6	7	8	9	10	11
12	13	14	15	16	17	18
19	20	21	22	23	24	25
26	27	28	29	30		

WEDNESDAY, SEPTEMBER 1, 1847

According to the *Quebec Mercury* and the *Quebec Gazette*, 1651 people (646 men, 593 women and 412 children) were in hospital on Grosse Île.

Twenty-two burials were recorded in the register of the Catholic chapel and three in that of the Protestant chapel.

SHIPS ARRIVING AT GROSSE ÎLE

Name of ship	Captain	Port of departure	Crossing time (in days)	Passengers Steerage	Cabin	No. of sick on arrival	No. of deaths during crossing
*Caledonia**	A. Greenhorn	Glasgow (Scotland)	34	38	7	0	0
Canada	McArthur	Glasgow (Scotland)	49	130	6	0	9
Julius Caesar	M. Flemming	Liverpool (England)	51	471	0	60	35
Kennedy	J. McArthur	Glasgow (Scotland)	49	129	6	20	12
TOTAL				768	19	80	

* It was probably this ship's second voyage of the season.

SHIPS LEAVING GROSSE ÎLE FOR QUÉBEC CITY

Name of ship	Quarantine time (in days)	Deaths in Grosse Île hospitals	Deaths on quarantined ships
Caledonia	A few hours	1	0
Haubet	1	0	0

THURSDAY, SEPTEMBER 2, 1847

Father Félix-Séverin Bardy, a curate at Cacouna, died at Hôtel-Dieu Hospital in Québec City, after having contracted typhus at Grosse Île. The *Quebec Mercury* also reported that Father F. Morin, brother of the Honorable Augustin-Norbert Morin, of Saint-Isidore, had returned to the city in ill health and that Father N. Bélanger was very sick.

The Reverend Charles Morris, a missionary from Portneuf, arrived at Grosse Île.

According to the *Quebec Mercury* and the *Quebec Gazette*, Drs. Stewart, Eastaff, Newton and Damours had all come down with typhus.

Father B. McGauran wrote to the Archbishop to say that the situation at Grosse Île was much improved since his previous visit. He brought it to his superior's attention that the missionaries were still in need of a horse. Dr. Douglas lent them his buggy to go to the sector for healthy emigrants once a day, but if they were called during the night, or if the medical superintendent failed to keep his promise, the priests were obliged to walk for half a league, which was unpleasant for those who had just spent two or three hours going about the hospitals on foot.

Sixteen burials were recorded in the register of the Catholic chapel and five in that of the Protestant chapel.

SHIPS ARRIVING AT GROSSE ÎLE

Name of ship	Captain	Port of departure	Crossing time (in days)	Passengers Steerage	Cabin	No. of sick on arrival	No. of deaths during crossing
*Cambria**	W. Birnie	Glasgow (Scotland)	43	59	8	0	1

* It was probably this ship's second voyage of the season.

SHIPS LEAVING GROSSE ÎLE FOR QUÉBEC CITY

Name of ship	Quarantine time (in days)	Deaths in Grosse Île hospitals	Deaths on quarantined ships
Cambria	A few hours	0	0
Horatio	2	1	0

FRIDAY, SEPTEMBER 3, 1847

The Executive Council committee recommended that Mr. Robert Symes be reinstated as deputy emigration agent at Grosse Île, given the high esteem in which he was held by the authorities on the island and considering his zeal and efficiency. (See August 31.)

Father J.-B.-A. Ferland wrote that few emigrants were arriving at Grosse Île, since most of the ships no longer stopped there. The tents had all been taken down, thanks to Mr. Casgrain, and the foul-smelling ditch in the cemetery was being cleaned, making the air more pleasant to breathe.

In a letter to Monsignor Turgeon, Father J. F. McDonnell declared the situation at Grosse Île greatly improved. At the time, no more that 20 to 25 people were dying per day. Only two vessels were anchored off the island and they had few cases of illness aboard.

The *Canadien* reported that Mr. Casgrain had visited Grosse Île to inspect the buildings and wharf which were under construction.

The *Quebec Gazette* published the report of the special committee appointed by the Legislative Assembly to inquire into the management of the Grosse Île quarantine station. The committee, formed on June 21, claimed that the shortness of the last session of Parliament had made it impossible to thoroughly investigate the major questions which it had been mandated to examine. Consequently, instead of submitting recommendations to the Assembly, it was presenting the testimonies recorded during the inquiry between July 13 and 23 of that year. The following people had testified at the inquiry: Father W. Moylan, Father B. O'Reilly, Father J.-B.-A. Ferland, Bishop Mountain of the Anglican Church, Dr. Morrin, Captain Boxer, chief emigration agent Buchanan, and medical superintendent Dr. George Douglas.

Twenty-four burials were recorded in the register of the Catholic chapel and two in that of the Protestant chapel.

SHIPS ARRIVING AT GROSSE ÎLE

Name of ship	Captain	Port of departure	Crossing time (in days)	Passengers Steerage	Cabin	No. of sick on arrival	No. of deaths during crossing
Dundonald	J. James	Milford (Wales)	63	31	1	0	0

SHIPS LEAVING GROSSE ÎLE FOR QUÉBEC CITY

Name of ship	Quarantine time (in days)	Deaths in Grosse Île hospitals	Deaths on quarantined ships
Canada	2	0	0
Dundonald	A few hours	0	0
Kennedy	2	0	0

SHIPS ARRIVING IN QUÉBEC CITY WITHOUT A STOP-OVER AT GROSSE ÎLE

Name of ship	Port of departure	Passengers Steerage	Cabin
Marquis of Normandy	Dublin (Ireland)	0	11

SATURDAY, SEPTEMBER 4, 1847

Death of James English, a sailor aboard the *Coromandel*, at age 16.

Nine burials were recorded in the register of the Protestant chapel.

A total of 1 570 people were in hospital at the quarantine station during the week of August 29 to September 4.

According to a list published in the *Quebec Morning Chronicle*, 191 people died at Grosse Île during that same week.

SHIPS ARRIVING AT GROSSE ÎLE

Name of ship	Captain	Port of departure	Crossing time (in days)	Passengers Steerage	Cabin	No. of sick on arrival	No. of deaths during crossing
Provincialist	D. Williams	Londonderry (Ireland)	47	205	0	0	0

SHIPS LEAVING GROSSE ÎLE FOR QUÉBEC CITY

Name of ship	Quarantine time (in days)	Deaths in Grosse Île hospitals	Deaths on quarantined ships
Julius Caesar	3	20	0
Provincialist	A few hours	0	0

EMIGRANTS ARRIVING IN THE PORT OF QUÉBEC DURING THE WEEK OF AUGUST 29 TO SEPTEMBER 4

Country of origin	Number
England	932
Ireland	3 316
Scotland	189
Germany	412
Canadian ports downstream from Québec City	8
Total	4 857
Previous total (as at August 27)	81 440
GRAND TOTAL	86 297*

* This represents an increase of 56 436 emigrants compared with the total reported by Buchanan up to the same period in 1846, i.e. 29 861.

SUNDAY, SEPTEMBER 5, 1847

The *Miscou*, commanded by Captain B. Coutson, brought 19 steerage passengers to Grosse Île from Miramichi, New Brunswick, where they had been rescued from a ship in distress, the *Loosthank*. Since no deaths or cases of illness were reported among its passengers and crew, the ship left the quarantine station that same day.

The *Quebec Morning Chronicle* reported that emigrants had died on board the *Lady Bagot* during the week of September 5 to 11. This vessel is not mentioned in either the list of ships that were inspected at Grosse Île or the list of those that arrived in Québec City.

SHIPS ARRIVING AT GROSSE ÎLE

Name of ship	Captain	Port of departure	Crossing time (in days)	Passengers Steerage	Cabin	No. of sick on arrival	No. of deaths during crossing
Highland Mary	D. Crosby	Cork (Ireland)	48	100	0	6	4

SHIPS ARRIVING IN QUÉBEC CITY WITHOUT A STOP-OVER AT GROSSE ÎLE

Name of ship	Port of departure	Passengers Steerage	Cabin
Dunbrody	New Ross (Ireland)	12	0

MONDAY, SEPTEMBER 6, 1847

The emigration agent, A. C. Buchanan, told the Governor General that experiments had been carried out at sea using a new chloride of zinc disinfecting fluid on the *Albion* and the *Henrietta Mary*, which had sailed from Cork, Ireland. Since ships from this port were among the most disease-ridden vessels of the 1847 season, Buchanan hoped that Dr. Douglas would pay special attention to the state of health of passengers on these two ships when they put in at Grosse Île.

Five burials were recorded in the register of the Protestant chapel.

TUESDAY, SEPTEMBER 7, 1847

The *Quebec Mercury* reported that patients had been removed from the chapels and that these buildings, which had been cleaned and fumigated, could once again be used for religious services.

Thomas O. Barter, the hospital apothecary at Grosse Île, requested a raise equivalent to that previously granted to the other medical staff at the quarantine station.

One burial was recorded in the register of the Protestant chapel.

SHIPS ARRIVING AT GROSSE ÎLE

Name of ship	Captain	Port of departure	Crossing time (in days)	Passengers Steerage	Cabin	No. of sick on arrival	No. of deaths during crossing
Superior	J. Mason	Londonderry (Ireland)	51	366	0	150	18

NOW IN PORT.
NOTICE TO PASSENGERS.

Those Persons who have taken their Passages by the First Class Coppered Ship

SUPERIOR,
CAPTAIN MASON,
FOR QUEBEC,

Are required to be in Derry on TUESDAY, the 13th of JULY, pay the remainder of their Passage Money, and go on Board, as the Vessel will sail first fair wind after that date. A few more Passengers will be taken, on moderate terms, if immediate application is made to **Mr. DAVID MITCHELL**, *Dungiven*, or the Owners,

J. & J. COOKE.

A June 1847 poster announcing the imminent departure of the *Superior* for Québec City. The *Superior* put in at Grosse Île on September 7. In all, 71 of her passengers died: 18 during the crossing, 8 on board while she lay in quarantine and 45 in hospital on the island. (Public Record Office, Northern Ireland. In Cecil J. Houston and William J. Smyth, *Irish Emigration and Canadian Settlement: Patterns, Links and Letters*, University of Toronto Press, Toronto, 1990, p. 111.)

WEDNESDAY, SEPTEMBER 8, 1847

A. C. Buchanan reported that a boat had arrived in Québec City with 343 military tents which were no longer required for the emigrants at Grosse Île; it had unloaded them onto the Queen's Wharf. The tents were badly damaged, however, and needed to be cleaned and repaired before the Ordnance or Commissariat in Québec City would accept them in their stores.

An army doctor recommended the following method for disinfecting the tents: first, the canvas should be soaked or thoroughly sprayed with a chloride of lime solution; then the tents should be left to soak in warm water with mild soap for 12 hours; lastly, they should be scrubbed, rinsed and allowed to dry completely.

The *Quebec Mercury* told its readers that the temporary hospitals set up in the old sheds at the west end of the island in late May no longer held patients. The 1 327 sick emigrants who had been there had been moved to real hospitals. Since 150 of these people were convalescents, they had been sent to the east end of the island, which now had separate "wards" for men and women.

Death of Frederick Knight, a sailor on the *Zealous*, at age 22, and of James McLean, a sailor on the *Brothers*, at age 24.

Four burials were recorded in the register of the Protestant chapel.

SHIPS ARRIVING AT GROSSE ÎLE

Name of ship	Captain	Port of departure	Crossing time (in days)	Passengers Steerage	Cabin	No. of sick on arrival	No. of deaths during crossing
Albion	R. Allan	Glasgow (Scotland)	31	57	7	0	0
Eliza	J. Jones	Glasgow (Scotland)	54	269	0	39	29
Ottawa	R. Spencer	London (England)	52	39	6	0	0
TOTAL				365	13	39	

SHIPS LEAVING GROSSE ÎLE FOR QUÉBEC CITY

Name of ship	Quarantine time (in days)	Deaths in Grosse Île hospitals	Deaths on quarantined ships
Albion	A few hours	0	0
Highland Mary	3	2	1
Ottawa	A few hours	0	0

THURSDAY, SEPTEMBER 9, 1847

Dr. John Bradley, an emigrant who had arrived on the *Herald*, demanded the sum of £ 30 for the expenses he had incurred while working at Grosse Île as a replacement for Dr. McGrath, when the latter was ill. On his arrival at Grosse Île on June 23, he had offered his services to Dr. Douglas. He had then continued on to Montréal, where he received a letter from Douglas asking him to come to work on the island. He had returned to Grosse Île, but on July 18, the superintendent informed him that his services were no longer required, since Dr. McGrath had recovered. He had waited 16 days to be paid and then incurred certain expenses in order to continue on his way.

FRIDAY,
SEPTEMBER 10, 1847

The *Canadien* published a shocking story, previously appearing in the *Journal de Québec*, about an emigrant woman who had been killed by one of the employees at Grosse Île. Apparently, this sick woman was getting out of a boat and was advancing slowly and cautiously along a narrow plank which had been laid between the shore and the boat. A man who worked in the sheds grew annoyed at the woman's slowness and, grabbing her by the shoulders, shoved her with his hands and feet. The poor woman stumbled and fell, splitting her skull on a jagged rock. She was buried at once with other emigrants, who had died of typhus. The newspaper demanded that the employee in question be prosecuted in court.

According to the *Quebec Mercury*, 483 men, 472 women and 352 children were in hospital on Grosse Île . One hundred and four deaths had been recorded between September 5 and 9.

Death of George Gordon, a sailor aboard the *Saguenay*, at age 32.

Thirteen burials were recorded in the register of the Catholic chapel and eight in that of the Protestant chapel.

SHIPS LEAVING GROSSE ÎLE FOR QUÉBEC CITY

Name of ship	Quarantine time (in days)	Deaths in Grosse Île hospitals	Deaths on quarantined ships
Maria Somes	18	33	0

SATURDAY,
SEPTEMBER 11, 1847

The authorities in charge of military supplies requested that, in future, all military equipment loaned to the quarantine station during the season be properly cleaned and disinfected on Grosse Île before being sent back to Québec City. They deplored the terrible condition in which the military tents had been returned.

According to the *Quebec Mercury*, the arrival of the *Superior*, from Londonderry, and of the *Eliza*, from Glasgow, clearly demonstrated that emigrants from the poverty-stricken classes of Ireland and the British Isles were still being sent to Canada. Typhus and dysentery were rampant on the first vessel, and no more than about twelve of the passengers who had been taken to the sector for healthy people on Grosse Île could actually be considered healthy. In general, the passengers from the *Superior* were among the filthiest, most wretched people who had arrived during the season. The situation on the second ship, the *Eliza*, which was filled with Scottish Highlanders, was just as pitiful.

The *Quebec Mercury* reported that the medical staff on Grosse Île had been cut back. Dr. McGrath, Dr. Sauvé and Dr. Jameson were no longer working at the quarantine station, and Dr. Watson was supposed to leave the following week. The nursing staff had also been reduced.

Death of a sailor by the name of Peter Kant.

One hundred and twenty burials were recorded in the register of the Catholic chapel and two in that of the Protestant chapel.

According to a list published in the *Quebec Morning Chronicle*, 143 people had died at Grosse Île during the week of September 5 to 11.

NUMBER OF PEOPLE IN HOSPITAL ON GROSSE ÎLE
DURING THE WEEK OF SEPTEMBER 5 TO 11

Emigrants	Patients hospitalized as at last report	Patients admitted (+)	Patients discharged (-)	Deaths (-)	New total
Men	590	74	106	57	501
Women	559	61	87	39	494
Children	421	95	82	46	388
TOTAL	1570	230	275	142	1383*

* Except in one case, where the person had smallpox, all of these patients were suffering from typhus.

SUNDAY,
SEPTEMBER 12, 1847

Dr. Douglas requested instructions on what to do with the sick people still left in hospital at Grosse Île at the end of the navigation season. The buildings on the island were not winterized. (See reply of September 22.)

Affidavits made by two Irish emigrants before Robert Symes, justice of the peace and deputy emigration agent, after they arrived at the quarantine station aboard the *Superior*:

Hugh Reilly, a stone cutter from County Fermanagh, had boarded in Londonderry with his wife and five children. He was a former tenant of a property owner named Collins. Bryan Prior, who was married and had four children, had also been a tenant of Collins and used to live in the parish of Drumreilly. Both families had fallen on hard times in Ireland, where they had no food or assistance and had been asked to leave their land by agents of their landlord.

Reilly and his family had been promised that their passage to America would be paid for and that they would be provided with

226

food and clothing. If they refused the offer, they would not receive any further assistance. Prior had been told that his land was not valuable enough for Collins to send him to America with his wife and children. Therefore, he had made the journey alone, and his family had remained behind in Ireland, where they were homeless. Reilly added that the captain of the *Superior*, Mr. Mason, had been very kind to his passengers.

(Robert Symes forwarded these statements to the emigration agent's office in Québec City on September 14; the Governor General read them on September 16.)

Death of Alexis Plante, a baker employed by Martin Ray, at age 19.

Nineteen burials were recorded in the register of the Catholic chapel and five in that of the Protestant chapel.

SHIPS ARRIVING AT GROSSE ÎLE

Name of ship	Captain	Port of departure	Crossing time (in days)	Passengers Steerage	Cabin	No. of sick on arrival	No. of deaths during crossing
Atalanta	J. Moore	Dublin (Ireland)	44	226	0	0	4
*Belleisle***	J. Reid	Glasgow (Scotland)	31	21	7	0	0
General Hewitt	J. Gateby	Bremen (Germany)	52	516	0	0	12
Heromanga	R. Ramsey	Glasgow (Scotland)	35	36	20	0	0
Spermaceti	D. [Doam]	Plymouth (England)	44	201	5	0	0
Wellington	J. Press	Liverpool (England)	46	438	1	0	27
TOTAL				1 438	33	0	

* It was this ship's second voyage of the season. Its captain and port of departure were the same as on the first voyage.

SHIPS LEAVING GROSSE ÎLE FOR QUÉBEC CITY

Name of ship	Quarantine time (in days)	Deaths in Grosse Île hospitals	Deaths on quarantined ships
Atalanta	A few hours	0	1
Belleisle	A few hours	0	0
General Hewitt	A few hours	0	0
Heromanga	A few hours	0	0
Spermaceti	A few hours	0	0

SHIPS ARRIVING IN QUÉBEC CITY WITHOUT A STOP-OVER AT GROSSE ÎLE

Name of ship	Port of departure	Passengers	
		Steerage	Cabin
Great Britain	London (England)	13	0
John Bull	London (England)	23	0
*Mersey**	Torquay (England)	8	0
Tottenham	New Ross (Ireland)	5	0
TOTAL		49	0

* It was this ship's second voyage of the season. It left from the same port as on the first voyage.

MONDAY, SEPTEMBER 13, 1847

The *Drabs,* commanded by Captain S. Simpsons, was inspected at Grosse Île; it had arrived from Amsterdam, Holland, with no emigrants aboard. Since no deaths or cases of illness were reported among its passengers and crew, the *Drabs* left the quarantine station that same day. It is not mentioned in the list of ships that arrived in the port of Québec.

Pierre Laurencel, the Board of Works agent, mentioned that problems had been encountered during excavations to install a water reservoir: the workmen had been obliged to abandon a 16- by 12-foot tank after encountering large boulders at a depth of 25 feet.

The *Canadien* reported that 35 ships had arrived in the port of Québec since Saturday, September 11. Most were carrying a large number of passengers. A little while before, it had been possible to remove all the sick from the tents and transfer them to the sheds that had just been erected on Grosse Île. However, since the arrival of more emigrants had substantially increased the number of patients, it was necessary to use the canvas shelters once again.

The *Quebec Mercury* revealed that 30 employees had been cut from the nursing staff at the quarantine station.

Fifteen burials were recorded in the register of the Catholic chapel and five in that of the Protestant chapel.

SHIPS ARRIVING AT GROSSE ÎLE

Name of ship	Captain	Port of departure	Crossing time (in days)	Passengers		No. of sick on arrival	No. of deaths during crossing
				Steerage	Cabin		
George Ramsay	W. Flavin	New Ross (Ireland)	53	26	0	0	0
Isabella	G. Robson	Killala (Ireland)	57	236	0	15	8
*Jane Black**	T. Gorman	Limerick (Ireland)	33	395	0	3	3
TOTAL				657	0	18	

* It was this ship's second voyage of the season. Its captain and port of departure were the same as on the first voyage.

SHIPS LEAVING GROSSE ÎLE FOR QUÉBEC CITY

Name of ship	Quarantine time (in days)	Deaths in Grosse Île hospitals	Deaths on quarantined ships
George Ramsay	A few hours	0	0

TUESDAY,
SEPTEMBER 14, 1847

Pierre Laurencel reported on the progress of construction work at Grosse Île . Now that Mr. Lapointe had finished the last two buildings, all 12 sheds that had been ordered were at the emigrants' disposal. Laurencel also mentioned that an 18- by 12-foot guardhouse and a 33- by 24-foot wash house, equipped with five boilers, were completed. He had found water at the base of a rocky outcrop on the farm and had ordered the excavation of a well for the use of a kitchen located near Green Bay (Cholera Bay), not far from the 408-foot hospital. The masons' services were no longer required since they had finished four chimney ovens on the farm, two others in the hospitals and one in the middle of the island. Rock-filling operations continued at the wharf.

The Governor General informed Bishop George Mountain of the Anglican Church that religious organizations of all denominations would receive the sum of 20s. (or £ 1) per month for every orphan taken into their care, as well as an additional allowance for the child's clothing. He reiterated that the aim of government policy in this regard was to place emigrant orphans with relatives or friends who claimed them, subject to the approval of the Governor General.

According to the *Quebec Mercury* and the *Quebec Gazette*, a total of 1 336 people were in hospital on Grosse Île.

Anglican baptism of Molly Murphy, born August 21 to Alexander Murphy and Jane McKay, passengers on the *Superior*, from County Antrim, Ireland. The Reverend R. Anderson drew up the baptismal certificate.

Fourteen burials were recorded in the register of the Catholic chapel and three in that of the Protestant chapel.

SHIPS ARRIVING AT GROSSE ÎLE

Name of ship	Captain	Port of departure	Crossing time (in days)	Passengers Steerage	Cabin	No. of sick on arrival	No. of deaths during crossing
Argyle	T. Brodbank	Newport (England)	40	362	2	43	5
Sir Robert Peel	J. Murray	Liverpool (England)	51	480	0	12	31
Virgilia	S. Bane	Liverpool (England)	54	208	0	3	12
TOTAL				1050	2	58	48

WEDNESDAY, SEPTEMBER 15, 1847

Death of Hugh Ferguson, a hospital steward, at age 43.

Death of John Benger, a sailor aboard the *Broom*, at age 42.

Thirteen burials were recorded in the register of the Catholic chapel and six in that of the Protestant chapel.

SHIPS ARRIVING AT GROSSE ÎLE

Name of ship	Captain	Port of departure	Crossing time (in days)	Passengers Steerage	Cabin	No. of sick on arrival	No. of deaths during crossing
Charles	S. Hanlon	Youghall (Ireland)	40	65	0	0	0

THURSDAY, SEPTEMBER 16, 1847

Mr. L. Laidley, the deputy commissary general, suggested that emigrants at Grosse Île be provided with potatoes instead of bread. He stressed that this would save money since one pound of bread cost 3.5d. while the equivalent in potatoes, i.e. 3 pounds, cost only 1.5d. Unless Dr. Douglas had objections, Mr. Laidley requested that the substitution be approved. (See reply of September 22.)

Father B. McGauran informed Archbishop Signay that only nine ships were anchored off Grosse Île on September 16. Three of them were disembarking their passengers, several of whom had smallpox. Relatively speaking, the number of deaths was still approximately the same as during the rest of the season.

The *Quebec Mercury* reported that the following physicians were still on duty at Grosse Île: Drs. Douglas, Jacques, Fenwick, Johnston, Allen, Dickinson, Jameson, Watt and Mr. Aylwin. Dr. Wallace had returned to Québec City.

The *Quebec Mercury* also reported that the emigrants in the sheds had suffered miserably during a recent storm with cold easterly winds. The newspaper said that there were still a large number of patients recovering from dysentery at the east end of the island.

The *Quebec Mercury* reported on the death of Alexis Plante from typhus. Apparently, this young man, who had worked as a baker on Grosse Île for Mr. Martin Ray, was the second Canadian to die at the quarantine station in 1847. The first was a nurse by the name of Mrs. Garneau, who had come down with typhus after returning from Grosse Île to take charge of a number of orphans in Québec City. She had died within the space of two weeks.

Eleven burials were recorded in the register of the Catholic chapel and three in that of the Protestant chapel.

SHIPS ARRIVING AT GROSSE ÎLE

Name of ship	Captain	Port of departure	Crossing time (in days)	Passengers Steerage	Cabin	No. of sick on arrival	No. of deaths during crossing
Emerald	A. Montgomery	Newry (Ireland)	40	82	3	0	1

SHIPS LEAVING GROSSE ÎLE FOR QUÉBEC CITY

Name of ship	Quarantine time (in days)	Deaths in Grosse Île hospitals	Deaths on quarantined ships	
Charles	A few hours	0	0	
Eliza	8	16	0	
Jane Black	3	0	2	

FRIDAY, SEPTEMBER 17, 1847

After consulting with Dr. Douglas and A. C. Buchanan, the Executive Council committee agreed to the request for a pay raise of 10s. per day for Mr. Barter, the apothecary at Grosse Île.

Four burials were recorded in the register of the Catholic chapel and eight in that of the Protestant chapel.

SHIPS LEAVING GROSSE ÎLE FOR QUÉBEC CITY

Name of ship	Quarantine time (in days)	Deaths in Grosse Île hospitals	Deaths on quarantined ships
Emerald	1	0	0
Isabella	5	4	0
Superior	10	45	8

SATURDAY,
SEPTEMBER 18, 1847

Fifteen burials were recorded in the register of the Catholic chapel and four in that of the Protestant chapel.

According to a list published in the *Quebec Morning Chronicle*, 133 people had died at Grosse Île during the week of September 12 to 18.

SHIPS ARRIVING AT GROSSE ÎLE

Name of ship	Captain	Port of departure	Crossing time (in days)	Passengers Steerage	Cabin	No. of sick on arrival	No. of deaths during crossing
Ann*	A. McFee	Limerick (Ireland)	39	116	0	3	0

* It was this ship's second voyage of the season. It had the same captain as on the first voyage.

SHIPS LEAVING GROSSE ÎLE FOR QUÉBEC CITY

Name of ship	Quarantine time (in days)	Deaths in Grosse Île hospitals	Deaths on quarantined ships
Sir Robert Peel	4	16	2

NUMBER OF PEOPLE IN HOSPITAL ON GROSSE ÎLE
DURING THE WEEK OF SEPTEMBER 12 TO 18

Emigrants	Patients hospitalized as at last report	Patients admitted (+)	Patients discharged (-)	Deaths (-)	New total
Men	501	73	31	66	477
Women	494	43	87	32	418
Children	388	29	90	26	301
TOTAL	1 383	145	208	124	1 196*

* Of this number, 1 183 had typhus and 13 smallpox. Nine of the emigrants who had disembarked in good health died in the tents during the same week.

SUNDAY,
SEPTEMBER 19, 1847

Death of James Kenny, a 36-year-old orderly, during the week of September 19 to 25.

Ten burials were recorded in the register of the Catholic chapel.

SHIPS LEAVING GROSSE ÎLE FOR QUÉBEC CITY

Name of ship	Quarantine time (in days)	Deaths in Grosse Île hospitals	Deaths on quarantined ships
Argyle	5	7	0
Wellington	7	17	0

SHIPS ARRIVING IN QUÉBEC CITY WITHOUT A STOP-OVER AT GROSSE ÎLE

Name of ship	Port of departure	Passengers	
		Steerage	Cabin
Pearl*	London (England)	12	0

* It was this ship's second voyage of the season.

MONDAY, SEPTEMBER 20, 1847

The Governor General asked Dr. Douglas to assist Colonel Calvert and Dr. Ledoyen, who were supposed to go to Grosse Île to test a disinfecting fluid.

Taking up a news item in the *Quebec Morning Chronicle*, the *Quebec Gazette* reported that Dr. Newton, who had returned sick from Grosse Île, was convalescing.

Twelve burials were recorded in the register of the Catholic chapel and seven in that of the Protestant chapel.

SHIPS LEAVING GROSSE ÎLE FOR QUÉBEC CITY

Name of ship	Quarantine time	Deaths in Grosse Île	Deaths on
	(in days)	hospitals	quarantined ships
Virgilia	6	5	0

TUESDAY, SEPTEMBER 21, 1847

In his report on the progress of construction work at Grosse Île, Pierre Laurencel said that 10 men (6 carpenters, 3 labourers and 1 carter) were employed on a daily basis. Work on the wharf was progressing well: stone-filling operations continued and 660 more feet of planking were needed to panel the stairs. The last hospital, which was supposed to have measured 240 feet in length, had been erected in two separate 120-foot sections because the ground was uneven.

Laurencel was about to cover over a ditch that cut through the cemetery and extended to the river, because of the foul odour emanating from it. Now that Dr. Douglas had enough iron beds, he no longer had to have wooden beds made. Laurencel mentioned that J.-B. Coursie had left the island after falling gravely ill and that several of the workmen who had helped to build sheds on the farm had died in Québec City. Louis Lefebvre, who had worked on the wharf, and a man by the name of Plante had also died.

The *Quebec Mercury* reported that the steamer *Neptune* had arrived in Québec City from Grosse Île with a large number of emigrants aboard, including 20 orphans. Convalescent patients ready to leave the quarantine station had departed for Montréal on the *Lady Colborne*.

The *Quebec Mercury* also mentioned that Dr. Johnston was seriously ill with typhus again and had come back to Québec City on the steamer *Lady Colborne*. In addition, Dr. Fortin had left his post on the island following a reduction in medical staff.

According to the *Canadien*, 1276 people (518 men, 429 women and 329 children) were in hospital on Grosse Île .

Seventeen burials were recorded in the register of the Catholic chapel.

WEDNESDAY, SEPTEMBER 22, 1847

Douglas recommended that the salary of hospital stewards be raised by 5s. per day and that the wages of cooks and nurses be increased by 3s. 6d. per day

In response to Douglas' request of September 12 regarding what should be done with the sick at Grosse Île after the navigation season, the Executive Council committee said that it would be unwise to consider preparing the buildings on the island to keep emigrants there in winter. It would be more expedient to send them to Montréal or Québec City, where they could be housed in buildings that would be erected for them and fitted out for that purpose.

The Executive Council committee agreed to the suggestion made by the deputy commissary general on September 16 that emigrants be provided with potatoes instead of bread. (The Governor General ratified this decision on September 24.)

Thirteen burials were recorded in the register of the Catholic chapel and six in that of the Protestant chapel.

THURSDAY, SEPTEMBER 23, 1847

Fourteen burials were recorded in the register of the Catholic chapel and eight in that of the Protestant chapel.

SHIPS ARRIVING AT GROSSE ÎLE

Name of ship	Captain	Port of departure	Crossing time (in days)	Passengers Steerage	Cabin	No. of sick on arrival	No. of deaths during crossing
Douce Davie	T. J. Renny	Sligo (Ireland)	44	305	2	10	6
Emigrant	J. Price	Liverpool (England)	44	528	1	150	46
Gentoo	J. Hokin	Plymouth (England)	37	49	3	0	0
*Nerio**	W. Gibson	Limerick (Ireland)	48	134	0	10	3
*Victoria**	J. Martin	Saint Ives (England)	45	44	0	0	0
TOTAL				1 060	6	170	

* It was the second voyage made by these ships during the season. Their captain and port of departure were the same as on the first voyage.

FRIDAY, SEPTEMBER 24, 1847

The Governor General agreed to the salary increase for hospital stewards requested by Dr. Douglas on September 22.

The Governor General's secretary informed Buchanan and Douglas that the sick on Grosse Île would be taken to Québec City or Montréal before the end of the navigation season. Emigration agent Buchanan would have to take whatever measures were necessary for that purpose.

According to the *Quebec Gazette*, Mr. Buchanan was still sick.

Death of Angus Angelis, a sailor aboard the *Emigrant*, at age 40.

Sixteen burials were recorded in the register of the Catholic chapel and one in that of the Protestant chapel.

SHIPS ARRIVING AT GROSSE ÎLE

Name of ship	Captain	Port of departure	Crossing time (in days)	Passengers Steerage	Cabin	No. of sick on arrival	No. of deaths during crossing
*Albion**	C. Daly	Cork (Ireland)	43	183	1	14	5
Chieftain	W. McEwan	Belfast (Ireland)	46	97	1	0	1
Henrietta Mary	J. Reid	Cork (Ireland)	37	266	1	22	12
Sophia	J. Bellord	Waterford (Ireland)	48	23	0	0	0
TOTAL				569	3	36	

* It was this ship's second voyage of the season. It had the same captain as on the first voyage.

SHIPS LEAVING GROSSE ÎLE FOR QUÉBEC CITY

Name of ship	Quarantine time (in days)	Deaths in Grosse Île hospitals	Deaths on quarantined ships
Chieftain	A few hours	0	0
Gentoo	A few hours	0	0
Sophia	A few hours	0	0
Victoria	A few hours	0	0

SHIPS ARRIVING IN QUÉBEC CITY WITHOUT A STOP-OVER AT GROSSE ÎLE

Name of ship	Port of departure	Passengers	
		Steerage	Cabin
Cherokee*	Glasgow (Scotland)	0	5
Florence	Plymouth (England)	11	0
TOTAL		11	5

* It was this ship's second voyage of the season.

SATURDAY, SEPTEMBER 25, 1847

Dr. Joseph Beardon, assistant surgeon for the Royal Navy, requested a salary for the period when he had fallen ill, shortly after resigning from his position as medical assistant at Grosse Île. He had tendered his resignation in August. (This request was rejected on December 8.)

Eleven burials were recorded in the register of the Catholic chapel and six in that of the Protestant chapel.

According to a list published in the *Quebec Morning Chronicle*, 121 people had died at Grosse Île during the week of September 19 to 25.

SHIPS ARRIVING AT GROSSE ÎLE

Name of ship	Captain	Port of departure	Crossing time (in days)	Passengers Steerage	Cabin	No. of sick on arrival	No. of deaths during crossing
Ariel	J. Stewart	Kilrush (Ireland)	47	119	0	0	0

SHIPS LEAVING GROSSE ÎLE FOR QUÉBEC CITY

Name of ship	Quarantine time (in days)	Deaths in Grosse Île hospitals	Deaths on quarantined ships
Ann*	7	0	0
Ariel	A few hours	0	0

* It is hard to understand why this ship was quarantined for such a long period, since it had only three sick passengers aboard when it arrived at Grosse Île.

SHIPS ARRIVING IN QUÉBEC CITY WITHOUT A STOP-OVER AT GROSSE ÎLE

Name of ship	Port of departure	Passengers	
		Steerage	Cabin
Emperor	Plymouth (England)	5	0
Florence	Cardiff (Wales)	1	0
TOTAL		6	0

COMPARISON OF EMIGRATION STATISTICS FOR THE PORT OF QUÉBEC IN 1846 AND 1847
(MAY 9 TO SEPTEMBER 25)

Country of origin	1847	1846
England	30124	8043
Ireland	50732	19934
Scotland	3264	1406
Germany	7129	887
TOTAL	91249*	30270

* To calculate the real number of arrivals in the port of Québec, the number of deaths that occurred during the crossing and in quarantine must be subtracted from this total.

NUMBER OF PEOPLE IN HOSPITAL ON GROSSE ÎLE
DURING THE WEEK OF SEPTEMBER 19 TO 25

Emigrants	Patients hospitalized	Patients admitted	Patients discharged	Deaths	New total
	as at last report	(+)	(-)	(-)	
Men	477	189	130	45	491
Women	418	135	64	41	448
Children	301	112	40	35	338
TOTAL	1196	436	234	121*	1277**

* Another 10 people died in the sector for healthy emigrants.

** Of this number, 1240 had typhus and 37 smallpox.

SUNDAY,
SEPTEMBER 26, 1847

Sixteen burials were recorded in the register of the Catholic chapel.

MONDAY,
SEPTEMBER 27, 1847

Death of Benjamin Evans, a sailor aboard the *Goliah*, at age 20.

Six burials were recorded in the register of the Catholic chapel and eight in that of the Protestant chapel.

TUESDAY,
SEPTEMBER 28, 1847

The Reverend John Butler, a missionary at Kingsey, arrived at Grosse Île ; the Reverend Richard Anderson and the Reverend Narcisse Guerout left for Québec City.

According to the *Quebec Mercury*, 473 men, 441 women and 349 children were in hospital on Grosse Île, representing a total of 1 263 patients.

Ten burials were recorded in the register of the Catholic chapel and five in that of the Protestant chapel.

SHIPS LEAVING GROSSE ÎLE FOR QUÉBEC CITY

Name of ship	Quarantine time (in days)	Deaths in Grosse Île hospitals	Deaths on quarantined ships
Albion	3	1	0
Henrietta Mary	4	7	0
Nerio	5	3	0

WEDNESDAY,
SEPTEMBER 29, 1847

According to Pierre Laurencel, rock-filling operations were continuing on the wharf; seven carts were being used to transport the extremely heavy type of granite that served as fill. The construction of the last hospital was going well. The soldiers' barracks had been shingled, and an extension had been built for Protestant missionaries.

Drs. E. Jacques, A. G. Fenwick, W. Cox, W. C. Allen and J. Dickinson asked the Governor General to grant them an allowance equal to one half of their present salary, as was customary in the army and the navy, over the coming winter or until their services were required once again. The physicians justified their request by saying that they had left a flourishing practice to perform arduous and dangerous duties on Grosse Île. To support this assertion, they mentioned that out of the 25 doctors who had worked at the quarantine station during the season, 24 had come down with typhus and 4 had died.

Anglican baptism of Thomas Renny, captain of the *Douce Davie*, at age 32. The Reverend J. Butler drew up the baptismal certificate.

Eleven burials were recorded in the register of the Catholic chapel and one in that of the Protestant chapel.

SHIPS LEAVING GROSSE ÎLE FOR QUÉBEC CITY

Name of ship	Quarantine time (in days)	Deaths in Grosse Île hospitals	Deaths on quarantined ships
Douce Davie	6	2	0

THURSDAY, SEPTEMBER 30, 1847

Some 400 convalescent patients left for Montréal on the steamer *Canada*.

The Archbishop of Québec asked the government to reimburse the cost of taking orphans in his care to various parishes in the archdiocese. (See reply of October 1.)

According to the *Quebec Mercury*, two men died while disembarking from the *Emigrant*. One hundred and sixty-two people from this ship had been hospitalized.

The *Journal de Québec* reported that Father Marquis, curate at Saint-Grégoire, had taken 19 emigrant orphans away from Grosse Île with him the week before. A few days earlier, Father Harper, parish priest of Saint-Grégoire, had left with 16. In addition, Father Fortier, parish priest of Nicolet, and Father Faucher, parish priest of Lotbinière, had each left recently with 14 orphans, for whom they had already found places in respectable families.

Nine burials were recorded in the register of the Catholic chapel and four in that of the Protestant chapel.

Dr. Douglas reported that an average of 1 330 people were in hospital per day from September 1 to 30 inclusively.

1847

OCTOBER

S	M	T	W	T	F	S
					1	2
3	4	5	6	7	8	9
10	11	12	13	14	15	16
17	18	19	20	21	22	23
24	25	26	27	28	29	30
31						

241

FRIDAY,
OCTOBER 1, 1847

Thirty-five convalescents left for Québec City aboard the steamer *Lady Colborne*.

Dr. Douglas proposed a series of measures to gradually prepare for the closing of the quarantine station, scheduled for the end of the month. He suggested that 400 convalescent emigrants be sent to Montréal once a week, until only those emigrants for whom the voyage would be too dangerous were left on Grosse Île . He suggested that the latter be sent to the Marine Hospital in Québec City rather than to Montréal. Douglas planned to reduce his medical staff as the number of sick declined; he had already discharged three medical assistants and several hospital employees.

The medical superintendent also thought that the services of the deputy emigration agent, as well as those of his boatman and cook, were no longer required at the quarantine station. Mr. Durmody, a clerk, could distribute travel passes to emigrants when necessary. Dr. Douglas also said that half of the detachment of troops could return to Québec City as of October 5, and the remainder the week after. Two policemen and two boatmen would also be able to leave. (See reply of October 25.)

In response to the request made by the Archbishop of Québec on September 30, the Governor General agreed to defray the expenses incurred in taking orphans to various parishes in the archdiocese.

Dr. Douglas wrote to the editor of the *Quebec Mercury* informing him of the discovery of the body of a drowned man on the rocks near Telegraph Hill. According to the medical superintendent, this man was evidently a worker from Québec City. Douglas therefore asked the editor to publish the description he had provided in the hope that it would help to identify the body. The man was given a decent burial on Grosse Île . The newspaper published the information the next day.

According to the *Quebec Mercury*, the Reverend R. Anderson had felt unwell after returning from Grosse Île on Tuesday, September 28; he had decided, therefore, to stay in Québec City in order to see a doctor.

The newspaper also announced that the Reverend C. J. Morris, who had recently come back from the quarantine station, was seriously ill with typhus.

The *Quebec Mercury* reported that 773 people (304 men, 253 women and 216 children) were in hospital on Grosse Île on October 1.

Catholic baptism of Catherine Carroll, born September 29 to Patrick Carroll, a labourer, and Bridget Waller, from County Roscommon, Ireland. Father F. McDonnell drew up the baptismal certificate.

Nine burials were recorded in the register of the Catholic chapel and one in that of the Protestant chapel.

SATURDAY,
OCTOBER 2, 1847

Four burials were recorded in the register of the Catholic chapel and two in that of the Protestant chapel.

According to a list published in the *Quebec Morning Chronicle*, 86 people had died at Grosse Île during the week of September 26 to October 2.

NUMBER OF PEOPLE IN HOSPITAL ON GROSSE ÎLE
DURING THE WEEK OF SEPTEMBER 26 TO OCTOBER 2

Emigrants	Patients hospitalized	Patients admitted	Patients discharged	Deaths	New total
	as at last report	(+)	(-)	(-)	
TOTAL	1 277	153	629	86	715*

* Of this number, 690 had typhus and 25 smallpox.

SUNDAY,
OCTOBER 3 1847

The *Quebec Morning Chronicle* reported that emigrants had died on the *Samson* during the week of October 3 to 9, 1847. This vessel is not mentioned in either the list of ships that were inspected at Grosse Île or the list of those that arrived in Québec City.

Nine burials were recorded in the register of the Catholic chapel and two in that of the Protestant chapel.

SHIPS LEAVING GROSSE ÎLE FOR QUÉBEC CITY

Name of ship	Quarantine time	Deaths in Grosse Île	Deaths on
	(in days)	hospitals	quarantined ships
Emigrant	9	40	2

Name of ship	Port of departure	Passengers	
		Steerage	Cabin
Favourite	Greenock (Scotland)	16	3

MONDAY, OCTOBER 4, 1847

Six burials were recorded in the register of the Catholic chapel and three in that of the Protestant chapel.

TUESDAY, OCTOBER 5, 1847

Dr. Douglas rejected the request made by Dr. Bradley on September 9 regarding the reimbursement of certain expenses he had incurred while working at Grosse Île .

According to a report on the condition of the tents used on the island during the season and left at the Queen's Wharf in Québec City, 291 of these canvas shelters not only needed washing but also required major repairs. Forty-one others were no longer usable, but should nevertheless be washed before being disposed of.

Father McGauran told Archbishop Signay that it might not be necessary to send more priests to Grosse Île that season since the number of sick had decreased considerably. Nonetheless, there were still 800 sick people at the quarantine station. Soon, the services of Father McDonnell would no longer be needed. Father McGauran said that the orderlies and caretakers were just as negligent as ever; however, he felt that it was impossible to remedy the situation.

The *Quebec Mercury* revealed that the Reverend R. Anderson, a missionary of the Quebec Church of England in the township of Ireland (Province of Québec) was seriously ill with typhus, which he had caught at Grosse Île. He had been admitted to a private hospital in Beauport and was not expected to survive the day. The *Quebec Gazette* reported that the Reverend C. J. Morris, an Anglican missionary from Portneuf, had died in the same hospital from typhus, which he too had contracted at the quarantine station.

According to the *Quebec Mercury*, the departure of 400 convalescents for Montréal on September 30 and of 35 others for Québec City on October 1 had enabled Douglas to close another hospital at the quarantine station and to discharge two physicians along with their orderlies and nurses.

According to the *Quebec Gazette*, 230 men, 124 women and 150 children were in hospital on Grosse Île, representing a total of 504 patients.

Nine burials were recorded in the register of the Catholic chapel and two in that of the Protestant chapel.

SHIPS ARRIVING AT GROSSE ÎLE

Name of ship	Captain	Port of departure	Crossing time (in days)	Passengers Steerage	Cabin	No. of sick on arrival	No. of deaths during crossing
Douglas	Douglas	London (England)	42	19	2	0	0
Sarah Milledge	P. McDonough	Galway (Ireland)	52	259	11	8	5
TOTAL				278	13	8	

SHIPS LEAVING GROSSE ÎLE FOR QUÉBEC CITY

Name of ship	Quarantine time (in days)	Deaths in Grosse Île hospitals	Deaths on quarantined ships
*Douglas**	A few hours	0	0

* It was this ship's second voyage of the season. Its captain and port of departure were the same as on the first voyage.

WEDNESDAY, OCTOBER 6, 1847

Father Cazeau, on behalf of the Archbishop of Québec, asked the Governor General for an additional sum of money to reimburse the expenses incurred in providing spiritual assistance to sick Catholic emigrants at Grosse Île and in the Marine Hospital in Québec City. These expenses were much higher than anticipated: they exceeded the sum of £ 500 which the Governor General had allocated three months earlier. (See reply of October 26.)

Dr. Bradley submitted another request for payment relating to services he had rendered at Grosse Île ; his first request had been rejected. This time he said that he was destitute, and merely asked for the sum of £ 10 to defray his expenses and travel to Pennsylvania, where he believed that he could find professional employment. (See reply of October 25.)

Death of Samuel Palmer, a policeman, at age 46.

Three burials were recorded in the register of the Catholic chapel and one in that of the Protestant chapel.

Name of ship	Captain	Port of departure	Crossing time (in days)	Passengers Steerage	Cabin	No. of sick on arrival	No. of deaths during crossing
Sir John Campbell*	J. Campbell	Belfast (Ireland)	42	381	4	0	2

* It was this ship's second voyage of the season. Its captain and port of departure were the same as on the first voyage.

SHIPS LEAVING GROSSE ÎLE FOR QUÉBEC CITY

Name of ship	Quarantine time (in days)	Deaths in Grosse Île hospitals	Deaths on quarantined ships
Sir John Campbell	A few hours	0	0

THURSDAY, OCTOBER 7, 1847

Dr. Douglas informed the secretary of the Board of Works, Thomas A. Begley, that he had cut down on construction costs by annexing his office to the farmhouse in the sector reserved for healthy emigrants at the east end of the island.

According to the *Quebec Mercury*, only three ships were anchored at the quarantine station.

The *Quebec Gazette* reported that about 90 convalescents had left the island on the *Lady Colborne* accompanied by two physicians whose services were no longer required at the quarantine facility.

Eight burials were recorded in the register of the Catholic chapel and seven in that of the Protestant chapel.

FRIDAY, OCTOBER 8, 1847

Eight burials were recorded in the register of the Catholic chapel.

An article in the *Quebec Morning Chronicle* presented emigration statistics for the port of Liverpool for the season as a whole. The following table shows the destination of these emigrants, 66 percent of whom were Irish. The remainder were mostly Scottish, English or German:

Destination	Number of emigrants
United States	77 403
Canada (Québec and Ontario)	27 666
New Brunswick	1 479
Nova Scotia	171
Prince Edward Island	444
Other	311
TOTAL	107 474*

* Obviously, this total includes emigrants other than those who arrived in the port of Québec.

SHIPS LEAVING GROSSE ÎLE FOR QUÉBEC CITY

Name of ship	Quarantine time (in days)	Deaths in Grosse Île hospitals	Deaths on quarantined ships
Sarah Milledge	3	3	0

SHIPS ARRIVING IN QUÉBEC CITY WITHOUT A STOP-OVER AT GROSSE ÎLE

Name of ship	Port of departure	Passengers Steerage	Cabin
Constance	Bristol (England)	9	0
Mary*	Glasgow (Scotland)	20	0
TOTAL		29	0

* It was this ship's second voyage of the season. Its captain and port of departure were the same as on the first voyage.

SATURDAY,
OCTOBER 9, 1847

Catholic baptism of Catherine Jane Vézina, born October 8 to Arsène Vézina, a labourer, and Anne Robinson, from Île aux Grues. Father F. McDonnell drew up the baptismal certificate.

Four burials were recorded in the register of the Catholic chapel and two in that of the Protestant chapel.

According to a list published in the *Quebec Morning Chronicle*, 61 people had died at Grosse Île during the week of October 3 to 9.

SHIPS ARRIVING IN QUÉBEC CITY WITHOUT A STOP-OVER AT GROSSE ÎLE

Name of ship	Port of departure	Passengers Steerage	Cabin
Peruvian	Glasgow (Scotland)	1	0

COMPARISON OF EMIGRATION STATISTICS FOR THE PORT OF QUÉBEC IN 1846 AND 1847 (MAY 9 TO OCTOBER 9)

Country of origin	1847	1846
England	30 157	8 422
Ireland	51 302	20 239
Scotland	3 304	1 455
Germany	7 129	887
TOTAL	91 892*	31 003

* To calculate the real number of arrivals in the port of Québec, the number of deaths that occurred during the crossing and in quarantine must be subtracted from this total.

NUMBER OF PEOPLE IN HOSPITAL ON GROSSE ÎLE DURING THE WEEK OF OCTOBER 3 TO 9

Emigrants	Patients hospitalized as at last report	Patients admitted (+)	Patients discharged (-)	Deaths (-)	New total
Men	286	9	120	24	151
Women	234	17	83	24	144
Children	195	10	123	13	69
TOTAL	715	36	326	61	364

SUNDAY, OCTOBER 10, 1847

Death of William Polk, a 22-year-old clerk employed by Mr. Ray, a sutler, during the week of October 10 to 16.

Six burials were recorded in the register of the Catholic chapel.

SHIPS ARRIVING AT GROSSE ÎLE

Name of ship	Captain	Port of departure	Crossing time (in days)	Passengers Steerage	Cabin	No. of sick on arrival	No. of deaths during crossing
*Earl Powis**	H. Waker	Dundee (Scotland)	52	12	8	0	0
John Hawkes	J. Richards	Limerick (Ireland)	48	111	3	2	5
Lord Metcalfe	W. Rosie	Aberdeen (Scotland)	52	36	15	0	0
TOTAL				159	26	2	

*It was this ship's second voyage of the season. Its captain and port of departure were the same as on the first voyage.

SHIPS LEAVING GROSSE ÎLE FOR QUÉBEC CITY

Name of ship	Quarantine time (in days)	Deaths in Grosse Île hospitals	Deaths on quarantined ships
Earl Powis	A few hours	0	0
Lord Metcalfe	A few hours	0	0

MONDAY,
OCTOBER 11, 1847

After being informed by Buchanan that all healthy passengers had left Grosse Île on October 4, Mr. A. B. Hawke, the chief emigration agent for Upper Canada, recommended that Mr. Symes and Mr. Durmody be relieved of their duties at the quarantine station in order to save money.

Three burials were recorded in the register of the Catholic chapel and two in that of the Protestant chapel.

SHIPS ARRIVING AT GROSSE ÎLE

Name of ship	Captain	Port of departure	Crossing time (in days)	Passengers Steerage	Cabin	No. of sick on arrival	No. of deaths during crossing
Messenger	Shields	Liverpool (England)	49	227	0	12	12

SHIPS LEAVING GROSSE ÎLE FOR QUÉBEC CITY

Name of ship	Quarantine time (in days)	Deaths in Grosse Île hospitals	Deaths on quarantined ships
John Hawkes	1	0	0

TUESDAY,
OCTOBER 12, 1847

Father McGauran wrote to the Archbishop of Québec, Joseph Signay, saying that he would keep Father McDonnell at Grosse Île for another eight days. He criticized the attitude of Dr. Douglas, describing him as a wily Scotsman who, in order to make a profit, would delay the departure of a few hundred emigrants from Grosse Île in violation of the orders he had received. The *Lady Colborne* was supposed to embark 230 emigrants the next day; of that number, barely two were able to make it to the steamboat without assistance.

According to the *Quebec Morning Chronicle*, there were no more than 400 emigrants at Grosse Île and the number of deaths had declined substantially. The newspaper mentioned that the Reverend R. Anderson and the Reverend C. J. Morris, ministers of the Church of England, were among those who had died from typhus over the past two weeks. These clergymen had caught the disease while fulfilling their ministerial duties among the emigrants at Grosse Île .

The *Quebec Mercury* reported that a detachment of troops had left the quarantine station and was returning to Québec City.

Four burials were recorded in the register of the Catholic chapel.

WEDNESDAY,
OCTOBER 13, 1847

According to Pierre Laurencel, all the sheds were finished. A fence still had to be built behind the hospitals near Green Bay (Cholera Bay). As well, the ditch in the cemetery had to be covered.

Three burials were recorded in the register of the Catholic chapel.

SHIPS ARRIVING AT GROSSE ÎLE

Name of ship	Captain	Port of departure	Crossing time (in days)	Passengers Steerage	Cabin	No. of sick on arrival	No. of deaths during crossing
Bryan Abbs	Donald	Limerick (Ireland)	61	179	0	0	5
*St. Lawrence**	W. Tullock	Aberdeen (Scotland)	46	23	5	0	0
TOTAL				202	5	0	

* It was this ship's second voyage of the season. Its captain and port of departure were the same as on the first voyage.

SHIPS LEAVING GROSSE ÎLE FOR QUÉBEC CITY

Name of ship	Quarantine time (in days)	Deaths in Grosse Île hospitals	Deaths on quarantined ships
Bryan Abbs	A few hours	0	0
Messenger	2	1	0
St. Lawrence	A few hours	0	0

THURSDAY,
OCTOBER 14, 1847

The Executive Council committee rejected the request for an allowance submitted by medical assistants at Grosse Île on September 29.

The *Quebec Mercury* reported that the quarantine station would be shut down in a few days. The medical personnel had been reduced to two physicians, Dr. Douglas and Dr. Jacques, and only one hospital was still in use. Some 250 invalids had been taken to Montréal on the *Lady Colborne*, accompanied by Dr. Fenwick. No more than 100 patients were still at the quarantine station, and most were suffering from chronic dysentery. The newspaper specified that the military detachment had returned to Québec City on October 12 and that the police force now included only two sergeants and two men; one of the latter, Mr. Lindsay, had typhus.

Four burials were recorded in the register of the Catholic chapel.

SHIPS ARRIVING AT GROSSE ÎLE

Name of ship	Captain	Port of departure	Crossing time (in days)	Passengers Steerage	Cabin	No. of sick on arrival	No. of deaths during crossing
Clio*	R. Easthorpe	Padstow (England)	47	226	1	0	0
Ninian	T. J. Elliot	Limerick (Ireland)	45	99	10	3	1
TOTAL				325	11	3	

* It was this ship's second voyage of the season. Its captain and port of departure were the same as on the first voyage.

SHIPS LEAVING GROSSE ÎLE FOR QUÉBEC CITY

Name of ship	Quarantine time (in days)	Deaths in Grosse Île hospitals	Deaths on quarantined ships
Clio	A few hours	0	0

FRIDAY, OCTOBER 15, 1847

Four burials were recorded in the register of the Catholic chapel.

SHIPS LEAVING GROSSE ÎLE FOR QUÉBEC CITY

Name of ship	Quarantine time (in days)	Deaths in Grosse Île hospitals	Deaths on quarantined ships
Ninian	1	0	0

SATURDAY, OCTOBER 16, 1847

Two burials were recorded in the register of the Catholic chapel.

According to a list published in the *Quebec Morning Chronicle*, 33 people had died at GrosseÎle during the week of October 10 to 16.

NUMBER OF PEOPLE IN HOSPITAL ON GROSSE ÎLE DURING THE WEEK OF OCTOBER 10 TO 16

Emigrants	Patients hospitalized as at last report	Patients admitted (+)	Patients discharged (-)	Deaths (-)	New total
Men	151	18	125	10	34
Women	144	26	112	15	43
Children	69	10	50	8	21
TOTAL	364	54	287	33	98

SUNDAY,
OCTOBER 17, 1847

Death of William Lindsay, a 24-year-old policeman, during the week of October 17 to 23.

Two burials were recorded in the register of the Catholic chapel.

MONDAY,
OCTOBER 18, 1847

Catholic marriage of Patrick Flood and Eliza Watters, from County Kilkenny, Ireland. Father B. McGauran signed the marriage certificate.

Two burials were recorded in the register of the Catholic chapel.

TUESDAY,
OCTOBER 19, 1847

In preparation for closing the quarantine station, transferring all remaining emigrants to Montréal and putting the buildings in order for the winter, Dr. Douglas requested authorization to leave four people on Grosse Île to keep an eye on the facilities once the season was over. Although in previous years, two caretakers had been equal to the task, Douglas said that more would be necessary in 1847 because of the larger number of buildings.

Two of these employees could live in the hospitals, one in the barracks and another at the east end of the island where the sheds had been erected. The medical superintendent proposed that one of the police sergeants and three of the boatmen be hired as caretakers; the latter would make it possible to reach the mainland in the event of an emergency. Douglas suggested that they be paid $10. per month, without rations. (See reply of October 25.)

Dr. Douglas informed the Governor General that the money which had been remitted to the chief hospital steward by emigrants who had since died at Grosse Île totalled £ 816 3s. 6 1/2d. Of that amount, £ 200 17s. had been entrusted to the emigration agent, to be handed over to relatives of the deceased. A sum of £195 10d. had been given to Anglican and Roman Catholic clergymen for the benefit of the orphans whom they had taken into their care. A balance of £ 149 16s. 6d. was still in the possession of the medical superintendent, who suggested that it be transferred to the emigration agent so that he might forward it to friends of the deceased in Europe.

Dr. Douglas suggested that an inventory be made of the contents of 204 boxes belonging to deceased emigrants. This would make it possible to remit valuable articles to people who might claim them in the future. As for the 23 feather beds and a large quantity of clothing belonging to the deceased, Douglas suggested that they be destroyed or burnt. (See reply of October 25.)

Four burials were recorded in the register of the Catholic chapel.

WEDNESDAY,
OCTOBER 20, 1847

Three burials were recorded in the register of the Catholic chapel.

THURSDAY,
OCTOBER 21, 1847

The *Quebec Gazette* reported that Mr. Julyan, a Commissariat employee stationed on Grosse Île, had had a hunting accident on Île Sainte-Marguerite; his hand had been shattered when his gun exploded.

According to Dr. Douglas, an average of 346 people were in hospital per day on Grosse Île from October 1 to 21 inclusively. (It may be concluded, therefore, that the last sick emigrant left hospital on October 21, 1847.)

FRIDAY,
OCTOBER 22, 1847

Pierre Laurencel told C.-E. Casgrain, the Public Works commissioner, that he hoped to complete construction work on Grosse Île the following week. Fenders had been installed on the wharf and the risers of the two stairways had been panelled. The fence behind the hospitals and the cover for the ditch in the cemetery were nearing completion. The hospitals still had to be closed for the winter. Only nine men were still working on the island: three carpenters were busy on the wharf, one carpenter and two labourers were covering the ditch in the cemetery and two carpenters were building the fence behind the hospital and doing other odd jobs. A carter was transporting materials when necessary.

SATURDAY,
OCTOBER 23, 1847

According to the *Quebec Mercury*, the Grosse Île quarantine station was closed, for all practical purposes. All emigrants, whether healthy or sick, had been removed, and only two patients remained. They were William Lindsay and a Mr. Hum, who were employees at the station. (As mentioned above, Lindsay died in the week of October 17 to 23.)

The *Quebec Mercury* found it disturbing that several nurses had returned from Grosse Île in apparent good health recently and had died of typhus shortly afterwards.

The *Quebec Mercury* published a long table with three columns, entitled «Return of Money and Effects left by the Emigrants, who died without relatives, at Grosse Isle, from the 16th of May to the 21st of October, 1847.» The table appeared again in subsequent issues, on October 28 and 30, and on November 2, 6, 9, 13 and 16. It identified some 200 people, gave the name of the vessel they had arrived on, and listed what each had left. The total amount of money remaining was £ 829; as well, there were around 200 boxes and trunks, and a number of feather beds and items of clothing. The *Quebec Gazette* reported that the sum of £ 129 had been left by a woman named Catherine Fraser, who had arrived on the *Broom*, and who apparently had relatives in Upper Canada.

According to a list published in the *Quebec Morning Chronicle*, 14 people had died at Grosse Île during the week of October 17 to 23.

NUMBER OF PEOPLE IN HOSPITAL ON GROSSE ÎLE DURING THE WEEK OF OCTOBER 17 TO 23

Emigrants	Patients hospitalized as at last report	Patients admitted (+)	Patients discharged (-)	Deaths (-)	New total
TOTAL	98	7	91	14	0

MONDAY, OCTOBER 25, 1847

The Executive Council committee agreed to the arrangement proposed by Dr. Douglas on October 19, namely, that four people should be left in charge of the quarantine station over the winter. The committee also approved the superintendent's suggestions concerning the money and personal effects left by the emigrants who died at Grosse Île during the season. However, it asked that the £ 200 17s. held by the emigration agent and the £ 149 16s. 6d. in the superintendent's possession be handed over to the deputy inspector general of public accounts, who had been recently appointed receiver of emigrants' monies and effects. The Governor General approved these proposals on October 27 and requested that an inventory of the boxes be made before a public notary.

The Executive Council committee recommended that Dr. Bradley be paid the sum of money he had asked for on October 6, as compensation for the services he had rendered at Grosse Île .

TUESDAY, OCTOBER 26, 1847

The Governor General replied to a request made by the Archbishop of Québec on October 6 for further assistance in paying for expenses related to bringing religious comfort to sick Catholic emigrants at

Grosse Île and at the Marine Hospital in Québec City. He said that he was postponing his decision until the accounts from the station were presented to him in their entirety.

WEDNESDAY, OCTOBER 27, 1847

The *Canadien* and the *Quebec Morning Chronicle* both published a table of the deaths recorded weekly at Grosse Île during the season which had just ended. A total of 3452 people were reported to have died.

In reply to a proposal made on October 11 by Mr. Hawke, the chief emigration agent for Upper Canada, the Executive Council committee said that it had approved the termination of the positions held by Mr. Symes and his staff on October 25; it agreed that the services of the clerk, Mr. Durmody, could also be dispensed with, if the medical superintendent of the quarantine station had no objections.

COMPARISON OF EMIGRATION STATISTICS FOR THE PORT OF QUÉBEC IN 1846 AND 1847 (MAY 9 TO OCTOBER 27)

Country of origin	1847	1846
England	30 557	8 672
Ireland	51 651	20 444
Scotland	3 381	1 521
Germany	7 129	887
TOTAL	92 718*	31 524

* To calculate the real number of arrivals in the port of Québec, the number of deaths that occurred during the crossing and in quarantine must be subtracted from this total.

THURSDAY, OCTOBER 28, 1847

The *Anteris*, commanded by Captain W. McRay, arrived at Grosse Île from Arichat, Nova Scotia, with 46 steerage passengers who had been rescued from the *Maria*, after it was shipwrecked off Cape Breton Island on its way from Galway, Ireland. No deaths or cases of illness were reported among its passengers or crew.

According to the *Quebec Mercury*, there were no longer any patients at Grosse Île, except for Mr. Hum, an employee at the quarantine station who was suffering from typhus. Mr. Lindsay, his fellow worker, had died. The newspaper also drew attention to the list of unclaimed money and personal effects left by deceased emigrants and said that the deputy inspector general of public accounts would be put in charge of the matter. This type of list had apparently been compiled every year since 1835.

The *Quebec Morning Chronicle* reported that the quarantine station was winding up its operations and would close for the winter on November 1 or 2. All the emigrants had left the island. Several doctors and other members of the hospital staff had gone back to Québec City and, surprisingly, a good number of them had come down with typhus since their return. All the doctors from Québec City had survived, however, except for one. He was Dr. Racey, who had taken to his bed about 10 days before and died on October 25.

FRIDAY, OCTOBER 29, 1847

Joseph Cary, the deputy inspector general of public accounts and receiver of emigrants' monies and effects, published a notice in the newspapers announcing that anyone who possessed or had custody of money, goods, chattels or effects belonging to dead or sick emigrants should deliver them to him at once, in accordance with the order of the Governor-General-in-Council, dated October 25. This notice appeared in the *Canadien* on October 29 and the *Gazette de Québec* on October 30.

At Grosse Île, a list of the deceased emigrants' goods, personal effects and money began to be drawn up before Saxton Campbell, a public notary of Québec City. The list included 203 batches of objects worth about £ 180 altogether, a few silver watches, and around £ 350 in cash. The inventory was completed on November 2, when Murdoch McKay, the chief hospital steward at Grosse Île, declared that all the personal effects received from the emigrants had been presented to the notary. McKay was then entrusted with the safekeeping of these belongings, until the chief emigration agent at Québec City, or any other authorized government official, should require them.

The money and valuable goods left by the emigrants were given to Dr. George M. Douglas, the medical superintendent of Grosse Île, so that he might turn them over to the deputy inspector general of public accounts.

According to the *Canadien*, there were no longer any sick people at Grosse Île; there were, however, still 247 patients at the Marine Hospital in Québec City.

SHIPS ARRIVING AT GROSSE ÎLE

Name of ship	Captain	Port of departure	Crossing time (in days)	Passengers Steerage	Cabin	No. of sick on arrival	No. of deaths during crossing
Lord Ashburton	E. Bell	Liverpool (England)	47	489	2	60	107

SATURDAY,
OCTOBER 30, 1847

The *Quebec Mercury* reported that the *Lord Ashburton* had arrived in a deplorable state. One hundred and seven passengers had died during the crossing and another 60 were ill with typhus or dysentery. The steamer *Alliance* had been sent from Québec City to embark all the emigrants, regardless of their state of health. Five more people died on the trip between Grosse Île and Québec City, and the newspaper wondered how many more victims there would be before the steamer reached Montréal. Five passengers had been required to remain on board the *Lord Ashburton* to help sail the vessel from Grosse Île to Québec City.

1847

NOVEMBER

S	M	T	W	T	F	S
		1	2	3	4	5	6
7	8	9	10	11	12	13
14	15	16	17	18	19	20
21	22	23	24	25	26	27
28	29	30				

MONDAY,
NOVEMBER 1, 1847

Dr. Douglas reported on the arrival of the *Lord Ashburton*, the last vessel inspected at Grosse Île. The passengers had been transferred onto the steamer *Alliance*, which took them directly to Montréal. These passengers were in as sickly and wretched a condition as any that had been seen during the past season. More than a quarter of the emigrants had died during the voyage and half the remaining passengers were either ill or convalescent when they arrived at Grosse Île . Four people had died on arrival and, just before writing his report, Douglas was informed that eight others had passed away during the night.

On account of the cold weather and the fact that the quarantine station's buildings were not winterized, Douglas had not taken any passengers ashore, but had transferred them to the steamer after summary

cleaning. The disinfecting fluid made by Messrs. Ledoyen and Calvert was sprinkled throughout the hold and this removed the offensive odour which had filled it. The medical superintendent had distributed fresh meat and bread to the poor passengers so that they would have food for the trip to Montréal, where they would arrive the next day.

Dr. Douglas informed the Governor General that he would leave the quarantine station on November 3. As agreed, a team of caretakers would be responsible for the buildings and stores. The superintendent was also leaving a washerwoman and two assistants on the island to wash some 4 000 articles of hospital bedding over the winter.

Reporting on the arrival of the *Lord Ashburton* and its numerous sick passengers, the *Quebec Gazette* was sharply critical of the British government's laxity in allowing a ship to leave with so many emigrants crammed into it. Such carelessness was a disgrace to the imperial government, caused unspeakable suffering and had ruinous consequences for the colony.

SHIPS LEAVING GROSSE ÎLE FOR QUÉBEC CITY

Name of ship	Quarantine time (in days)	Deaths in Grosse Île hospitals	Deaths on quarantined ships
*Lord Ashburton**	2	0	0

* No passengers disembarked at the quarantine station.

On ship, emigrants were packed into overcrowded steerage quarters. In 1847, the applicable legislation was the *Passengers Act* of 1842, which provided that each steerage passenger must have an area of 10 square feet and that the height between decks must be not less than 6 feet. (*Illustrated London News*, May 10, 1851, McGill University, McLellan Library.)

WEDNESDAY,
NOVEMBER 3, 1847

Indignant about the arrival of the *Lord Ashburton* in such a horrible condition, the *Canadien* denounced the British government's negligence in permitting passenger ships to leave at such a late date. The vessel was now at Québec City, even though it had not been inspected, quarantined and fumigated, as required by law. Two or three more ships full of passengers were still expected. These facts alone, said the *Canadien*, demonstrated the immediate and urgent need for a bill that would control emigration, both in England and in Canada.

The *Quebec Gazette* reported that the steamer *Alliance* had arrived in Montréal with passengers from the *Lord Ashburton* who had embarked at Grosse Île. Six people had died during the trip up the river.

The quarantine station was closed completely and definitively.

THURSDAY,
NOVEMBER 4, 1847

Dr. Douglas wrote a letter to the editor of the *Quebec Mercury* to reply to an accusation that he had inflicted inhumane treatment on the passengers on board the *Lord Ashburton*. To begin with, the superintendent could not help the fact that the vessel had arrived at such a late date, in a season when the weather was inclement. Nor was he responsible for the wretched state of the emigrants, who had arrived sick and totally destitute on an overcrowded ship.

Instead of disembarking them at Grosse Île, where the buildings were not designed to receive patients during the cold season, Douglas had transferred them onto one of the finest steamers on the St. Lawrence, distributed an ample supply of food to them, allowed a Catholic priest to visit them and then sent them on to Montréal, where there was a hospital that could take in sick people during the winter months.

At Grosse Île, the *Lord Ashburton* was then cleaned: the berths and everything used by the sick emigrants were thrown overboard, and the ship was washed and disinfected with the fluid made by Messrs. Ledoyen and Calvert. Douglas concluded his letter by asking, somewhat sarcastically, if he would have earned the thanks of the city's residents if he had allowed these emigrants to land at Québec City.

SHIPS ARRIVING IN QUÉBEC CITY WITHOUT A STOP-OVER AT GROSSE ÎLE

Name of ship	Port of departure	Passengers	
		Steerage	Cabin
Douglas	Hull (England)	10	0

FRIDAY,
NOVEMBER 5, 1847

Dr. Douglas informed the Governor General that the quarantine station had closed on November 3. Following the instructions sent to him, the buildings and various stores on the island had been left for the winter under the supervision of Murdoch McKay, Charles Langlois, Arsène Vézina and Charles Métivier. The medical superintendent asked that these employees be given the same extra allowance of food as they had received during the summer, that is, one pound of bread and one pound of meat per day. He had omitted to request this in recommending that the caretakers be paid $10 a month. Douglas reminded the Governor General that these men were all married and had children, and that their wages were insufficient to support their dependents. (See Executive Council committee's reply of November 12.)

The *Quebec Gazette* published a letter, signed «W.», in response to the justifications given by Dr. Douglas in the *Quebec Mercury* the day before. According to the writer, there was still no satisfactory explanation for the fact that both healthy and sick passengers from the *Lord Ashburton* had been placed on the same steamer to be taken to Montréal.

MONDAY,
NOVEMBER 8, 1847

A. C. Buchanan reported that four sick passengers from the *Richard Watson* were hospitalized at the Marine and Emigrant Hospital in Québec City. He said that these emigrants were «encumbrances» (or dependents) on the estate of Lord Palmerston in County Sligo, Ireland. Lord Palmerston had paid for their passage and provided them with a good supply of food. Clothes were to have been given to the poorest of them on embarking, but there had not been enough to go around. These emigrants were among the most destitute of any who had arrived this season; they had no specific destination and had been sent on to Montréal that morning at government expense.

SHIPS ARRIVING IN QUÉBEC CITY WITHOUT A STOP-OVER AT GROSSE ÎLE

Name of ship	Port of departure	Passengers	
		Steerage	Cabin
*Richard Watson**	Sligo (Ireland)	169	1

* This ship did not stop at Grosse Île because the quarantine station had been closed since November 3.

WEDNESDAY,
NOVEMBER 10, 1847

Dr. Mahoney, the inspector general of hospitals, suggested that the provincial government, at whose request troops had been sent to the quarantine station, should defray the costs related to medical care given by Dr. Douglas to the soldiers of the 93rd Highlanders Regiment stationed at Grosse Île . For the period between May 31 and October 12, these expenses came to £ 9 4s. 5d., covering 135 days of treatment, as shown in the table below. (See Executive Council committee's reply of November 24.)

MEDICAL CARE FOR SOLDIERS STATIONED AT GROSSE ÎLE

Period	No. of people treated	No. of days
May 31 - July 19	28 men, 1 woman and 1 child	50
July 20 - August 30	29 men, 1 woman and 1 child	42
August 31 - October 12	50 men, 3 women and 2 children	43
TOTAL		135

Pierre Laurencel left Grosse Île after preparing all the buildings for winter and closing them up. He wrote a report on the work he had supervised during the season:

On the farm at the east end of the island, there had been built: 12 sheds 204 feet in length, a 33-foot-long wash house, a 30-foot-long house for the police superintendent, a guardhouse 18 feet in length, a storehouse and a kitchen (both 13 feet long) for Mr. Symes' use, four

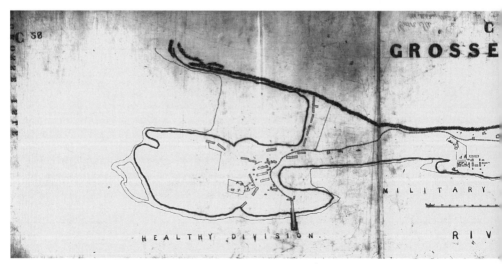

A MAP SHOWING QUARANTINE FACILITIES IN THE THREE SECTORS OF GROSSE ÎLE IN 1850. EXCEPT FOR THE FACT THAT THE EASTERN AND WESTERN SECTORS HAD EXCHANGED ROLES WITH RESPECT TO THE ACCOMMODATION OF HEALTHY VERSUS SICK EMIGRANTS, THIS MAP PROVIDES A GOOD INDICATION OF THE PHYSICAL LAYOUT OF THE QUARANTINE STATION IN THE FALL OF 1847. (NAC, H2/340; NMC-53839(2))

24-foot-long kitchens, three 15-foot privies for the sheds, a house for the policemen and a small kitchen, and an 18-foot extension for the superintendent's office.

Laurencel also noted that the privy pits had been lined with two-inch thick planks to prevent the earth walls from falling in. A cistern had been dug and a pump installed in it. Two small bridges wide enough for carts had been constructed. All construction work had been done by day labourers, except in the case of the sheds.

In the administrative sector at the centre of the island, the Board of Works agent reported that the following buildings had been constructed: an 18- by 12-foot office for the commissary general, a 7- by 12-foot pump house, a 12-foot-long kitchen and an 11-foot-long privy for the troops. The roofs of three barracks, each measuring 45 feet by 10 feet 3 inches, had been reshingled. A number of minor repairs had been carried out on the barracks as well, and a pump had been installed.

At Dr. Douglas' residence, a kitchen measuring 22 feet by 8 feet 3 inches had been added, as well as a dining room measuring 18 feet 6 inches by 10 feet, a 15- by 9-foot lean-to, a small passageway and a fence around the house. An 18- by 12-foot extension with a covered veranda had been built onto the Protestant missionaries' residence.

In the sector for the sick at the west end of the island, Laurencel had overseen the construction of 10 hospitals: one 150 feet long, three 120 feet long, two 100 feet long, one 132 feet long, one 408 feet long, one 204 feet long and one 118 feet long. Other new buildings included

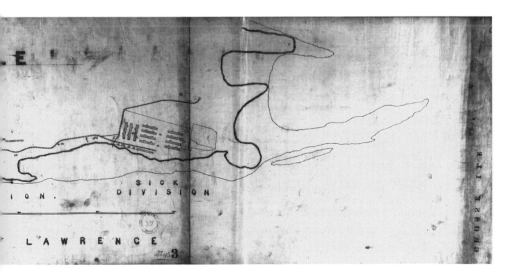

265

six kitchens (three 24 feet in length and the rest 12 feet long), a 30-foot-long apothecary's office with a 12-foot lean-to, two privies (one 16 feet long and the other 18 feet long), a dairy, a doctors' residence and another lean-to. Laurencel concluded by mentioning that the wharf at Grosse Île had been substantially renovated.

THURSDAY,
NOVEMBER 11, 1847

The *Quebec Morning Chronicle*, following the example of other Québec City newspapers, denounced the late arrival of vessels crammed with wretched emigrants, like those on the *Lord Ashburton* and the *Richard Watson*. Transporting such people to a northern country at this time of the year was an act of cruelty or ignorance. The newspaper predicted that the harshness of Canadian winter would make their existence miserable and said that many might die of cold and hunger.

The *Quebec Morning Chronicle* also mentioned that Mr. Buchanan, the indefatigable and attentive emigration agent, was recovering from a severe attack of typhus. His colleague in Toronto, Mr. McEldery, had been less fortunate, since the same disease had claimed his life.

COMPARISON OF EMIGRATION STATISTICS FOR THE PORT OF QUÉBEC IN 1846 AND 1847*

Country of origin	1847	1846
England	32 328	9 163
Ireland	54 329	21 049
Scotland	3 752	1 645
Germany	7 697	896
TOTAL	98 106**	32 753

* Statistics for 1847 were published by the *Quebec Mercury* and the *Quebec Morning Chronicle* on November 11 and by the *Quebec Gazette* on November 17.

** 65 353 more emigrants arrived in 1847 than in 1846.

FRIDAY,
NOVEMBER 12, 1847

The Executive Council committee refused the request made by Dr. Douglas on November 5 concerning a food allowance for the four caretakers on Grosse Île during the winter. The committee was of the opinion that the salary of $10 was sufficient in that part of the country, considering that the employees received free lodgings. (Douglas was informed of this decision by the provincial secretary on November 17.)

SATURDAY,
NOVEMBER 13, 1847

Mr Filder, the commissary general, asked that payment be made to one of his subaltern officers, a certain Mr. Julyan, who had been employed as a clerk at Grosse Île . (See reply of November 24.)

TUESDAY,
NOVEMBER 16, 1847

Dr. Douglas requested financial compensation for the expenses he had incurred and the extra responsibilities he had assumed during the past quarantine season in his capacity as medical superintendent at Grosse Île. (See reply of November 24.)

THURSDAY,
NOVEMBER 18, 1847

Captain E. Bell, who had commanded the *Lord Ashburton*, died of typhus in a private hospital in Beauport. This ship was the last to visit the quarantine station during the 1847 navigation season.

WEDNESDAY,
NOVEMBER 24, 1847

The Executive Council committee agreed that Dr. Douglas should be paid the extra compensation he had requested on November 16. From the time he had been appointed to the position of medical superintendent at Grosse Île in 1840 to the beginning of the 1847 season, the doctor's salary had been £ 50 per month for six months each year, starting May 1 and ending October 31.

The previous March, he had asked to be paid for April, November and December as well (and thus receive £ 150 more) since during these months he also worked for the government, preparing the quarantine station or writing up his report and closing accounts. His request was also motivated by forecasts of increased emigration and higher incidence of disease, which would make the coming season particularly difficult, and by the fact that he would probably have to rent a house in Québec City for his family. At the time, the committee had recommended this request favourably to the Governor General, who had given it his consent.

During the season, the responsibilities and work of the medical superintendent at Grosse Île had increased to a degree that was quite unforeseeable. Consequently, the committee, recognizing the doctor's tireless efforts and assiduity in a time of great danger and hardship, recommended to the Governor General that the superintendent of Grosse Île be granted a bonus of £ 100 for additional services. This amount would also cover the unpaid professional fees for medical care provided by Dr. Douglas to soldiers in the detachment posted at Grosse Île in the summer of 1847. These fees, for which Dr. Douglas had already presented a bill, came to £ 9 4s. 5d.

The Executive Council committee agreed to grant a compensation of 15s. per day to Mr. Julyan, the commissary general's clerk at Grosse Île, as had been requested on November 13. This was the same amount as that granted to Mr. Studdert, a subaltern officer in the 93rd Highlanders Regiment.

THURSDAY, NOVEMBER 25, 1847

Dr. Aylwin, who had worked at the quarantine station as a medical assistant from July to October 5, asked that his salary be extended to cover the time he was sick. Only a few days after leaving his job at Grosse Île, he had become seriously ill with typhus and had been confined to his bed until November 20.

TUESDAY, NOVEMBER 30, 1847

Stephen E. De Vere, a nobleman who had sailed to Canada in steerage class on an emigrant ship in 1847, wrote a letter about his stay at Grosse Île to F. Elliot, the chairman of the Board of Colonial Land and Emigration Commissioners in Great Britain:

In June, when De Vere was at Grosse Île, medical services and hospital facilities were quite inadequate. Medical examinations on board vessels were brief and hasty; practically no questions were asked. The physician walked along the row of passengers on deck and picked out those who looked unwell, and, after a cursory examination, had them taken to shore and sent to hospital. This hastiness meant that certain healthy passengers were detained and hospitalized, while a good number of others, although sick with typhus, were free to continue their journey.

With respect to the general management of the hospitals, De Vere did not feel qualified to give an opinion. The sheds were miserable; they were so flimsily built that they kept out neither heat nor cold. There was not enough care given to separating the sick from the healthy, or to disinfecting and cleaning the buildings once sick people had been removed to hospital. Often the same straw on which the sick emigrants had lain became a bed for the next occupant, and De Vere knew of many poor families who preferred to burrow under stones piled up along the shore rather than take shelter in the infected sheds.

De Vere had only praise for those who carried out the task of bringing food to the sheds and thus offered the emigrants some passing relief. It was dangerous and difficult work, requiring much judgment, and it was done with enthusiasm, humanity and discernment.

1847

DECEMBER

S	M	T	W	T	F	S
				1	2	3	4
5	6	7	8	9	10	11
12	13	14	15	16	17	18
19	20	21	22	23	24	25
26	27	28	29	30	31	

WEDNESDAY,
DECEMBER 1, 1847

The *Canadien* announced that the navigation season at Québec City was now closed. Not a single vessel from overseas remained in the port.

FRIDAY,
DECEMBER 3, 1847

The Executive Council committee agreed to the request for financial compensation made by Dr. Aylwin on November 25. He was granted the sum of £ 25 for the time he lost because of his illness. The committee also took into account the fact that Dr. Aylwin, as an employee at Grosse Île, was prevented from maintaining his regular practice and depended entirely on the government for income.

SUNDAY,
DECEMBER 5, 1847

Dr. Douglas wished to receive instructions as to how he should dispose of certain sums of money, coming to £ 150 in all, which remained in his keeping. The money was the remainder of the extra pay granted to the orderlies at Grosse Île . Some of these employees had left their jobs before the extra funds were authorized; others had not claimed their due. Dr. Douglas also held another £ 28 6d., which represented the unpaid wages of nine nurses and orderlies who had died; this money had not been claimed by their relatives. (See reply of December 15.)

MONDAY,
DECEMBER 6, 1847

Father Cazeau wrote once more on behalf of the Archbishop of Québec to request compensation for the expenses incurred in providing spiritual comfort to sick Catholic emigrants at Grosse Île and at the Marine Hospital in Québec City. He said that a complete account of these expenses would be submitted to the government. (See reply of December 15.)

WEDNESDAY,
DECEMBER 8, 1847

Dr. Douglas sent a letter to the Governor General about the disinfecting fluid made by Messrs. Ledoyen and Calvert. To begin with, he said that he was unable to form an opinion on the basis of personal observation, since when Ledoyen and Calvert arrived at Grosse Île, the season was advanced, the hospitals were no longer overcrowded, and all the sick emigrants had been removed from the tents to the new buildings.

In constructing these buildings, a great deal of attention had been given to the ventilation system, so that it was difficult to detect any offensive smell; Ledoyen and Calvert had therefore decided not to use their disinfecting fluid there. As a result, Douglas stated that he could give no opinion on the efficacy of the fluid in neutralizing "contagious miasmas" (or disease-causing emanations) in hospitals, preventing the spread of disease and protecting those whose work brought them into contact with sick people.

Douglas pointed out that the two men had contracted typhus when they were using the fluid in the wards of the Marine Hospital in Québec City. It was therefore reasonable to conclude, he said, that the fluid did not possess the protective properties attributed to it. In any case, the superintendent did not believe that a chemical agent could replace good ventilation, which, when properly achieved, made it possible to remove all unhealthy air.

WEDNESDAY,
DECEMBER 15, 1847

In reply to the inquiry made by Douglas on December 5, as to how he should dispose of certain sums of money remaining in his keeping, the Executive Council committee recommended that Douglas deposit the £ 150 in the Savings Bank and transmit the £ 28 6d. to Joseph Cary, the deputy inspector general of public accounts and receiver of emigrants' monies and effects, who would keep it with the other sums of money belonging to dead emigrants.

The Executive Council committee recommended that a bank draft for £ 300 be made out to Father Cazeau to cover expenses incurred in providing spiritual comfort to sick Catholic emigrants at Grosse Île and at the Marine Hospital in Québec City, as mentioned in his letter of December 6.

Table of illustrations